Contents

New Headway Intermediate – the NEW edition

Introduction

PHOTOCOPIABLE MATERIALS

Introduction

Why a new edition of *New Headway Intermediate*?

Following the recent publication of *New Headway Elementary* and *Pre-Intermediate*; and *New Headway Beginner*, it became apparent that a new edition of *New Headway Intermediate* was necessary to match the fresher, more international feel of the new lower levels. This new edition has provided the opportunity not only to refresh and update both content and design, but also to give an even clearer, more streamlined approach to the whole course, while maintaining the key elements central to its success.

Every aspect of the book has been reviewed. There are small changes, which help activities to run more smoothly, as well as more major changes to bring texts and topics up-to-date.

What remains the same?

The basic *Headway* methodology is the same. Proven traditional approaches are used alongside those which have been developed and researched more recently.

- **Grammar**
  The clear, systematic and effective grammatical syllabus remains largely the same, modified where necessary for greater clarity. Each unit starts with a brief *Test your grammar* section designed both to revise and promote students' grammatical knowledge. The Grammar Reference at the back is cued, as before, from the units.

- **Practice**
  There is still a wide variety of practice tasks and activities covering all the skills. Many have been amended and shortened and some replaced. There is even greater emphasis on personalized speaking.

- **Skills work**
  This remains integrated and balanced, with a mix of accuracy and fluency-based activities. As previously, all the texts for listening and reading come from authentic sources with the necessary adaptations to suit the level.

- **Everyday English**
  This section has been adapted from the *Postscripts* section of *New Headway Intermediate* and focuses primarily on aspects of spoken English.

What are the differences?

Over the years there has been much feedback from *Headway* users all over the world. This has contributed hugely to the new edition.

- **Design**
  As with *New Headway Elementary* and *Pre-Intermediate* Student's Books, units are shorter, at eight pages. The design is clearer, more appealing, with clearly divided sections making the units easier to navigate. Every text, activity and task has been reviewed and revised. Photographs and illustrations have been carefully chosen not only to enhance and clarify activities, but also to inform and stimulate students.

- **Grammar treatment**
  There are now *Grammar Spots* at pertinent points throughout the units. These replace the *Language Reviews*. They highlight areas of grammar, requiring students to analyse both form and use, work out rules for themselves and do some exercises for reinforcement. Grammar tasks generally have been reviewed, and demonstrate more clearly what is new and what is revision for the intermediate student. The Grammar Reference section has also been reviewed. Introductions are given to new related areas, with cues to practice activities in the Workbook.

the NEW edition

New Headway

Intermediate Teacher's Book

Liz and John Soars
Mike Sayer

OXFORD
UNIVERSITY PRESS

UNIVERSITY PRESS

Great Clarendon Street, Oxford OX2 6DP

Oxford University Press is a department of the University of Oxford.
It furthers the University's objective of excellence in research, scholarship,
and education by publishing worldwide in

Oxford New York

Auckland Bangkok Buenos Aires Cape Town Chennai
Dar es Salaam Delhi Hong Kong Istanbul Karachi Kolkata
Kuala Lumpur Madrid Melbourne Mexico City Mumbai Nairobi
São Paulo Shanghai Taipei Tokyo Toronto

Oxford and Oxford English are registered trade marks of
Oxford University Press in the UK and in certain other countries

© Oxford University Press 2003

The moral rights of the author have been asserted

Database right Oxford University Press (maker)

First published 2003
Third impression 2004

ISBN 0 19 4387534

Printed and bound in Hong Kong

Acknowledgements

The authors and publisher are grateful to those who have given
permission to reproduce the following extracts and adaptations of
copyright material:

p79 *Who Wants To Be A Millionaire?* Words and Music by Cole Porter © 1956
Buxton Hill Music Corp, USA. Warner/Chappell Music Ltd., London W6
8BS. Reproduced by permission of International Music Publications Ltd. All
Rights Reserved.
p123 *California Dreamin'.* Words & Music by John Phillips & Michelle
Phillips © Copyright 1965 Wingate Music Corporation, USA. Universal/
MCA Music Limited. Used By Permission Of Music Sales Limited. All Rights
Reserved. International Copyright Secured.
p124 *Why Does It Always Rain On Me?* Words by Francis Healy ©1998 Sony
Music Publishing. Reproduced by permission of Sony Music Publishing.

Photocopiable pages designed by Bryony Newhouse.

- **Reading and listening texts**

  These are generally shorter, yet still challenging. There is a great variety of preparation and comprehension tasks, all of which integrate much speaking practice, often personalised. The replacement texts generally have a more global feel, and try to reflect our changing world.

- **Writing**

  The development of the writing skill is now in a separate section at the back of the book. This comprises twelve complete writing lessons cued from the unit, but which can be used at the teacher's discretion. The writing syllabus itself is fuller, providing models for students to complete, adapt, and follow in order to produce a satisfying piece of writing.

  Throughout *New Headway Intermediate – the NEW edition*, students are required to draw from their own culture and experience to put topics and language into a personal context.

What's in the Teacher's Book?

- **Full teaching notes**, answers, and possible problems

- *Don't forget!* **section** which refers to relevant exercises in the Workbook, and to the Word list.

- **Tapescripts** in the main body of the teaching notes

- **Word list**

  There is a list of words that appear unit by unit in *New Headway Intermediate – the NEW edition*. Photocopy the Word list for each unit as you go through the book and give a copy to each of your students. It is probably best given towards the end of each unit as an aid to revision.

  Encourage students to write in the translation if they feel it is necessary.

- **Extra ideas and songs section** with notes on how to use them for use after Units 1–3, 4–6, 7–9, and 10–12. You will find the songs on the recording at the end of each section, i.e. at the end of Units 3, and 6.

- **Stop and check tests**

  There are four Stop and check revision tests which cover Units 1–3, 4–6, 7–9, and 10–12. These can either be set in class, or given for homework (preferably over the weekend) and then discussed in the next lesson. Students can work in small groups to try to agree on the correct answer, then you can go over it with the whole class, reminding students of the language items covered. It is important that, in the translation sentences which come at the end of each Stop and check test, students translate the ideas and concepts, and not word by word. There is an interactive version of the Stop and check tests online on the Student's website.

- **Progress tests**

  There are two progress tests, which cover Units 1–6, and 7–12.

What's in the Workbook?

The Workbook is an important component to the course as it revises the grammatical input of the Student's Book. Many of the exercises are on the Student's Workbook recording, for use in class or at home.

What's in the Teacher's Resource Book?

The Teacher's Resource Book contains photocopiable games and activities to supplement the main course material.

VIDEO

There is an optional accompanying video in two parts.

- A light-hearted drama in six episodes called *Wide Open Spaces*, about a couple who get tired of the town and try country life.
- Six short factual reports on a range of topics of general interest: seven wonders of Britain, crime writer Agatha Christie, WOMAD (the World Organization of Music and Dance), London taxi drivers, Rugby (one of the most famous public schools in Britain), and the importance of the sea for Britain.

Headway online

There is a teacher's website with additional materials for teachers: **www.oup.com/elt/teacher/headway**, and a student's site with interactive practice exercises for students and interactive versions of the Stop and check tests: **www.oup.com/elt/headway**.

Finally!

We actually try to guide students to an understanding of new language, rather than just have examples of it on the page. We attach great importance to practice activities, both controlled and free, personalized and impersonal. The skills work comes from a wide range of material – newspapers, magazines, biographies, short stories, radio programmes, songs – and features both British and American English. We hope you and your students enjoy using the books, and have success with them whether using *Headway* for the first time or having learned to trust its approach from previous use.

Tenses • Auxiliary verbs
Short answers • What's in a word?
Social expressions

It's a wonderful world!

Introduction to the unit

As you begin *New Headway Intermediate – the NEW edition,* you may be starting a new course with a new group of students. If so, make sure that everyone gets to know each other and you. Learn each other's names and find out a little bit about each other's backgrounds and interests.

One warm-up idea is to put students in pairs and ask them to interview each other until they find three things in common. Then ask one person in each pair to introduce him/herself and his/her partner to the class. For example, *I'm Jaime, this is Yoko, and we both like learning English, swimming, and watching old films.*

The *Test your grammar* section, which starts the unit, is designed to help students learn a little about each other as well as testing them on their use of auxiliary verbs.

The theme of the first unit is our world. The reading text is about the seven wonders of the modern world, and in the *Listening and speaking* section, three people discuss their ideas about modern wonders. The *Writing* section at the back of the book practises correcting mistakes in the context of a letter.

Language aims

It is often a good idea to remind yourself of the language in each unit before you prepare your lessons. One way you can do this is to read the appropriate *Grammar Reference* section at the back of the Student's Book. Many of the units contain an introduction to the grammar topic. These can be read before moving on to each specific point.

Grammar – auxiliary verbs   A global view is taken of the language in Unit 1 by focusing on the auxiliary verbs which help form the different tenses. This allows you to assess students' knowledge of familiar verb forms that can sometimes cause difficulty. In particular, we look at the Present Simple and Continuous, Past Simple and Continuous, Present Perfect Simple and Continuous, future forms, active and passive, and short answers. Expect students to make mistakes in all these areas at this level!

The emphasis in Unit 1 is on the formation of the tenses. All of them are revisited in later units and examined in greater depth to explore similarities and differences of meaning, and to provide extensive discriminatory practice.

Obviously there is some focus on meaning as well as form in Unit 1 because students are using language in context. But remember that you are reminding learners of what they should or might know, so when mistakes occur, don't try to teach the whole of the English language in the first few lessons.

Note that the passive voice is not dealt with in its own unit. It is presented along with the active equivalent in Units 2, 3, and 7. There is an introduction to the passive on p137 of the *Grammar Reference* section.

Question forms   Learners have perennial problems forming questions in English. They need to use an auxiliary verb, and if there isn't one in the statement, they need to use *do/be/have.* In many languages, questions can be formed simply with a rising intonation, but in nearly all questions in English, the subject and verb are inverted. There are a number of activities in Unit 1 that practise question formation.

Vocabulary   The exercises in the *Vocabulary* section are designed to make students think about how they learn vocabulary. It has exercises on guessing meaning, spelling and pronunciation, word formation and collocation, and keeping vocabulary records.

Everyday English   Various social expressions, some informal and some not, are introduced and practised. They have been selected in the hope that they will be used during the rest of the course, as normal day-to-day interactions that take place between all the people in the class. Encourage students to use some of them: *I'm sorry I'm late. I got stuck in traffic. I'm sick and tired of this weather. Take care.*

Remember that the *Everyday English* section can be used at any point in Unit 1.

Notes on the unit

TEST YOUR GRAMMAR (SB p6)

This *Test your grammar* section aims to get students talking to each other from the very beginning. It gives them an opportunity to get to know each other as they ask their partners the questions and talk about themselves. It also challenges students to form questions, which they often find difficult, and it tests students in their understanding and use of basic tenses, such as the Present Simple and Continuous, Present Perfect Simple and Continuous, and Past Simple.

POSSIBLE PROBLEMS
1 Students may still be very uncertain in their use of these tenses, particularly in forming questions. Reassure the student who says, 'I no understand present, past …' by saying 'Don't worry. That's why we're studying this book.'
2 Students often say *I born* or *borned* rather than the passive *I was born* …

1 Ask students to work individually to form the questions. Go round monitoring carefully to see how well students can use these forms and to help them with problems. When they have finished, ask them to check their answers in pairs.

Answers
2 Where were you born? When were you born?
3 Where do you live?
4 How many brothers and sisters have you got?
5 Why are you studying English?
6 How long have you been studying English?
7 Which countries have you been to?
8 When did you go to Canada?

To help students practise their pronunciation, you may want to say the questions and ask students to listen and repeat.

Get various students to ask you the questions, so you can check that they have formed them correctly. Answer the questions about *you*, so the new students can learn about their teacher.

As the students ask you the questions, correct their mistakes carefully, including pronunciation and intonation mistakes. Remember that *Wh-* questions must start high and then fall, for example:

Where do you come from?

A good way of prompting for self-correction is not to answer a question until it is formed correctly. You can help students by indicating the part of the sentence that isn't correct.

2 Students work in pairs to ask and answer the questions. Allow them plenty of time to get to know each other if they don't already. Go round monitoring and helping as necessary.

3 Ask one student to tell the class about his/her partner. Remind the class that they are now using the third person – *he* and *she*. Correct, but don't overcorrect because you don't want to spoil the flow. Students will probably be very interested to learn about each other.

Ask a few other students to do the same. If you have a large class, you probably won't be able to work with everyone. If that's the case, keep track of those who don't get a chance, so you can ask them the next time students contribute in front of the whole class.

As an optional homework activity, ask students to write a short biography of their partner.

WHAT DO YOU KNOW? (SB p6)

Tenses and auxiliary verbs

1 Put students in pairs or small groups to do the quiz. Encourage them to use dictionaries for unknown words. Or, if you prefer, check understanding of words such as *ray, leap, on stage,* and *assassinate* before they begin.

T 1.1 Students listen and check their answers.

Answers and tapescript
1 b
2 a
3 taking his first steps on the moon
4 b
5 meat
 Note: Some vegetarians do not eat fish either.
6 World Wide Web
7 b
8 five
9 c
10 b
11 because he was in prison for 27 years
12 b

Note: The basic email message *send-and-read* software was written in early 1972, and expanded later that year to become the largest network application for over a decade. This was the forerunner of the huge variety of 'people-to-people' traffic that we see on the Web today.

T 1.1
1 The modern Olympic Games started in 1896.
2 It takes eight minutes for the sun's rays to reach the Earth.
3 He was walking on the moon.
4 If you are flying over the International Date Line, the Pacific Ocean is below you.
5 A vegetarian doesn't eat meat.

6 www. stands for World Wide Web.
7 Glasses were invented in Italy around 1300 AD.
8 Brazil has won the World Cup five times.
9 John Lennon was returning to his apartment when he was assassinated.
10 Chinese is spoken by the most people in the world.
11 Nelson Mandela didn't become President of South Africa until he was 76 years old because he was in prison for 27 years.
12 People have been sending emails since the 1970s.

GRAMMAR SPOT (SB p7)

1 Ask students to look back at the quiz and find examples of the tenses. The aim here is diagnostic. Some students will know all of the tenses, some may know very few.

Answers
Present Simple: 2 does ... take; 3 that's; 4 is; 5 doesn't ... eat; 6 does ... stand for
Past Simple: 1 did ... start; 3 said; 11 didn't ... become, was
Present Perfect Simple: 8 has ... won
Present Continuous: 4 are flying
Past Continuous: 3 was ... doing; 9 was ... doing
Present Perfect Continuous: 12 have ... been sending
Present Simple passive: 10 is spoken
Past Simple passive: 7 were ... invented; 9 was assassinated

2 Ask students to find and underline the auxiliary verbs in the quiz. Then put them in pairs to discuss the questions.

Answers
We use *do/does/did* to make the question and the negative of the Present and Past Simple.
We use *have* to form the Present Perfect Simple and Continuous.
We use *be* to form the Present and Past Continuous and passive forms.

SUGGESTION
If you prefer to look at auxiliaries as a class, before doing Part 2 of the *Grammar Spot*, you could do the following.
Write seven sentences on the board, for example:
We <u>are</u> learning English.
English <u>is</u> spoken all over the world.
I <u>don't</u> like maths.
<u>Do</u> you smoke?
Why <u>didn't</u> you come to the party?
I <u>haven't</u> had anything to eat today.
What <u>does</u> your father do?

Ask students what is special about the underlined words. Ask if they mean anything. Elicit the fact that they are all auxiliary verbs. Ask *What do auxiliary verbs do?* (They help other verbs.) If you have a multilingual class and you suspect they don't know what an auxiliary verb is, get them to check the definition in their dictionaries.

Focus attention on *had* and *do* in the last two sentences. Ask *Are they auxiliary verbs?* (No).

Refer students to Grammar Reference 1.1–1.3 on SB pp134–135.

2 Put students in pairs or groups of four to think of some general knowledge questions. Write some categories on the board to get them started, for example, *History, Different countries, The natural world, Famous people, Sports, Food and drink*. Monitor and help.

When students are ready, mix the pairs or groups. If they prepared in groups of four, then mix two from one group with two from another. Ask them to ask and answer each other's questions.

PRACTICE (SB p7)

Negatives and pronunciation

The aim of this exercise is to practise forming the negative of various verb forms and to look at contrastive stress.

1 Read through the example as a class, then ask students in pairs to correct the information in the other sentences.

T 1.2 Students listen and compare their answers.

Ask three or four students to repeat the sentences.

The sun doesn't rise in the west! It rises in the east!

Exaggerate the stress pattern yourself, and encourage students to copy you. Repeat the process with some of the other sentences. Alternatively, play the recording and ask students to repeat.

Put students in twos or threes to practise saying the sentences. Go round monitoring and correcting. You may need to push students to get the correct stress.

Answers and tapescript
1 The sun doesn't rise in the west! It rises in the east!
2 Cows don't eat meat! They eat grass!
3 Mercedes-Benz cars aren't made in Canada! They're made in Germany!
4 Neil Armstrong didn't land on the moon in 1989! He landed in 1969!
5 John Lennon wasn't performing on stage when he was assassinated! He was returning to his apartment!
6 The Pyramids weren't built by the Chinese! They were built by the Egyptians!

7 We haven't been in class for five hours! We've been in class for one hour!

8 We aren't studying Italian! We're studying English!

Talking about you

2 Ask students in pairs to complete the questions. When they have finished, elicit the answers from the class. Help students with their pronunciation. Once a question is established, ask someone to direct the question to another student in the class, and get that student to answer with real information.

T 1.3 Students listen and check their answers.

Students ask and answer the questions in their pairs. Correct carefully.

Answers and tapescript

1 A What **did you** do last night?
  B I stayed at home and watched television.
2 A What kind of books **do you** like reading?
  B Horror stories and science fiction.
3 A **Have you** ever been to the United States?
  B Yes, I have. I went there last year.
  A **Did you** like it?
  B Yes, I really enjoyed it.
4 A What**'s** the teacher **doing**?
  B He's helping Maria with this exercise.
5 A **What does** your mother do?
  B She works in a bank.
6 A Why **didn't you** do your homework last night?
  B Because I didn't feel well.
7 A What **are you** doing next weekend?
  B I'm going to a party.
8 A **Have** you **got** a TV in your bedroom?
  B No, I haven't. Just a CD player.

is or *has*?

3 **T 1.4** Students listen to the recording and write *is* or *has* in the gaps. Play the recording again so that they can check their answers.

Answers and tapescript

1 is	4 has	7 is
2 is	5 has	8 has
3 is	6 is	

T 1.4

1 My sister's a teacher.
2 She's on holiday at the moment.
3 She's in France.
4 She's never travelled to Europe before.
5 She's been there for two weeks.
6 She's going back to work next week.
7 Her husband's a builder.
8 He's got his own business.

MAKING CONVERSATION (SB p8)

Short answers

Students will undoubtedly have come across short answers before but probably don't use them because they are too complicated. They require too much analytical thought to use correctly, by which time the moment has passed. Students won't be using them at the end of this lesson either! Short answers should come from a spontaneous, instinctive source, and this will only happen at a much later stage of language learning.

However, consciousness-raising is important. Most items of language are recognized long before they are produced. Short answers, along with reply questions and question tags, are a very important part of the language, especially the spoken language, and mastery will only come through extensive exposure.

1 Ask one or two students about the picture in the book: *Who are the people? What time is it?*, etc. Then focus students on the question *How does Emma feel?*

T 1.5 Play the recording. Ask students to read and listen to the conversation.

Sample answer

Perhaps Emma doesn't feel well or is bored with her father's questions. She gives short answers. She is quite rude.

2 **T 1.6** Ask students to listen to a similar conversation and identify the differences.

Sample answer

Emma's voice sounds a lot nicer, but she also uses short answers to sound more friendly and polite, rather than just saying *yes* and *no*.

3 Students work in pairs to complete the conversation.

T 1.6 Play the recording again so that students can check their answers.

Answers and tapescript

Dad Good morning! Did you have a nice time last night?
Emma Yes, **I did**. I went round to Bill's house.
Dad Do you want breakfast?
Emma No, **I don't**, thanks. I'm not hungry.
Dad Have you had any coffee?
Emma Yes, **I have**. I don't want any more, thanks.
Dad Is Bill coming round tonight?
Emma No, **he isn't**. He's going out for dinner with his family.
Dad OK. Are you leaving for school soon?
Emma Yes, **I am**. I'm going right now. Bye!

4 Give students two minutes to read the conversation and memorize as much as they can. Then tell them to close their books. Put students in pairs to see how much of the conversation they can remember.

1 Read the information about short answers as a class. Alternatively, write the first line of the mini-conversation on the board, and elicit the correct short answer. Point out that we use the auxiliary verb, not the full verb, in the short answer. Elicit extra information phrases from students. Some suggestions: *It was fantastic/awful/boring./ We won!/ We lost!*

2 Ask students in pairs to reply to the questions using short answers. Remind them that the auxiliary verb in the short answer must agree with the auxiliary verb in the question.

> **Sample answers**
> Yes, I have. My brother's 22, and my sister's 16.
> No, it isn't. It's quite warm.
> Yes, I am. I need a holiday.
> No, I didn't. I stayed in and watched TV.
> No, I haven't. But I've been to Tokyo.

Model the correct intonation pattern for the example conversation. Students listen and repeat. Point out that the question starts high and ends with a fall-rise, while the short answer falls.

Did you watch the match last night?   *Yes, I did.*

Ask students to practise the conversations in pairs. You could then get them to change partners. When you come together as a group, ask one or two pairs to repeat one of their conversations to the class. Alternatively, do the activity as a mingle – give each student one of the six questions to ask, and ask them to walk around the classroom starting short conversations with different people.

Refer students to Grammar Reference 1.4 on SB p135.

5 **T 1.7** Students listen and answer the questions with a short answer. This can be done orally or in writing.

> **Sample answers and tapescript**
> 1 Is it hot today? **Yes, it is./No, it isn't.**
> 2 Is it raining? **Yes, it is./No, it isn't.**
> 3 Are you wearing trainers? **Yes, I am./No, I'm not.**
> 4 Do you usually come to class by bus? **Yes, I do./No, I don't.**
> 5 Are you going out tonight? **Yes, I am./No, I'm not.**
> 6 Did you have a good day yesterday? **Yes, I did./No, I didn't.**
> 7 Have you got a dictionary? **Yes, I have./No, I haven't.**
> 8 Have you got any pets? **Yes, I have./No, I haven't.**

Conversations

1 Read through the example, then ask students in pairs to complete the exercise.

  T 1.8 Play the recording so that students can check their answers.

> **Answers and tapescript**
> 1 A Do you like studying English?
>   B Yes, I do. It's my favourite subject.
> 2 A Is it a nice day today?
>   B No, it isn't. It's freezing.
> 3 A Have you seen my pen?
>   B No, I haven't. You can borrow mine if you want.
> 4 A Are you staying at home this evening?
>   B Yes, I am. Do you want to come round?
> 5 A Did you go on holiday last summer?
>   B No, I didn't. I couldn't afford to.

Ask students to practise the conversations in pairs.

2 Read through the survey with students and ask them to think of two more *Yes/No* questions. Then give them a few minutes to think of what they are going to say in response to each question.

When they are ready, ask them to stand up and ask three other students the questions. Model the activity briefly by interviewing a strong student. Go round monitoring and correcting.

Getting information

This information-gap activity practises a wide range of question forms, and aims to develop students' fluency.

3 Read through the introduction as a class, and ask students if they know any famous people from their countries who have been Goodwill Ambassadors. Put students in **A** pairs or **B** pairs, and then ask **A** pairs to look at SB p151 and **B** pairs to look at SB p152. Ask students to read their passage carefully and work with their partner to make questions from the prompts. When students are ready, split the pairs so that there is an **A** student with a **B** student. Students then ask and answer questions to complete their information.

Monitor the activity closely and note any errors. In the class discussion, check that students have all the answers, and write any errors on the board for students to correct.

ADDITIONAL MATERIAL

Workbook Unit 1
Exercises 1–7 Auxiliary verbs
Exercise 8 *have/have got*

Wonders of the modern world

The aim of this reading exercise is to develop students' ability to read for gist and specific information, to expand vocabulary around the topic of discoveries and inventions, and to encourage lots of fluency-based speaking practice.

1   A good way of leading into the lesson is to write *Wonders of the modern world* on the board, and elicit as many wonders as students can think of. Give one or two examples of your own to get them started. Some ideas include television, mobile phones, and impressive modern architecture like the Petronas Towers in Kuala Lumpur.

Ask students to look at the chart, and check that they understand the topics in **A** by referring them to the photos. Ask students in pairs to match the topics in **A** with the items in **B**. Encourage them to use their dictionaries.

Answers
International travel: airlines, abroad
Medical science: health care, penicillin
The Internet: online, website
Agriculture: corn, famine
Space travel: solar system, galaxies
The Olympic Games: competition, drug abuse*

Drug abuse could, of course, go under medical science. Point out that there have been many recent cases of Olympic athletes abusing drugs to gain a physical advantage in their sports. You may want to explain that abusing drugs means using them for bad reasons.

2   Ask students to read the text quickly and match each paragraph with one of the topics in exercise 1. This is a reading for gist task, so students should be able to do it quickly without reading every word. Set a time limit of five minutes. In pairs, students compare their answers before going over the answers with the whole class.

Answers
1   The Internet
2   Space travel
3   Medical science
4   International travel
5   The Olympic Games
6   Agriculture

3   Read through the questions as a class, then ask students to work individually to find the answers in the text. Tell them to find the correct paragraph then look for the answer to the question in the paragraph. They should try to pick out specific pieces of information, not read the text word by word. Let them compare their answers in pairs before checking with the whole class.

Answers
1   The way we live and work. There will be more interactivity between the user and the website, and we will be able to give instructions using speech.
2   Space probes have been to Mars, Jupiter, Saturn, and the sun.
3   Average life expectancy has risen dramatically.
4   The number of people in aeroplanes at any one moment.
5   **Good:** a competition in which every country takes part, coming together in peace and friendship. We feel hope for the future.
   Bad: commercialization, greed, drug abuse.
6   Farmers grow food that feeds the world but politicians don't seem capable of making decisions which will prevent famine.
7   We haven't used nuclear weapons to destroy the world yet.
8   **100 million:** the yearly increase in the number of people who use the Internet
   a few hundred: the number of web pages in 1994
   1969: when Neil Armstrong walked on the moon
   millions of people: have benefited from aspirin
   47: average life expectancy worldwide in 1900
   four: the number of years between Olympic Games
   1709: when whole villages in France died of hunger
   50: the number of years we have had nuclear weapons

SUGGESTION

There are a number of words in the text that students may not know. Since the aim is to read for gist as well as specific information, there is no need to spend time explaining new words. However, if you want to do a vocabulary-in-context exercise to check the words, write the following on the board.

Find the word or phrase that means:
1   *goes up* (paragraph 1)
2   *completely changed* (paragraph 1)
3   *three terms for a machine that travels in space* (paragraph 2)
4   *a space machine that does not carry people* (paragraph 2)
5   *got something good from* (paragraph 3)
6   *small and unimportant* (paragraph 3)
7   *has gone up very fast* (paragraph 3)
8   *people guess* (paragraph 4)
9   *used to sell things and make money* (paragraph 5)

Answers
1 increases	5 benefited
2 revolutionized	6 humble
3 space capsule/probe/ observatory	7 has risen dramatically
4 space probe	8 It is estimated
	9 commercialized

Alternatively, design your own vocabulary matching exercise on a handout.

A FURTHER SUGGESTION

Here is an idea for more vocabulary work to revise and extend vocabulary about the topics.

Write the following words on the board, then ask students to decide which topics of the reading text they go with, for example *tractor* goes with *Agriculture*.

tractor	wheat	free time	combine harvester
rocket	marathon	moon	stadium
screen	towel	mouse	jet lag
operation	farm	CD-ROM	nurse
medal	surgeon	sprinter	planets
beach		antibiotic	program
		astronaut	

Answers

International travel: beach, towel, free time, jet lag
Medical science: operation, surgeon, antibiotic, nurse
The Internet: screen, mouse, CD-ROM, program
Agriculture: tractor, wheat, farm, combine harvester
Space travel: rocket, moon, astronaut, planets
The Olympic Games: medal, marathon, sprinter, stadium

Talking about you

4   Give students a few minutes to read through the questions and think of things to say. Let them make notes, but tell them not to write whole sentences.

Put students in groups of three or four to discuss the questions. It is a good idea to make one student the chairperson. It is the chairperson's job to ask other students the questions, make sure everyone has a chance to speak, and report on what people said in the whole-class discussion.

Monitor and listen, but don't correct too much. The aim here is fluency.

LISTENING AND SPEAKING (SB p12)

My wonders

1   Tell students that they are going to listen to three people of three different generations discussing their ideas about the wonders of the modern world. Read through the chart with the whole class. Ask which wonders they think Kelly and Peter will mention.

T 1.9   Students listen and complete the chart.

Answers and tapescript

	What is the wonder?	What's good about it?	Are there any problems?
Sam	dishwasher	It's marvellous. Every time you use a cup, etc. you just fill it up, turn it on, and it's clean.	Not really. Sadly, it doesn't tidy the rest of the house.
Kelly	mobile phones	You can call and text friends, and they can call and text you. If you need a lift or if you're going to be home late or if you're staying late at school you can let people/your parents know.	People use them too much. When people shout into the phone in a public place, it's really annoying. It's dangerous to use them when driving. Teachers go mad if they ring or beep in class.
Peter	the Internet and email	It's changed the world and business. Most business is done through email.	You're glued to the computer. People will forget how to communicate face to face.

T 1.9

K = Kelly   S = Sam   P = Peter

K We were doing the wonders of the world in school today. You know, the seven ancient wonders, the pyramids and such like and we got to talking about what modern wonders would be and well we all thought that …

S Huh! I know what the best modern wonder is for me. I know what's changed *my* life more than anything else …

P What's that, Dad?

S The dishwasher.

K Uh? What d'you mean – the dishwasher?

S I mean the dishwasher. I think it's marvellous! Every time I use something – cups, plates, dishes, knives, forks, you know, I just put it in, and after a few days it fills up, I turn it on and 'bingo' – all clean, bright and sparkling and I start again. Helps keep my kitchen tidy. I'm not very good at tidyi …

K Yeah, and the rest of the house is a mess! Come on Grandpa, be a bit more serious, we …

S I *am* serious!

K Well, anyway, *we* all said at school the very best thing was the mobile phone …

P I knew it!

S Huh! I don't even know how to use one.

K Oh, I couldn't live without mine. It's brilliant. I can call or text my friends all the time …

P Don't I know …

K ... from wherever I am and they can call or text me. Or if I need a lift from you or Mum ...

P You mean like when you need picking up from a friend's house in the evening?

K Yeah, that kind of thing ... or if I'm going to be home late, or like staying late at school or whatever – I can just let you and Mum know what's happening.

S OK, OK that's good, but the problem is that people use them too much for every little thing, you're never alone ...

K You're never alone with a mobile phone, you're never alone ...

P (laughs) All right, all right Kelly you can stop that. What *I* really hate is when people shout into them in public places and *everyone* has to listen to their boring conversations – you know the kind of thing – er 'Hello sweetheart, it's me. I'm on the train, you can put the dinner in the oven.'

S Sometimes it's not just boring, it's really dangerous, you know, when people use them when they're driving – I've seen lots of ...

K And teachers go absolutely mad if we forget to turn them off and they ring in class or you hear the 'beep' 'beep' 'beep' of a text message.

S I'll bet they do. Good manners certainly aren't a wonder of the modern world!

P Well, I have to say for me the most amazing wonder is an obvious one ... it's the Internet and email. It's changed the whole world and it's totally transformed *my* business. Everyone at work is always on the computer, checking emails, sending emails. It's where most of our business is done nowadays.

S Yeah, but the bad part is that you're glued to your computer all day – er I reckon people'll forget how to communicate face to face soon, it'll all be through machines. Just because you've got all these different ways to communicate doesn't mean there's any more to say! I'm glad I didn't have emails and texting in my day.

K Ah, but Grandpa, the way things are going, you'll probably be able to send messages through your dishwasher soon!

S Huh, not in my lifetime I hope!

Ask students to check their answers in pairs. Monitor to see how well they have completed the chart.

T 1.9 They will probably need to listen to the recording a second time.

During the feedback, ask whether students agree with any of the speakers' choices.

SUGGESTION

If students found the listening very difficult, it is a good idea to introduce some of the more demanding vocabulary before playing the recording a second time. Write on the board: *'Bingo!', go mad, glued to your computer, transform a business, face to face.* Check the meaning of the words, or ask students to check the words in their dictionaries, then ask which wonders these words may be used to describe.

---

2 Ask students in pairs to put the inventions in order of importance.

3 Match each pair of students with another pair, and ask them to work together to agree on the three most important inventions.

4 As a class, ask each group which they thought was the most and least important invention. Ask if they can think of any other machines, inventions, or discoveries they could add to the list.

VOCABULARY (SB p12)

What's in a word?

The aim here is to get students to think about how they learn vocabulary. Ask students how they record and remember new words. List their ideas on the board. Add your own ideas, or the suggestions below, to make a useful handout for students.

SUGGESTIONS

- Guess meaning from context: what part of speech is the word? What does it probably mean?

- Don't just translate words.

- Draw pictures in your book and label them.

- Record words in useful groups under topic headings like *Travel* or parts of speech headings like *Adjectives*.

- Write new words in personalized sentences so that you remember how to use them. Don't just write *interested*, write *I'm not interested in getting a job.*

- Write words that go together – collocations. For example, *delicious food.*

- Mark the stress in a word. For example, *computer.*

- Learn and use the phonetic symbols.

- Write new words on cards, with their definition or translation on the back, and keep them in a card filing system. Look at the first five cards every day. If you remember the words without looking on the back, put them at the back of the file. If you don't, keep them at the front.

- Write a handful of new words on pieces of paper, and carry them in your left pocket all day. Take them out and look at them. When you know them, put them in your right pocket.

- Design vocabulary tests. Find ten words or phrases that your teacher has taught in the last two or three weeks, and prepare questions to ask the other students. You could start the lesson by doing a vocabulary test with the other students. For example, you ask *When a plane arrives late at an airport, we say it is what?* The other students should write *delayed.*

Parts of speech and meaning

1 Start by writing a sentence with *uggy* on the board, for example, *I always have uggy for breakfast*. Ask students if *uggy* is a real word. Ask them if it is a noun, verb, or adjective. How do they know? Is it countable or uncountable? Is it likely to be food?

Ask students in pairs to look at the sentences and decide what part of speech *uggy*, or its related word, is in each case. Go over the answers with the class, then ask students to guess what *uggy* means in each sentence. Finally, let them match the real words with the nonsense words in the sentences. Students should have a good idea by now what the real words mean, although they might want to check them in a dictionary. Explain that they can use this idea not just with nonsense words but with any unknown words they come across when they are reading. They should try to guess meaning from part of speech and context, rather than just looking up words in their dictionaries.

Answers
1 A noun. It means *popcorn*.
2 A verb in the past. It means *skidded*.
3 An adverb. It means *passionately*.
4 An adjective. It means *hectic* (very busy).

Spelling and pronunciation

2 As an example, read out the four words in 1. Ask the students which word has a different vowel sound. Then ask students in pairs to read the words in each group aloud, and underline the vowel sound that is different. If your students are unfamiliar with phonetic symbols, refer them to the list and examples on SB p159.

T 1.10 Play the recording so that the students can check their answers.

Answers and tapescript
1 /ʊ/ or /uː/?
good <u>food</u> wood stood
2 /iː/ or /e/?
bread head <u>read</u> (present) read (past)
3 /eɪ/ or /e/?
paid made played <u>said</u>
4 /ʌ/ or /əʊ/?
done <u>phone</u> sun won
5 /eə/ or /ɪə/?
dear hear <u>bear</u> near
6 /ɜː/ or /ɔː/?
<u>work</u> fork walk pork

English spelling is not phonetic. The same combination of letters can be pronounced in different ways.

3 Do the first as an example, then ask students in pairs to read the phonetics aloud and write down the word.

T 1.11 Play the recording so that the students can check their answers.

Answers and tapescript
1 food   5 read
2 near   6 work
3 stood   7 phone
4 paid   8 walk

Word formation

4 Ask students in pairs to complete the sentences. In the feedback, point out that a good way to increase vocabulary is to think about how words can be formed by using prefixes and suffixes. You could extend this activity by giving students other verbs and asking them to look in their dictionaries and find out how many words they can make.

Answers
1 act**or**   3 act**ion**   5 act**ivities**
2 act**ive**   4 **Act**ing

Words that go together

5 Ask students in pairs to match the words. As you discuss the answers, ask students if they can think of any other collocations.

Answers
strong coffee   film star   fall in love
full-time job   drive carefully try on a jumper

Keeping vocabulary records

6 The aim here is to have a brief class discussion and to share ideas about how to record vocabulary.

Put students in small groups to show each other their vocabulary notebooks (if they have one), and to tell each other what methods they use to record words. In the feedback, ask which methods they would like to borrow from other people in their group.

You may wish to elicit the following ideas, or copy them on to a handout for your students to refer to.

ORGANIZING A VOCABULARY NOTEBOOK

- Record words in groups. The two most common ways of grouping are *topics* and *parts of speech*. So, one page of your notebook might be headed *Sport*, the next page *Adjectives to describe people*, etc.

- Leave space at the bottom of each page so you can add new words or phrases as you come across them.

- Devote a regular time when you transfer new words into your notebook. Think about which words you remember, and which you need to check in your dictionary. Don't write in words you already know, or words that you don't think you need to learn.

- Try to organize words visually, rather than just using translation. So, draw pictures and label them, draw spidergrams so you can see how words connect.
- Make the pages of your vocabulary notebook interesting and therefore memorable by using different coloured pens, and pictures and diagrams.
- Enjoy writing in your vocabulary notebook. Treat it like your diary, not like homework.
- Think about how best to record the meaning, use, and pronunciation of a word or phrase. Look at these examples:

rugby = a sport played with an oval ball (*definition*)

cȧterpillar = *bruco* (*translated with stress marked*)

I'm looking forward to <u>going</u> on holiday soon. I can't wait! (*example sentence showing meaning in context with* going *underlined to show that* look forward to *is followed by* -ing).

cosy = warm, comfortable, e.g. a cosy cottage/flat/fire/sofa/bed (*synonyms and collocations*)

ADDITIONAL MATERIAL

Workbook Unit 1
Exercise 9 Vocabulary – Word formation
Exercise 10 Vocabulary – Words that go together
Exercise 11 Vocabulary – Grammar words
Exercise 12 Pronunciation – Word stress
Exercise 13 Pronunciation – Phonetic script

WRITING (SB p103)

Correcting mistakes (1)

This exercise introduces students to symbols commonly used to point out errors in written work. The aim of using them is to pinpoint errors in a piece of work, thus prompting the student to self-correct. This exercise should get students to think about the sort of errors they make, and to take responsibility for editing and correcting their own work.

1 Read through the symbols as a class and make sure the students understand them. Then ask the students to read the letter and correct the mistakes. Ask them to check in pairs before checking with the whole class. You may wish to copy the answers below on to an OHT or handout.

Answers

> 23, St. Mary's Road,
> Dublin 4,
> Ireland
> Tuesday, 10 May

Dear Stephanie

How are you? I'm very well. I came **to** Dublin two weeks ago **to** study at a language school. I want **to** learn **English** because **it** is a very important language. I'm **staying** with **an** Irish family. They've got two **sons** and a daughter. Mr Kendall is **a** teacher, and Mrs Kendall **works** in a hospital. The Irish **are** very kind, but they speak very quickly!

I study in the morning. My **teacher's** name is Ann. She **told** me that my English is OK, but I **make** a lot of mistakes. Ann **doesn't** give us too much homework, so in the afternoons I **always go** sightseeing. Dublin is much **bigger** than my town. I like **painting very much**, and I'm very **interested in** modern art, so I visit galleries and museums. I've met a girl called Martina. She **comes** from Spain, and (she) **goes** to Trinity College. Last night we **went** to the cinema, but the film wasn't very **exciting**.

Would you like to visit me? Why don't you come for a weekend?

I'd love to see you.

Write to me soon.

Love,

Kati

2 Ask students in pairs to answer the questions.

Answers

1 She is in Dublin. She is staying with the Kendalls, an Irish family.
2 She is studying English at a language school.
3 She studies in the morning, and goes sightseeing in the afternoon.
4 She goes sightseeing, and she visits galleries and museums.
5 She has met Martina.

3 Prepare the students for the writing task in 4 by asking them to imagine that they are a student in another town and to answer the questions in 2. Make sure they write full sentences, which they can use when they write their letter.

4 Ask the students to write a similar letter to the model to a friend back home. This exercise could be set up in class and done for homework.

SUGGESTION

Sometimes, before students hand in homework, ask them in pairs to swap their work. They should try and find mistakes in their partner's work and use the correction symbols if they can. Ask them to write in pencil rather than pen, as they might make another mistake!

EVERYDAY ENGLISH (SB p13)

Social expressions

The aim of this section is to introduce students to useful expressions for actual classroom use. Expressions will be used for the rest of the course. Students will sometimes be late, buy new clothes, arrange to meet outside class, etc. With a little encouragement from you, these expressions could be used naturally and appropriately on many occasions in day-to-day interactions.

1 Read the introduction as a class. Explain that *Hang on a sec* and *I need to go to the loo* are informal and familiar expressions that are used when with friends.

Ask students in pairs to match a line in **A** with a line in **B**. This is more difficult than it seems. Some students will think that this is an easy exercise and race through it. Monitor and check their answers. If there are mistakes, tell them how many there are without saying what they are.

T 1.12 Students listen and check their answers.

Answers and tapescript
1 A Sorry I'm late. I got stuck in traffic.
   B Never mind. You're here now. Come in and sit down.
2 A Bye, Mum! I'm off to school now.
   B Take care, my love. Have a nice day!
3 A Have you heard that Jenny's going out with Pete?
   B Really? I don't know what she sees in him!
4 A How long did it take you to do the homework?
   B Ages! How about you?
5 A I don't know about you, but I'm sick and tired of this weather.
   B So am I. I can't stand all this rain.
6 A Who was that I saw you with last night?
   B Mind your own business!
7 A I'm tired. I'm taking next week off.
   B That sounds like a good idea. The break will do you good.
8 A Let's go for a run in the park!
   B Me? Run? You must be joking!
9 A Can we get together this afternoon at 3.00?
   B I'm sorry. I can't make it then. What about a bit later?
10 A What a gorgeous coat! Was it expensive?
   B Yes, it cost a fortune!

Go over any problems. Ask students to memorize some of the conversations, then practise them in pairs with their books closed.

2 **T 1.13** Play the recording. Students listen to the sentences and reply using one of the lines from **B** in exercise 1.
A good way to do this is to play a sentence, pause the recording, and nominate two or three individuals to reply.

Sample answers and tapescript
1 A I'm taking this Friday and next Monday off. We're going away for a long weekend.
   B That sounds like a good idea. The break will do you good.
2 A Can we meet at about 7 o'clock?
   B I'm sorry. I can't make it then. What about a bit later?
3 A I'm really sorry I'm late. I overslept.
   B Never mind. You're here now. Come in and sit down.
4 A John's going to take Sue to the party next week.
   B Really? I don't know what he sees in her.
5 A Dad, how much do you earn?
   B Mind your own business!

3 Read through the example with the class, then put students in new pairs to choose one or two of the conversations in exercise 1 and continue them. Monitor and prompt, but the aim is fluency, so don't correct too much. Ask one or two pairs to act out their conversations for the class at the end.

Don't forget!

Workbook Unit 1
Exercise 14 Verb + preposition
Word list
Photocopy the Word list for Unit 1 (TB p154) for your students. Ask them to write in the translations, learn them at home, and/or write some of the words in their vocabulary notebooks.

Present tenses • Simple or continuous?
Passive • Sport • Numbers and dates

Get happy!

Introduction to the unit

The theme of this unit is happiness. The topic provides suitable contexts for practising the main linguistic aim of the unit: the use of the present tenses. The focus is not only on the differences between the Present Simple and Continuous but also on state verbs which cannot be used in the continuous. The topic allows for practice of present active versus present passive.

The reading text is about a clown doctor. In the *Vocabulary and listening* section, students listen as three people describe why they like a particular sport or activity. There are many opportunities for both controlled and free speaking practice throughout the unit.

The *Writing* section at the back of the book practises beginning and ending letters and emails.

Language aims

Grammar – present states and actions   At this level students should be familiar with the forms and most of the uses of the Present Simple and Continuous. The assumption is that work on these tenses will be revision; therefore the tasks are quite challenging, and there are many opportunities for students to offer their own explanations of form and use. The language is introduced through a text about a lawyer's lifestyle in which students are asked to recognize and manipulate the form, in particular looking at auxiliary verbs used to form questions, negatives, and passives. This is followed by activities to contrast the use of the Present Simple and Continuous and focus students' attention on state verbs, such as *understand* and *like*.

> **POSSIBLE PROBLEMS**
>
> Intermediate students often feel they already fully 'know' the Present Simple and Continuous. In practice, however, they still make frequent mistakes when trying to use them. The aim here is to overcome any complacency or resistance by challenging students to 'show off' their knowledge in the *Discussing grammar* sections before exploring new language, such as action versus state verbs and the passive.
>
> The main form problem here is the use of *does* in the third person when forming questions and negatives. The pronunciation of *do* and *does* in questions is worth drilling and practising. In terms of use, trying to choose which of the two tenses to use is often difficult. Stick with the basic rule that we use the Present Simple to talk about something that is always true (states and facts) or happens repeatedly (habits), and we use the Present Continuous to talk about something that is in progress and not yet finished (even if it is not occurring at the moment of speaking) or something that is happening now. Students at this level usually know these rules. The confusion comes when the use in their language is different. This is particularly true with state verbs like *understand. *Are you understanding me?* seems quite logical because it is talking about now. The exception posed by state verbs is covered comprehensively in the unit.
>
> If you have a monolingual class, it is often a good idea to make a list of common errors made with these tenses. You can give students your list of typical errors and ask them to correct them. Why not have a class discussion on how present tenses are used in your students' language and in English?

Vocabulary   The main lexical area is sport and leisure. The task encourages students to use their dictionaries to extend their vocabulary in their chosen sports and leisure activities.

Everyday English Students always make mistakes with numbers, so the recognition and production of a variety of these is reviewed here.

Notes on the unit

TEST YOUR GRAMMAR (SB p14)

This activity is designed to find out how much your students know about the use of present tenses in English. It is an opportunity for you and them to find out how much work needs to be done and in which areas.

Ask students to work in pairs. Emphasize that you want them to do the exercise quickly. You may want to set a time limit. Go through the answers with the whole class, asking for the correct answer and a brief explanation from different pairs.

Do not give lengthy explanations as to why the sentences are correct or incorrect. If students have questions, tell them that you are going to be studying these tenses later in the lesson. Also, don't worry about how your students give their explanations as long as they have the correct general idea.

Answers
1 *They have a teenage son* is correct. *Have* = possession is a state verb and cannot be used in the continuous.
2 *She speaks five languages* is correct. *She's speaking five languages* is impossible – you can't speak five languages at the same time!
3 *Don't turn off the TV! I'm watching it* is correct. The watching is happening at this moment. *I watch it* means that you do this regularly, habitually. It is incorrect in this context.
4 *Oh no! It's raining!* is correct. It's raining now, at the moment. *It rains* is used to describe typical weather for a place or season, e.g. *It never/often/always rains here in winter*.
5 *We think opera is boring* is correct. *Think* = opinion is a state verb and cannot be used in the continuous. You can use *think* in the Present Continuous when it is something that is happening now, for example *I'm thinking about my girlfriend*; *I'm thinking of going to Spain on holiday*.
6 *English is spoken all over the world* is correct. *People speak English* is also possible, but *English* itself can't speak, and so must be used passively.

Present tenses

1 Lead in by asking students *What makes people happy?* Elicit ideas and write them on the board. Then ask students to look at the list of 'ingredients' in the Student's Book. Check that they understand vocabulary (*supportive* = helpful and sympathetic). Then ask students to give each 'ingredient' a grade between 1 and 5. Let them compare their answers in pairs before checking briefly with the whole class.

Answers
Students' own answers.

2 Focus attention on the pictures. Elicit vocabulary to describe the ages shown, for example, *child/childhood, teenager/youth/adolescence, middle-aged person/middle age, senior citizen/old age/retirement*.

Ask questions to get them talking, for example *Who looks happiest? What's good/bad about being a teenager/an adult/elderly?*

Alternatively, put students in groups of three to look at the pictures and discuss the questions in the book. In the feedback, find out who thinks which age is the happiest. If you have a class of mixed ages, you could ask students to tell each other what's so great about being their age.

3 Ask students to look at the pictures of Sidney Fisk. Ask what they can predict about his lifestyle.

T 2.1 Play the recording and ask students to read the text as they listen. (Note: An *interior designer* is a person whose job it is to plan the colour, style, and furnishing for the inside of a house.)

SUGGESTION
We often suggest that students read and listen at the same time because many of them appreciate the reinforcement that each skill gives to the other. However, you should feel free to vary the procedure to suit your class. You might want your students to listen first, then read, or simply to read without listening at all. It is up to you.

Ask students in pairs to discuss the questions, then have a whole-class discussion.

Possible answers
1 **Good:** well paid, travels, married with a family, beautiful big house, busy.
  Bad: doesn't see his children much, often away from home, not much time to relax, too busy.
2, 3 Students' own answers

The aim here is to review the form of the Present Simple and Continuous in a student-centred recognition exercise. It focuses on the way auxiliary verbs are used. It should be an opportunity for students to show off some grammatical knowledge.

1 Ask students to work individually to find the words in the text.

Answers
1 They are all adverbs of frequency.

2–3 Check that students remember what an auxiliary verb is, then put them in pairs to work through the questions. Write the answers on the board, with some examples provided by students, and go over them with the whole class.

Answers
2 The Present Simple. The verbs are mostly in this tense because the general lifestyle and daily habits of Sidney Fisk are being described.
3 Present Continuous: *He's working in Mexico. He's travelling to France.*
Present Simple passive: *He's paid very well. ... his time is spent ... .* The auxiliary verb *be* is used to form the passive.

4 Do the first as an example, then put students in pairs to complete the questions and answers.

Answers
a **Does** he travel a lot? Yes, he **does**.
b **Does** she work in a bank? No, she **doesn't**.
c **Do** they play golf? Yes, they **do**.
d **Do** you play tennis? No, I **don't**.
e **Is** he paid a lot? Yes, he **is**.
f **Is** he working in France at the moment? No, he **isn't**.

Refer students to Grammar Reference 2.1 and 2.2 on SB pp135–136.

4 Ask students to complete the questions individually and then check in pairs. Monitor and help as much as possible at this stage. Ask students to practise asking and answering the questions. Students will have to remember or refer to the passage to answer correctly. Monitor and correct all errors here.

T 2.2 When students are ready, play the recording so that they can check their answers. You may want to play the recording a second time and ask your class to listen and repeat. The pronunciation of *does he?* /ˈdəzi/ is particularly difficult.

Answers and tapescript
1 **Is he** married? **Yes, he is.**
2 What **does he** do? **He's a lawyer.**
3 Where **does he** live? **In a big house in Dallas, Texas.**
4 Has **he got** any children? **Yes, he's got two.**
5 What **does** his wife do? **She's an interior designer.**
6 Which sports **does he** play? **He sometimes plays golf.**
7 Where **is he** working at the moment? **In Mexico.**
8 **Is he** paid very well? **Yes, he is.**

5 The activity now changes from practice of the third person to practice of the first and second persons. Give students a few minutes to work in their pairs to prepare some questions. Tell them they can use the ideas in exercise 4, or use their own ideas for questions.

IDEAS FOR OTHER QUESTIONS
- How do you relax after work/school?
- How much do you spend per week? (You could review *Mind your own business!* in response to this. See Unit 1 *Everyday English* SB p13.)
- What do you do at the weekend/at weekends?
- How often do you go on holiday?
- How often do you do homework?

Model the activity with a strong student by asking three or four questions from exercise 4. Put students in new pairs to ask each other the questions. Then ask some students to briefly describe their partners to the class.

Alternatively, you could do this as a mingle. Set a time limit. Students walk around the room, asking as many people as possible.

ADDITIONAL MATERIAL

Workbook Unit 2
Exercises 1–4 Present Simple
Exercise 5 Pronunciation – *-s* at the end of a word

PRACTICE (SB p16)

Listening and speaking

This section further compares and contrasts the uses of the Present Simple and the Present Continuous in a series of accuracy-focused speaking and writing activities.

1 Before you play the recording, ask students to look at the headline and the photos and describe Jeff Norman's lifestyle. Ask *What do you think he does? Do you think he likes his job?* You could compare the pictures of Jeff Norman with those of Sidney Fisk. They are exactly the same age. *Do they look similar? Do they have the same jobs? What's Jeff's job?*

Pre-teach new vocabulary from the listening by writing the following on the board and asking students to say how they might be part of Jeff's lifestyle: *tips, joggers, a marriage counsellor.*

T 2.3 Play the recording. Students listen and answer the questions.

Answer and tapescript

He's a 45-year-old man with a college (UK = university) degree who works as a paperboy, a job that is usually done by teenagers.

T 2.3

People think it's a joke that a man my age with a college degree is a paperboy! But, hey, it's great. I'm paid good money – $60,000 a year for four hours' work a day. On top of that I often get $50 a week in tips. Not bad!

My job isn't easy. I get up at 2.00 a.m. every day, seven days a week. The first newspaper is delivered at 2.30 a.m. I finish four hours, 65 miles, and 1,000 newspapers later. I drive a red Chevy Blazer and the newspapers are packed into the back.

I love the peace and quiet in the early morning. Most of the time I have the world to myself. Occasionally, I meet a jogger. I usually get back home by 7.00 a.m. Then I have the rest of the day to be with my family and do what I want.

I have two teenage children and my wife works at the University of Iowa. Some days I coach my kids' baseball team, other days I play golf. I'm also studying for my master's degree at the moment. I want to be a marriage counsellor eventually, but I'm not in a hurry. I'm enjoying life too much. Some people think it's not much of a job but, hey, when they're sitting in an office, I'm playing golf! So I ask you – who has the better life?

2 Ask students in pairs to try to remember what Jeff said and to complete the sentences.

T 2.4 Play the recording. Tell your students to listen carefully to check their answers. Make sure they write the exact words that Jeff uses. You may need to pause the recording to give students time to write. Ask them to compare their answers with a partner's.

Answers and tapescript

1 **I'm paid** good money – $60,000 a year. And I often **get** $50 a week in tips.
2 I **get up** at 2.00 a.m. The first newspaper **is delivered** at 2.30 a.m.
3 I **drive** a red Chevy Blazer and the newspapers **are packed** into the back.
4 I **love** the peace and quiet.
5 Occasionally, I **meet** a jogger.
6 I usually **get back** home by 7.00 a.m.
7 My wife **works** at the University of Iowa.
8 Some days I **coach** my kids' baseball team, other days I **play** golf.
9 I'm also **studying** for my master's degree at the moment. I **want to** be a marriage counsellor.

10 Some people **think** it's not much of a job, but, hey, when they**'re sitting** in an office, I**'m playing** golf.

3 Give students a few minutes to write notes about Sidney and Jeff in the chart. Ask them to try to remember as much as they can, then look back to the passage about Sidney on SB p15 and the sentences about Jeff on SB p16 to check their work. Alternatively, you could put students in pairs, and ask one student to write about Sidney while the other writes about Jeff.

Answers

	Sidney Fisk	**Jeff Norman**
Work	lawyer; works for international company; paid well; travels a lot	paperboy; makes $60,000 a year; works 7 days a week; gets up 2 a.m.; starts work 2.30 a.m. and gets home 7.00 a.m.; wants to be marriage counsellor
Home and family	married; two children, 11 and 14; rarely sees children; beautiful big house; wife is interior designer	spends most of day with family; married; two teenage children
Free time	not much free time; plays golf with wife at weekends	lots of free time; coaches kids' baseball team; plays golf; studying for master's degree

Ask students in pairs to make sentences comparing the lifestyles of the two men. Introduce one or two useful expressions to help them compare. Write on the board:

Sidney is a lawyer, <u>but</u> Jeff is a paperboy.

<u>Both</u> *Sidney <u>and</u> Jeff play golf.*

They <u>both</u> play golf.

Jeff is happi<u>er</u> <u>than</u> Sidney.

WHAT DO YOU DO? (SB p17)

Simple or continuous?

This section provides controlled speaking practice in contrasting the Present Simple and Present Continuous.

1 **T 2.5** Write two general comprehension questions on the board: *What does she do? What's she doing at the moment?* Then play the recording and elicit answers to the questions. Play the recording again, and ask students to read and listen at the same time.

Put students in pairs and give them a few minutes to practise and memorize the dialogue. Then ask them to close their books and see how much they can remember. It can be both challenging and satisfying for students to memorize occasionally, especially for stress and intonation practice. Monitor the pairs as they practise, and correct any errors, especially in the use and pronunciation of the tenses.

2 This is a semi-controlled roleplay. Check that students know all the jobs. Ask them in their pairs to choose two or three and make up conversations similar to that in exercise 1. Monitor and correct or just note errors. Then ask selected pairs to roleplay their conversations for the whole class.

3 This personalized activity can be short. Put students in small groups to find out about each other, or let students walk around the room, talking to several different partners.

Students could write some of the conversations for homework.

GRAMMAR SPOT (SB p17)

The aim here is to explore some of the verbs that cannot be used in the continuous.

1–2 Read 1 and 2 to the class. Ask students to give you more examples of action and state verbs.

3 Look together at the example. Students underline the other six state verbs, then check with a partner. Monitor and help.

> **Answers**
> <u>like</u> <u>know</u> <u>understand</u> work enjoy <u>think</u> (= opinion)
> come play <u>have</u> (= possession) <u>love</u> <u>want</u>

NOTE
The fact that *enjoy* is an action verb can seem strange to students, especially as *like* is not. You may need to point out that *like* expresses an opinion, *I like parties*, but with *enjoy* you can be active in an experience, *I enjoy parties*, and *I'm enjoying this party very much*. Note that *think* is an action verb when it is a thought process, *I'm thinking about my holiday*, and *have* is an action verb when it describes an activity, *I'm having lunch*.

Refer students to Grammar Reference 2.3 on SB p136.

PRACTICE (SB p17)

Discussing grammar

This is the first *Discussing grammar* section in *New Headway Intermediate – the NEW edition*. In these activities, encourage students to work things out for themselves and revise what they already know.

1 Go through the examples as a class, then ask students to work individually to complete the exercise. Monitor and help. Ask students to check their work in pairs before going through the answers as a class.

> **Answers**
> 3 ✗ I love you a lot.
> 4 ✓
> 5 ✗ I'm sorry. I don't know the answer.
> 6 ✓
> 7 ✗ I think you speak English very well.
> 8 ✓

2 Ask students to work individually to complete the pairs of sentences. Monitor and help. Ask them to check their work in pairs, then go over the answers as a class. This exercise could also be given for homework and discussed in the next class.

> **Answers**
> 1 They **come** from Paris.
>   They**'re coming** by car.
> 2 She**'s having** dinner now.
>   She **has** (= possession) a beautiful new car.
> 3 I **think** (= opinion) that all politicians tell lies.
>   **I'm thinking** about my girlfriend at the moment.
> 4 We**'re not enjoying** this party at all.
>   We **don't enjoy** big parties.
> 5 Be quiet! I**'m watching** my favourite programme.
>   I always **watch** it on Thursday evenings.
> 6 He**'s seeing** (= visiting) the doctor at the moment.
>   I **see** (= understand) your problem, but I can't help you.
> 7 This room **is** usually **used** for big meetings.
>   But today it **is** being **used** for a party.

ADDITIONAL MATERIAL

Workbook Unit 2
Exercises 6 and 7 Present Simple and/or Present Continuous
Exercises 8 Adverbs of frequency

READING AND SPEAKING (SB p18)

I'm a clown doctor!

The aim of this section is to develop students' ability to read for gist and specific information, to introduce the

Present passive, and to practise further the Present Simple and Present Continuous.

The first two exercises set the scene, create interest in the topic, and introduce key vocabulary.

1 Elicit one or two suggestions from students of what doctors and clowns do. Then put students into groups of three or four and give them a few moments to make their lists. Ask each group to tell the class their ideas. Build up a full list of ideas on the board. You could get half the groups to think about what doctors do, and half to think about what clowns do.

Sample answers
(Note that other possible answers are in the answers for exercise 2 below)
Doctors: treat patients, take your temperature, give advice on general health, prescribe medicine
Clowns: make people laugh, entertain people

2 Ask students in their groups, or in pairs, to match the phrases in the box with clowns or doctors. You could let the students use a dictionary for this, although it is often a good idea to get them to guess first. One student usually has a good idea what each phrase means, and encouraging them to guess meaning and explain words to each other is part of the learning process. In the feedback, you could check most of these words with a mime. For example, check *give injections* by pretending to use a syringe.

Answers
Clowns: wear funny clothes, make children feel better, wear red rubber noses, tell jokes, do magic tricks, make funny faces
Doctors: make children feel better, perform operations, wear white coats, give injections, give medicine

3 Ask students to look at the pictures and predict what a clown doctor does.

4 Ask students to read the introduction and answer the focus question.

Answer
Laughter

5 Ask students to read the rest of the article. Then in pairs to answer the comprehension questions. Encourage them to look again at the article to find the answers.

Answers
1 Lucy is Dr LooLoo. Dr Chequers is her colleague.
2 They make funny faces, tell jokes and do magic tricks. They blow bubbles, shake hands with the kids and make up nonsense songs. They take special balloons to make 'balloon animals' and tell funny stories.

3 She's always been a clown. She worked with her father, who was a clown, when she was eight.
4 It's a great way to cheer up sick, frightened children in hospital.
5 She wears a fancy coat, a yellow shirt and tights with big stripes. She has a red rubber nose and wears her hair in crazy plaits.
6 Showing your feelings.
7 Because they meet the nurses and doctors, and they tell them about particular kids who they think will benefit from a clown doctor visit.
8 Sometimes she has a night out with friends, to unwind.
9 The *Theodora Children's Trust*. It's a charity; so she is paid with the money people give.
10 She arrives in the hospital with her colleague, Dr Chequers. Then she goes into the wards and meets the children. She makes funny faces, tells jokes, and does magic tricks. She blows bubbles, shakes hands with the kids, and makes up nonsense songs for them. At lunchtime she eats in the hospital cafeteria where she meets the nurses and doctors. At about six o'clock she takes off her make-up and changes her clothes. Sometimes she has a night out with friends. When she falls into bed, she crashes out.

GRAMMAR SPOT (SB p18)

1 Ask students to complete the sentences by looking back at the text and finding the missing words.

Answers
All over the world, children in hospital **are being treated** with a new kind of medicine.
It's a charity; so we **are paid** with the money people give.
The first sentence is the Present Continuous passive. The second sentence is the Present Simple passive.
Check the form:
... are being treated ...   *be* + *-ing* + past participle
... are paid ...   *be* + past participle

2 Ask students in pairs to complete the passive sentences.

Answers
1   Clowns **are loved** by people of all ages.
2   She's **being** given an injection.

Refer students to Grammar Reference 2.4 on SB p137.

Language work

6 Ask students in pairs to find the vocabulary in context. Encourage them to guess first. They can check in their dictionaries later. These are likely to be difficult phrases for your students – they only need to be understood passively at this level.

Answers

1 They're racing about yelling.
2 I'm naturally a very cheerful person.
3 We'd be useless.
4 She's always on my mind.
5 I have a night out with friends.
6 It helps me unwind.
7 I fall into bed and crash out.
8 I feel privileged to do this job.

7 The aim here is to use the reading as a springboard for further practice of the Present Simple and Present Continuous. If you don't think your students need any further guided work in this area, you could move straight on to the *What do you think?* section that follows.

Ask students in pairs to complete the interviewer's questions. They may need to look back at the text.

T 2.6 Play the recording. The full interview is recorded so that students can develop their listening skills whilst checking their answers. Ask them to listen and find out if their questions are exactly the same as on the recording. Answer any questions.

Sample answers and tapescript

I = Interviewer   L = Lucy

I Do you like your job?
L Oh yes, I do. I enjoy my job very much.
I Why do you like it so much?
L Because I love working with children and making them laugh.
I What do you wear to work?
L I wear crazy clothes. A fancy coat and stripy tights.
I Who are you working with now? Anyone special?
L Well, at the moment I'm working with a very sick little girl from Bosnia. She's had so many operations. She's very special to me.
I Does she speak any English?
L No, she doesn't. We communicate through laughter.
I Isn't it tiring?
L Yes, it is. It's very tiring indeed. I'm exhausted at the end of each day.
I What do you do in the evenings? Do you just go home and relax?
L No, I don't. I often go out with friends. I have the best friends and the best job in the world.

What do you think?

Round off the lesson with a personalized discussion on happiness and lifestyles. Give students a few minutes to read the questions and think about what they are going to say. Then put them in groups of three or four to discuss. You could make one person group leader – they have to ask the questions and make sure everybody has a chance to speak. You could make another student secretary – they have to write brief notes about what each person says, and report on what was said to the class at the end.

ADDITIONAL MATERIAL

Workbook Unit 2
Exercises 9 and 10 Present passive

VOCABULARY AND LISTENING (SB p20)

Sport and leisure

1 Start the lesson by brainstorming all the sports and activities your students can think of and writing them on the board. Then put students in pairs or threes to look at the pictures and add to their lists.

2 Ask students in pairs to decide whether the sports go with *play*, *go*, or *do*. Check the answers with the whole class.

Answers

go snowboarding	play golf	do yoga
do aerobics	go jogging	go mountain biking
play volleyball	play basketball	
go fishing	play football	

The rules are as follows:
• We use *play* with a game which uses a ball, often in teams.
• We use *go* with a sporting activity, ending in *-ing*.
• We use *do* with a sporting activity, often an exercise activity, not ending in *-ing*.
Note that there are some exceptions to these rules. For example, *do boxing*.

3 Ask students to fill in the chart. Encourage them to choose sports that most interest them. You may need to go round and help them use their dictionaries and sometimes for speed give them the words yourself. Be careful with the timing of this activity. If it goes on too long your students may become overloaded with new vocabulary. It is a good idea to leave enough time for them to be able to tell you and each other a bit about their chosen sports.

4 Introduce the activity by focusing the students on the photographs and asking which sports or activities they are. You could pre-teach some vocabulary by asking students to tell you what equipment is needed for each. Try to elicit the following:
aerobics: *trainers, music*
skiing: *skis, boots, poles, ski suit, goggles, socks, gloves*
football: *shorts, shirt, football boots, shin pads, tracksuit*

T 2.7 Play the recording. Ask students to listen and take notes about Mary, Jenny, and Thomas.

Alternatively, if you have three recorders and enough room, you can do this as a jigsaw activity. Divide the class into three groups and ask each group to listen to one person, answer the questions and then swap information with the other groups. Round off the activity by playing all three to the whole class.

Answers and tapescript

	Mary	Jenny	Thomas
1 Which sport/ activity … ?	aerobics	skiing	football
2 How often do they do it?	once a week on Thursday mornings	once or twice a year for two weeks	Friday evenings and Sunday mornings. Practice on Tuesday evening.
3 Where do they do it?	local old people's day centre	France, Italy or Austria	school football pitch
4 What equipment and clothes do they need?	loose-fitting clothes and trainers, music	skis, boots, poles, ski suit	special kit: a football shirt with a number on the back, shorts, socks, football boots, shin pads, team tracksuit
5 Are they good at it?	quite good	very good	team isn't very good

T 2.7 **Mary**

I'm 85 years old, but I've always been interested in keeping fit. Recently, I started doing aerobics. I go once a week – on – erm – a Thursday morning to the local old people's day centre. It's really nice there. They run a special aerobics class for us. Erm – first thing we do is exercise … for about three quarters of an hour. We go through all the exercises to music. There are between four and eight of us depending on the weather, really. We just wear loose-fitting clothes and comfortable shoes or trainers and, – erm – apart from the music, and Julianne, our lovely instructor, we don't need anything else! I'm quite good at it now. I can do most of the exercises, although there are one or two that are a bit energetic for me at my age – erm – I'm one of the oldest – erm – some of the others are just babies of about sixty! Afterwards we all go for a cup of tea and a piece of cake in the coffee bar. It's a really nice morning.

Jenny

I didn't start skiing until my mid 40s. Now I go once or twice a year for two weeks, usually in early spring. I live in London, so I go to ski resorts in Europe – in France, Italy, or Austria. At first it was really difficult, starting in my 40s. I spent most of the time on my bottom! But I was determined to learn so I took some classes. My husband thought I was mad – but my children said 'You go for it, Mum!' so I did and now my

husband's taken up skiing, too. I have my own skis, ski poles, and boots and stuff – that I take with me, and of course all the latest clothes – it's important to be fashionable on the ski slopes, you know. I have a lovely ski suit – I like to look good. Now my instructor says I'm a very good skier and in fact I even give lessons to friends – and my husband! If you've never been skiing, you should try it. Hey, I could give you your first lesson!

Thomas

I absolutely love football. I'm crazy about it. It's the best! I love watching it but I 'specially enjoy playing it. I am nine years old and I play for the local team at my school's football pitch. I play matches twice a week – on Friday evenings after school and on Sunday mornings. And we also have football coaching on Tuesday evenings when we just practise all our football skills. It's brilliant! Er – we all have a special kit – a football shirt with a number on the back – er – I'm number 7, it's my lucky number! And we wear shorts, socks and stuff, all in matching colours and of course our football boots – oh – and we also have to wear shin pads for protection, you know. We have a team tracksuit, too – but we only wear this before and after matches and for training. Erm – my mum always comes to support us – even when it's raining. Mmm – my team isn't very good, in fact, we nearly always lose – but we don't care! Er – our football coach, Martin, says winning doesn't matter – it's taking part that counts – mmm – maybe he's right, but d'you know what I think? I think it's just fantastic when we win! Yeah.

5 This short personalized activity, picks up from exercise 1 where students may have said which sports they like.

Model the activity by interviewing a reliable student, then ask students in pairs to interview each other. In the feedback, ask some students to briefly summarize what their partners said.

Alternatively, you could do this as a mingle, or you could ask the students to ask you the questions so that they can find out about *your* sporting activities.

WRITING (SB p104)

Letters and emails – beginnings and endings

Lead in by asking students a few questions about letters and emails. *How often do you email your friends? When do you write letters? When did you last write a letter? What is different about writing letters and writing emails?*

1 Ask students in pairs to make phrases. Do one or two as examples to get them started.

Possible answers
Starting: Dear Sir/Madam; Hi!
Ending: Best wishes; Yours sincerely; Yours faithfully; Lots of love; All my love; Love; All the best

2 Ask students in pairs to decide which extracts are beginnings and which are endings.

Answers
B = beginning   E = ending
1 B   2 B/E   3 E   4 B   5 B   6 E   7 B   8 E   9 B
10 E   11 E

3   Ask students in pairs to look again at the sentences in exercise 2 and decide which are formal/informal, and which words and phrases helped them decide.

Answers
1 **Informal** Just a note to say thank you so much for having me to stay last weekend.
2 **Formal** Thank you for your letter of 16th April. Please find enclosed a cheque for £50.00.
3 **Informal** Write or better still, email me soon.
4 **Informal** How are you doing? You'll never guess who I saw last week at Dan's.
5 **Formal** I am writing in response to your advertisement in yesterday's *Daily Star*.
6 **Formal** We trust this arrangement meets with your satisfaction.
7 **Informal** I'm sorry I haven't been in touch for such a long time.
8 **Formal** I look forward to hearing from you at your earliest convenience.
9 **Informal** I thought I'd write rather than email for a change.
10 **Formal** Give my regards to Robert.
11 **Informal** Take care and thanks again.

4   Ask students in pairs to match the beginnings and endings of five different letters and emails.

Answers
1 Let me know asap ...
2 It would be lovely to see you ...
3 Many thanks. I look forward ...
4 Can't wait to see you ...
5 We apologize for the inconvenience ...

5   Ask students in pairs to continue the beginnings of the letters and emails by adding the next lines. Do one as an example.

Answers
3 Could you please send me your brochure ...
2 I've changed my job a few times ...
5 Unfortunately this amount did not include ...
1 We've got four tickets ...
4 We'd love to come.

6   Discuss the answers as a class.

3 asks for information: *Could you please send me*
1 invites: *Any chance that you two are free*
5 asks for further payment: *this did not include*
4 accepts an invitation: *We'd love to come.*
2 gives news: *I've changed ... I've moved ...*

7   Give students a few minutes to write brief notes under the headings, *news*, *things done recently*, and *future plans*. Ask which phrases from the lesson they could use in their email, then ask them to write it for homework. You could ask them to email it to you! Correct it and email it back.

NOTE
Friends Reunited is a popular website which enables people to post news about themselves and find out what old school or college friends are doing.

EVERYDAY ENGLISH (SB p21)

Numbers and dates

These exercises can be done at any point in the unit, for example, as a warm-up at the beginning of a lesson. They should all be revision and so covered quickly.

1   **T 2.8**   Ask students to say the numbers, moving quickly around the class. Check that they are putting the stress on the correct syllable (*fifteen* but *fifty*) and that they are using *and* correctly. Then play the recording and ask students to listen and repeat.

Answers and tapescript
fifteen, fifty, four hundred and six, seventy-two, a hundred and twenty-eight

ninety, nineteen, eight hundred and fifty, thirty-six, one thousand five hundred and twenty

two hundred and forty-seven, five thousand, one hundred thousand, two million

Note that *and* is used with the *last* figure after hundreds, thousands, and millions. For example, *one thousand six hundred and twelve,* or *ten thousand and sixteen.*

2   Ask students to say the numbers in pairs. Note which numbers they are having trouble with. Give extra practice for these numbers when you play the recording.
    T 2.9   Play the recording so that students can listen and repeat. Alternatively, ask them to say the number first, then listen and check.

Tapescript
Money
four hundred pounds, fifty pence, nine euros and forty cents, forty-seven euros ninety-nine, five thousand yen, one hundred dollars
Fractions
a quarter, three quarters, two thirds, seven eighths, twelve and a half

Decimals and percentages
six point two, seventeen point two five, fifty per cent, seventy-five point seven per cent, one hundred per cent

Dates
nineteen ninety-five; two thousand and twenty; seventeen eighty-nine; the fifteenth of July, nineteen ninety-four; the thirtieth of October, two thousand and two

Telephone numbers
Oh one eight six five double five six eight nine oh
Eight hundred four five one seven five four five
Nine one nine six double seven one three oh three

3 The aim of this exercise is to practise listening to numbers in context.

[T 2.10] Play the recording so that students can listen and write down the numbers. Then ask them to discuss with a partner what each number refers to. Play the recording again, pausing after each conversation to discuss the answers.

Answers and tapescript
(Students can also write the figures)
1 fifteenth, twenty-fourth (dates)
2 four point two per cent, fifteen thousand (people out of work)
3 two (number of tickets); thirty-five pounds (the price of a ticket); 4929 7983 0621 8849 (Visa credit card number)
4 £39.99/thirty-nine ninety-nine/thirty-nine pounds and ninety-nine pence (the sale price of the shoes)
   half (everything is half price in the sale);
   £79.99/seventy-nine ninety-nine (the original price of the shoes)
5 tenth (wedding anniversary); seven o'clock (time)

[T 2.10]
1 'When are you going away on holiday?'
   'On the fifteenth.'
   'And when do you get back?'
   'On the twenty-fourth. I'll give you a ring when we get home.'
2 And now the business news. The unemployment rate has risen slightly this month. The national unemployment rate is now 4.2%, and in our area, an estimated 15,000 people are out of work.
3 'Thank you for calling the Blackpool Concert Hall. This is Matt speaking. How can I help you?'
   'Oh, hi. Erm – do you still have seats for tonight's concert?'
   'Yes, we do.'
   'Great. I'd like two tickets, please. Can I reserve them by phone?'
   'Yes, that's fine. Erm – tickets are £35 each. Could I have your name, please?'
   'Yes, Sarah Dawson.'
   'Thanks.'
   Can I pay by Visa?'
   'Yes, that's fine. Erm – what's your card number, please?'
   'It's 4929 ... 7983 ... 0621 ... 8849.'

'Let me read that back. 4929 ... 7983 ... 0621 ... 8849.'
   'That's right.'
4 'Hey, I really like your shoes! Where d'you buy them?'
   'At that new shop in town.'
   'Oh yeah? Next to the post office?'
   'Yeah.'
   'How much were they, if you don't mind me asking?'
   '£39.99 in the sale. Everything's half price, you know, so they were reduced from £79.99.'
   'What a bargain!'
5 'Hello?'
   'Hi, Jim. How're things?'
   'Fine. Listen – we're having a party this Saturday, and we were wondering if you'd like to come. It's our tenth wedding anniversary.'
   'Congratulations. When is it?'
   'It starts at seven o'clock.'
   'Saturday at seven? Sounds good.'

4 Students work with their partner to think of and explain five significant numbers in their lives.

Don't forget!

Workbook Unit 2
Exercise 11 Opposite adjectives
Exercise 12 Phrasal verbs – *look* and *be*
Word list
Photocopy the Word list for Unit 2 (TB p155) for your students. Ask them to write in the translations, learn them at home, and/or write some of the words in their vocabulary notebooks.

Past tenses
Passive • Art and literature
Giving opinions

Telling tales

Introduction to the unit

The theme of this unit is telling stories, both fictional and factual. This provides the means of illustrating and practising both form and pronunciation of the narrative tenses – the Past Simple, Past Continuous, Past Perfect, and the passive voice.

The *Reading and speaking* section includes biographies of Pablo Picasso and Ernest Hemingway. In the *Listening and writing* section students talk and write about a favourite book or film.

The *Writing* section at the back of the book practises using linking words and adding ideas to write an interesting story.

Language aims

Grammar – past tenses By the intermediate level, students will have some familiarity with narrative tenses but will still benefit from revising them, particularly in activities where they are required to discriminate between them. Therefore, in this unit, the Past Simple, Past Continuous, and Past Perfect are contrasted in the context of a traditional story from a Native American tribe and practised in a variety of accuracy-focused activities. The passive voice is also featured in the reading texts and practised in the language work which follows.

POSSIBLE PROBLEMS

1 The Past Simple has to be used in English for completed actions in the past where other languages can employ the Present Perfect.
*I bought it last year. *I have bought it last year.*
The Present Perfect is covered in depth in Unit 7. Until then, just remind students, if they make this mistake, that we use the Past Simple when we say *when* – when we refer to a specific past time.

2 Many common verbs are irregular. Refer to the list of irregular verbs on SB p157. They are also practised in several exercises in the Workbook.

3 There are three possible pronunciations of -*ed* at the end of regular Past Simple verbs and past participles: /t/ *washed* /d/ *lived* /ɪd/ *wanted* These are practised fully in the unit.

4 As in the Present Simple with the use of the auxiliary *do, does, don't,* and *doesn't* in questions and negatives, students may have questions about the use of *did* and *didn't* in the Past Simple. The connection between these should be pointed out.

Common mistakes:
*I did see *I didn't went *When you saw him? *She no come yesterday*

5 The use of the Past Continuous for interrupted past actions is usually clear when contrasted with the Past Simple.
I was having a bath when the phone rang.
However, the use of the Past Continuous as a descriptive, scene-setting tense can be more difficult to explain. It is best illustrated in context.
The sun was shining, the birds were singing – and then something terrible happened!

6 Overstressing the pronunciation of *was* and *were* can sound very unnatural in the Past Continuous as they are normally weak in context. /wəz/ *He was coming.* /wə/ *They were sitting.*

7 The Past Perfect tense has the problem of the contracted form *'d* because it is also the contracted form of *would.* It can be difficult for students to recognize the difference.
He'd (had) *said he'd* (would) *come.*
Exercise 10 in Unit 3 of the Workbook deals with this.

Vocabulary The *Vocabulary* section is a categorizing task on art and literature which sets the scene and introduces some necessary vocabulary for the reading texts.

Everyday English Giving opinions was chosen so that students can give their opinions about books, music, films, etc.

Notes on the unit

TEST YOUR GRAMMAR (SB p22)

The aim here is to preview the key language area of the unit, and find out how much the students know. If the students are unsure, don't spend time trying to explain at this stage. These uses are fully explained in context in later exercises.

Ask students to describe what they can see in the pictures. Mark is wearing an *apron* – this will probably be a new word and worth teaching.

Ask students in pairs to match the sentences with the pictures. Monitor, listen in on their discussions, and find out how clear the students are about their uses. In the feedback, keep your explanations brief.

> **Answers**
> a 3 – (The dinner is on the table)
> b 1 – (Mark is putting on his apron, ready to start cooking)
> c 2 – (Mark is at the cooker, cooking)

Ask the class if anybody can explain the difference in meaning between the tenses. If you have a monolingual class, you could do this briefly in L1. If not, it is a good idea to ask more specific check questions with reference to the pictures. This avoids long-winded explanations in English from students, and, hopefully, guides them to see rules they might be a little unsure of. For example, ask *In which picture did Mark start cooking before Carol arrived? In which picture did Mark start cooking after she arrived? In which picture did Mark finish cooking before she arrived?*

> **Answers**
> We use the **Past Simple** to show a sequence of past events – *arrived* then *cooked*.
> We use the **Past Continuous** to show a long action that started before *arrived*, and was interrupted by it or continued after it.
> We use the **Past Perfect** to show an earlier past event. *Carol arrived*, but *Mark had cooked* earlier.

A NATIVE AMERICAN FOLK TALE (SB p22)

Past tenses

In this section, the form and use of the Past Simple, Past Continuous, and Past Perfect are illustrated in the context of a story from the Algonquian /ael'gɒŋkwɪən/ tribe of North America.

> **NOTE**
> The Algonquian Indians lived in the area around the Ottawa River, Canada. Their descendants, now called Ottawa Indians, live in villages in Quebec and Ontario.

Begin by telling students that they are going to read a traditional story from a North American Indian tribe. Ask *Do you know any stories from ancient peoples who once lived in your country? What are they typically about? Why did people tell these stories?*

1 Ask students to look at the pictures. Ask *What can you see?* Pre-teach key vocabulary, such as *warrior, boast, teepee, war dance, scream, fearless, terrified.* Ask students in pairs to predict what the story is about.

2 Ask students to check their predictions by reading the story quickly, without worrying about the missing phrases.

Read through the phrases as a class. Students work individually to put the phrases in the correct place in the story, then check their answers in pairs.

T 3.1 Students listen and check their answers. Let students come up with their own interpretations as to what the moral or lesson of the story is.

> **Answers and tapescript**
> 1 b 2 f 3 e 4 d 5 a 6 c
>
> **T 3.1**
> Gluskap the warrior was very pleased with himself because he had fought and won so many battles. He boasted to a woman friend: 'Nobody can beat me!'
> 'Really?' said the woman. 'I know someone who can beat you. His name is Wasis.' Gluskap had never heard of Wasis. He immediately wanted to meet him and fight him. So he was taken to the woman's village. The woman pointed to a baby who was sitting and sucking a piece of sugar on the floor of a teepee.
> 'There,' she said. 'That is Wasis. He is little, but he is very strong.' Gluskap laughed and went up to the baby. 'I am Gluskap. Fight me!' he shouted. Little Wasis looked at him for a moment, then he opened his mouth. 'Waaah! Waaah!' he screamed. Gluskap had never heard such a terrible noise. He danced a war dance and sang some war songs. Wasis screamed louder. 'Waaah! Waaah! Waaah!' Gluskap covered his ears and ran out of the teepee. After he had run a few miles, he stopped and listened. The baby was still screaming. Gluskap the fearless was terrified. He ran on and was never seen again in the woman's village.

1 Look at the two sentences as a class, and ask students to name the tense and say which verbs are regular and which irregular. Then ask them to find other examples in the story. Let them check their answers in pairs before discussing them with the whole class.

Answers
The tense used is the Past Simple.
Laughed and *danced* are regular past forms.
Went and *sang* are the irregular past forms of *go* and *sing*.
Regular past forms in the story: *boasted, wanted, pointed, shouted, looked, opened, screamed, danced, covered, stopped, listened*.
Irregular past forms in the story: *was, ran*

2 Ask students in pairs to label the tenses and to discuss the difference in meaning. Alternatively, you could do this as a board presentation. Write the three sentences on the board, underline each tense, and elicit the names of the tenses from the class. Then draw these timelines, and elicit the rules of use for each tense from students.

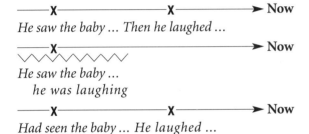

He saw the baby ... Then he laughed ...

He saw the baby ...
he was laughing

Had seen the baby ... He laughed ...

Answers
The first sentence is in the Past Simple. It means that he saw the baby and then he laughed.
The second sentence uses the Past Continuous then the Past Simple. It means that he started laughing before he saw the baby.
The third sentence uses the Past Simple then the Past Perfect. It means he started laughing after he saw the baby.

3 Ask students in pairs to find two examples of the Past Simple passive in the text. In the feedback point out the form: *to be* (in the Past Simple form) + past participle.

Answers
was taken, was (never) seen (again)
Note: *Was ... pleased* and *was terrified* are examples of the past participle used as an adjective.

Refer students to Grammar Reference 3.1–3.4 on SB pp137–139.

Pronunciation

This is a short exercise to help students pronounce the regular past tense ending -*ed*. It is also relevant to the regular past participle endings.

3 Demonstrate an example of each -*ed* ending so that students can hear the different pronunciation: /t/ *washed*, /d/ *lived*, /ɪd/ *wanted*. Students complete the exercise in pairs.

T 3.2 Play the recording. Students listen and check their answers. Ask them if they can see any rules.

Answers and tapescript

/t/	/d/	/ɪd/
laughed	covered	wanted
stopped	listened	shouted
looked	opened	boasted
danced	screamed	pointed

The rules are as follows:
Pronounce the -*ed* ending as /t/ after any unvoiced consonant except *t*.
Pronounce the -*ed* ending as /d/ after any voiced consonant except *d*.
Only pronounce -*ed* as /ɪd/ after the letters *t* and *d*, for example, *boast*.

T 3.2 Play the recording again. Ask students to listen and repeat.

Encourage correct pronunciation of -*ed* endings in the practice activities.

What was she doing?

This section gives students practice in using Past Continuous and Past Perfect forms, and in using auxiliary verbs in forming questions correctly. The emphasis is on spoken accuracy practice.

1 Read the introduction. Ask students to look at the photograph and read about Judy's day. Begin by asking *What does she do in her job? What can you say about her lifestyle?*

Ask students in pairs to describe Judy's day to each other by referring to the diary, for example *She got up at 6.30, and then she packed her suitcase.*

2 This activity provides controlled oral practice of the third person of the Past Continuous. First, check that students know why the Past Continuous is used here. Write on the board *She was packing her suitcase at 7 a.m.* Then ask questions like *Did she start packing before 7?* and *Did she continue packing after 7?* to show that this is an activity *in progress* at a particular time in the past.

Model the question and answer by asking around the class *What was she doing at ...?* Students should use the Past Continuous in their answers. Put students in pairs to practise. Go round monitoring and correcting. Pay particular attention to the weak form of *was* /wəz/.

SUGGESTION

Alternatively, you could do a prompt drill on form and pronunciation. Keep the pace quick and lively.

First say *What was she doing at seven o'clock yesterday morning?* Exaggerate the rhythm and the stress.

Students repeat as a class. Then get individuals to repeat.

Model and drill the question again with different times.

Then say *eight o'clock.*

Students ask the question from the prompt.

Say different times to different students and get them to produce the whole question. Make sure they are using the weak form /wəz/.

Then get students to ask you *What was she doing?* questions. Model the correct answers:

S1 *What was she doing at ten o'clock?*
T *She was flying to Glasgow.*

Once students have got the idea, let them ask and answer across the class in open pairs. Finally, put them in pairs to practise. Monitor and correct any errors.

NOTE

If you keep up the pace, drilling is a good way to build students' confidence and improve their pronunciation. You can use prompt drills with other structures as they are introduced in other units.

T 3.3 Play the recording while students listen and check.

Answers and tapescript
1 What was she doing at 7 o'clock yesterday morning?
  She was packing her suitcase.
2 What was she doing at 8 o'clock?
  She was driving to the airport.
3 What was she doing at 10 o'clock?
  She was flying to Glasgow.
4 What was she doing at half past eleven?
  She was having a meeting.
5 What was she doing at half past one in the afternoon?
  She was having lunch.
6 What was she doing at 3 o'clock?
  She was visiting Dot Com Enterprises.
7 What was she doing at 6 o'clock?
  She was writing a report on the plane.
8 What was she doing at half past eight in the evening?
  She was putting the baby to bed.

9 What was she doing at 10 o'clock?
  She was relaxing and listening to music.

3 This is the same activity as above, but personalized to give practice of *you* and *I*. Give students a few minutes to write a list of what they did yesterday. You could suggest the same time intervals as in Judy's diary. Model the activity with a strong student, then put students in pairs to ask and answer. Draw attention to the pronunciation of the weak form of *were* /wə/. Monitor and correct any errors.

Alternatively, you could do this as a mingle activity to change the pace and focus of the lesson.

End this part of the lesson with students asking you what you were doing at different times yesterday.

Had you heard it before?

This activity provides accuracy practice in context using the Past Perfect tense.

4 Put students in pairs, and ask Students **A** and **B** to read the sentences in their box. Answer any vocabulary questions.

Briefly model the activity with a strong student, then ask the pairs to complete the activity.

T 3.4 Students listen and check their answers. Ask students to listen again and repeat, paying attention to the stress and intonation.

Answers and tapescript
1 **A** I didn't laugh at his joke.
  B Why? Had you heard it before?
2 **A** Were you surprised by the ending of the film?
  B No, I'd read the book, so I already knew the story.
3 **A** I went to the airport, but I couldn't get on the plane.
  B Why? Had you left your passport at home?
4 **A** I was homesick the whole time I was living in France.
  B That's really sad! Had you never lived abroad before?
5 **A** The hotel where we stayed on holiday was awful!
  B That's a pity. Hadn't you stayed there before?
6 **A** I met my girlfriend's parents for the first time last Sunday.
  B Really? I thought you'd met them before.
7 **A** My grandfather had two sons from his first marriage.
  B Really? I didn't know he'd been married before.

5 Ask students to read the example conversation. In pairs they should choose two of the situations from exercise 4 and prepare longer conversations to present to the class.

An amazing thing happened!

6 This is an information gap activity that requires students to ask questions using the Past Simple and Past Continuous.

Pre-teach *sunbathing, wave, sunglasses, furious.*

Put students in pairs and ask Student **A** to look at SB p151 and Student **B** to look at SB p152. Ask students to read the story and think of questions to ask their partners to find the missing information. Give them a few minutes to do this before they begin interviewing each other. Students must work together to complete the missing parts of both stories.

Completed text

Last summer, Wanda and Roy went on holiday to Florida. Every day, they went swimming and lay in the sun.
One morning, they were at the beach near their hotel, swimming in the sea, when a huge wave knocked Wanda's expensive Italian sunglasses into the water. Wanda was very upset because Roy had given her the sunglasses for her birthday.
The next day, they were sunbathing on the same beach and Wanda was wearing a new, cheap pair of sunglasses, when suddenly there was another huge wave, which totally covered Wanda. She was furious, but then she looked down and to her amazement, she saw the expensive sunglasses that she had lost the day before.

7 This exercise gives further practice of Past Simple and Past Continuous forms by getting students to use the information in the texts in exercise 6 to improvise a conversation. A good way to make this work is to write a few conversation prompts on the board to help the student who is listening to the story:
So what happened next? Then what did you do? So then what happened? I don't believe it! You're joking! That's amazing! How awful! Oh no!

In pairs, ask one student to tell the story, while the other encourages the telling by using the prompts. When they have finished, they should change roles.

T 3.5 Students listen and compare their conversations.

Tapescript
N = Nicola W = Wanda

N Hi, Wanda. Did you have a good holiday?
W Oh, yeah, we had a great time. But I have to tell you – the most amazing thing happened.
N Really? What was that?
W Well, Roy and I were at the beach near the hotel and we were swimming in the sea – it was our first day – and this huge wave came along and knocked my sunglasses into the water. I ...
N Why were you swimming in your sunglasses?
W Oh, I don't know. I'd just left them on top of my head. I'd

forgotten they were there. Anyway, they were gone. I couldn't find them anywhere. I was really upset. You know Roy had given me those sunglasses for my birthday and they were really expensive.
N I remember – nearly £100.
W Yeah. Anyway, I had to have sunglasses, so I bought a new pair – just a cheap pair this time. The next day, I was lying on the beach, sunbathing. Then, suddenly another huge wave ...
N You didn't lose another pair of sunglasses?
W No, no. You'll never believe this – there was another huge wave. It completely covered me. I was so wet and ...
N Are you sure this was a good holiday?
W Yeah – but listen! When I looked down, there on the sand, right next to me, were my expensive sunglasses. The ones I had lost the day before! I couldn't believe my eyes!
N You're joking! That is *amazing*!

Discussing grammar

8 Ask students to complete the exercise individually then discuss their answers with a partner.

Answers

1 **were** eating = I arrived in the middle of the barbecue, so there were still some sausages left for me!
   'd (had) eaten = The sausages were finished when I arrived. There were none left for me!
2 **was** doing = They haven't taken the test yet.
   'd (had) done = They have taken the test and passed it.
3 **were** staying = They are staying at the Carlton now.
   had stayed = They stayed at the Carlton at some time in the past.
   (Number 3 is an example of reported speech.)
4 **Did** you learn = At the time you were in Italy
   Had you already learned = before going to Italy
5 **Did** Shakespeare write = a past event
   Was *Hamlet* written = a past event – Past Simple passive form

WRITING (SB p106)

A narrative (1)

Lead in by asking students to look at the picture. What do they think the story is about?

1 Ask students to read the story of the farmer and his sons. Is it similar to their predictions? You may need to check the words, *vineyard*, *grapes*, and *upset*.

Ask students in pairs to read the story again and decide where the clauses go.

2 Ask students in pairs to complete the sentences with linking words from the box. Do one as an example.

3 Ask students to compare the sentences with those in the story and to say what the differences are.

Ask students to continue rewriting the story adding more detail and making it more interesting.

A nice interactive way of doing this is to put students in pairs and ask them to copy the two sentences in the Student's Book onto a blank sheet of paper. Then ask them to write the next sentence. Pass the sheets of paper on, so that each pair has a new sheet. Ask the pairs to write the next sentence then pass it on, and so on, until the story is complete.

4 Ask students to write a folk tale or fairy story that they know. Set this for homework. Collect it and mark it. You could put the marked stories on the classroom wall so that all the students can read each other's stories. Alternatively, bind the stories in an anthology, entitled *Folk Tales from around the World*, and leave it in the classroom or school library for students to read in their free time.

Workbook Unit 3
Exercises 1–5 Past Simple and Past Continuous
Exercise 6 *while*, *during*, and *for*
Exercises 7–10 Past Perfect

VOCABULARY (SB p25)

Art and literature

This *Vocabulary* section is a categorizing task. It sets the scene and introduces some vocabulary for the reading texts which follow.

1 Ask students in pairs or small groups to complete the exercise. Make sure they realize that all the words are used as nouns (*act*, *play*, and *sketch* are of course also verbs). Check answers with the whole class.

2 This is a collocation activity. Students work in pairs to match the verbs with the nouns from exercise 1. Check answers as a class by asking individual students to come up and write answers on the board.

3 This exercise puts some of the collocations into context. Encourage students to do it quickly in pairs, then discuss it with the whole class.

3 I love **reading** about the lives of famous people so I always buy **biographies**.
4 **Fairy tales** often begin with the words 'Once upon a time'.
5 My friend's a great artist. He **painted/drew** my **portrait** and it looked just like me.
6 He **drew** a quick **sketch** of the trees.
7 We **went to** an **exhibition** of Picasso's paintings and sculptures.

READING AND SPEAKING (SB p26)

The painter and the writer

This is a jigsaw reading activity. Half the class reads a text about Pablo Picasso, while the other half reads about Ernest Hemingway. They then swap information about their person. This provides practice in asking questions in the past tense and builds students' ability to communicate with each other in English.

There are a number of difficult words and phrases in the texts. Some of them are connected with art and literature and are dealt with in the *Vocabulary* section. Others that may cause problems include:
Picasso: *genius, a spoiled child, a pet pigeon, he was honoured by an exhibition, spilled some paint*
Hemingway: *a strict family, graduated from school (UK = left school), he was wounded in the war, a successful book*
You could ask students to guess unknown words as they read and check them in their dictionaries. Alternatively, you could write these phrases randomly on the board when they do exercise 3. Check their meanings, then ask students to guess which text they come from, thus combining them with the prediction task in exercise 3.

1 If your class is of the same nationality, write up the names of a few famous writers and painters that students will be familiar with, and ask them to tell you what they know about each person. If students are of different nationalities, ask them to think of a famous writer or painter from each of their countries. Give them a few minutes to think of three or four interesting things to say about their famous people, then put them into groups to discuss them.

2 Introduce students to Picasso and Hemingway by asking them to look at the pictures in the Student's Book. They then discuss the questions in their groups.

> **NOTE**
> The picture by Picasso shown is his masterpiece, *Guernica*. Guernica, or *Gernika* in the Basque language, is a small Basque town in northern Spain that was almost totally destroyed by a bombing attack in 1937 during the Spanish Civil War. Picasso's painting of the scene is now in the Centro de Arte Reina Sofia, in Madrid.

3 Read through the sentences as a class, and explain any difficult vocabulary, for example students may not have come across *features* meaning *parts of the face*, or *poor* with the meaning *not very good*. Then put students in pairs to try to guess which sentences go with which man.

Answers
1 P 2 H 3 P 4 H 5 H 6 P

4 When students are ready, ask half the class (Students **A**) to read about Picasso and the other half (Students **B**) to read about Hemingway. The best way to organize this is to leave students in their pairs. For example, if you have a class of 12, ask three of the pairs to read about Picasso and three to read about Hemingway. Ask students to read and check their answers to exercises 2 and 3, then discuss their answers with their partner.

5 Ask students to read through the questions and discuss them with their partners. They will need to refer back to the text to find the answers. Make sure they write brief notes to answer each question. Monitor and help, but don't go through the answers as a class yet.

Answers
Picasso
1 Born: Málaga, Spain, on October 25, 1881
  Died: heart failure in 1973
2 Probably. He was the only son in the family, so he was spoiled.
3 His father was an art teacher, and gave him his first palette and brushes.
4 Watching his father paint, and being given his father's palette and brushes.
5 1904. Gertrude Stein.
6 The Spanish Civil War inspired his masterpiece, *Guernica*.
7 Twice.
8 1891: his father got a job as an art teacher
  1937: he painted *Guernica*, his masterpiece
  1949: his last child, Paloma, was born

Hemingway
1 Born: Oak Park, Illinois, on July 21, 1899
  Died: killed himself with a shotgun on July 2, 1961
2 We don't really know. He was one of six children in a strict, religious family.
3 His father taught him a love of nature, the outdoor life, hunting, fishing. His mother taught him a love of music and art.
4 Working as a journalist, and being wounded in Italy during the First World War.
5 After the war, probably in 1919 or 1920. Gertrude Stein.
6 He worked as an ambulance driver in the First World War and a war correspondent in the Spanish Civil War and World War II. He used these experiences in some of his novels.
7 Four.

8 1917: he graduated from school.
   1918: he was wounded.
   1927: his first wife divorced him.
   1928: his father committed suicide.
   1940: he wrote *For Whom the Bell Tolls*.
   1954: he had two plane crashes and was awarded the Nobel Prize for literature.

6 Ask students to work in **A/B** pairs so that each has read a different text. Then ask them to discuss the questions in exercise 5. When they have finished, ask them to work together to write three or four sentences to describe similarities and differences between the two men. Go through the answers to exercise 5 in detail with the whole class. However, if you feel students have a good understanding of the two texts, you can just ask two or three pairs to describe similarities and differences that they found.

Possible answers
Similarities
• They were both born in the nineteenth century.
• They both had a love of art.
• Hemingway got a shotgun at about the same age that Picasso got a paintbrush.
• They both went to Paris and met Gertrude Stein.
• Their greatest works were both influenced by the Spanish Civil War.
• They both had more than one wife.
• They were both honoured in their lifetimes.
Differences
• Picasso was spoiled, but Hemingway's parents were strict.
• Hemingway did well at school, but Picasso hated it.
• Hemingway killed himself, died young, suffered from bad health and depression, but Picasso was very old when he died and probably had a healthier, happier life.

GRAMMAR SPOT (SB p27)

1 Read out the examples from the texts. Elicit the answer, then ask students to find other examples in the texts and underline them.

Answers
The verbs are in the Past Simple passive form.
Pablo Picasso
was born, was blown, was spoiled, was allowed, was recognized, were shocked, were made up of, was honoured
Ernest Hemingway
was born, was given, was fascinated, was sent, was wounded, was encouraged, was written, was not mirrored, wasn't helped, was awarded, were taken up

2 Ask students to complete the sentences, then discuss their answers with a partner.

Answers
a Pablo's father left the room. When he returned, Pablo **had** completed the picture.
b Picasso **was** given his father's palette and brushes.
c Both Hemingway and Picasso **were** living in Paris when they met Gertrude Stein.
d Both men **were** honoured in their lifetime.

Refer students to Grammar Reference 3.5 on SB p139.

ADDITIONAL MATERIAL

Workbook Unit 3
Exercises 11 and 12 Past Simple active and passive
Exercise 13 *was, were, did,* or *had*?

LISTENING AND WRITING (SB p28)

Books and films

The aim here is to get students talking about books and films in a personalized spoken-fluency activity that practises the past tenses. The ideas and vocabulary necessary to set up a personalized writing task are also introduced. The listening task asks students to listen for the main ideas.

1 Begin by briefly modelling the task. Talk about a book or film you like. Bring in a copy of the book, or the film on video/DVD, or even a poster. Briefly say the title, what it is about, and why you like it. Then give students a minute or two to think about their favourite book or film before describing it to the other students in groups of four or five.

2 Ask students to look at the list of books and films. Ask them to tell the others in their group which of the books and films they have read or seen.

Answers
They are all both book and film. However *Spiderman* started as a comic; and books based on the films *Titanic* and *Star Wars* are just spin-offs.

3 **T 3.6** Play the recording. Ask students to listen and put a tick next to the titles mentioned.

Answers
Harry Potter and the Philosopher's Stone
Captain Corelli's Mandolin
Dracula
Frankenstein
The Sun Also Rises

Ask students to discuss in small groups what each person on the recording said about these books. You will probably need to play the recording again so students can expand on their answers.

Answers and tapescript

Vinnie says that *The Philosopher's Stone* is terrific, J K Rowling's a really good writer, and it is not just for kids. Maeve says that the film *Captain Corelli's Mandolin* is very sad. Sue says she could not read the book. Will says you have to skip the first 100 pages, but then it is a great love story. Sue says her best book of all time is *Dracula*. She says it is brilliant and better than any film. Will saw a Dracula film starring Tom Cruise. Vinnie thinks it is scarier than *Frankenstein*. Maeve prefers *Frankenstein* because you feel sorry for the monster. Vinnie says that *The Sun Also Rises* is about Hemingway's travels in France and Spain, and his drinking.

T 3.6

V = Vinnie   W = Will   S = Sue   M = Maeve

V   Hey, I just read a great book.

W   A book? Hey Vinnie, we're impressed! What was it?

V   *The Philosopher's Stone.*

M   Isn't that a Harry Potter book?

V   Well, yeah, yeah, but … . No, no, come on you guys, – really, it was terrific. I was so amazed. J K Rowling's a really good writer. Lots of adults read her books, they're not just for kids.

W   Sure, Vinnie. You believe that, if you want.

S   No, come on, he's right. I mean, I've seen people reading Harry Potter on the Underground and I've seen the video – my nephew has it – it's excellent!

M   Actually, I've just bought *Captain Corelli's Mandolin* on DVD. Has anyone read that book?

S   Oh no, no, please! Not *Captain Corelli's Mandolin*. I could *not* read that book. Everybody said it was great. I could *not* read it.

W   You have to skip the first hundred pages and after that it's great.

V   Hey guys! Call me old-fashioned but I like to begin a book at the beginning.

W   But it is a great story, though – 'specially when it, y'know, moves to him and the girl on the Greek island.

M   Yeah, it's a fantastic love story. But sooo sad! Actually, I read it on holiday, on a beach on a Greek island – would you believe – and I just cried and cried. People kept asking me if I was OK!

V   Hey, didn't Nick Cage star in the film?

W   Yeah, with Penelope Cruz … she is just so lovely …

M   Er well right so … what *is* your favourite book then, Sue?

S   Oh … well … my all time best is … right, you'll never believe this … it's – it's *Dracula*!

M   *Dracula*? You're kidding!

S   No, – no, I'm not. I know everybody's *heard* of *Dracula* and *seen* Dracula films, but I bet not many people have read the book. It's by a man called Bram Stoker and it's brilliant.

W   Yeah – there are loads of *Dracula* films. Er, I saw one not long ago actually, with – er – Tom Cruise.

V   Yeah, yeah, I love horror movies – the scarier the better!

M   Well, actually, I think *Frankenstein*'s a much better horror movie. You feel really sorry for that poor monster.

S   Well, it's good but not that good. I mean that's only *my* opinion of course.

V   *Dracula* is more scary … with huge teeth that he sinks into the necks of beautiful women. Aaargh!

M   Aaargh! That's disgusting!

S   OK Vinny. OK. So what else do *you* read – I mean other than Harry Potter, that is.

V   Hey – come on, come on! I had to read Ernest Hemingway at school and I quite enjoyed it … oh … what was it called? Oh yeah, yeah, yeah, *The Sun Also Sets*.

W   *Rises*. – *The Sun Also Rises*.

V   Whatever.

M   No, I read it years ago – it's a great read, actually. It's all about Hemingway's travels through France and Spain, isn't it? Oh, … and his drinking.

W   Yeah, Hemingway drank a lot, didn't he? Well, we're going on holiday to Florida next month. Maybe we can hang out in the bars where he used to drink and …

V   What? What? Hemingway lived in Florida?!

W   You're the American!

V   Well …

W   Yeah, in – in Key West, but we'll only visit *some* of the bars he went to!

4   Set up the activity by asking different students to tell you what their favourite book or film is. Then give the students a few minutes to write notes to answer the questions. Put the students in pairs or threes. Ask them to take turns to ask and answer the questions in the Student's Book. In feedback, ask several students to summarize for the whole class what their partners said.

5   For homework, ask students to use their notes from exercise 4 to write a paragraph about their book or film.

EVERYDAY ENGLISH (SB p29)

Giving opinions

This could be done at any stage in the unit after the reading texts. It provides practice in giving opinions about books, films, people, food, etc.

1   Read through the example with the class, then put students in pairs to discuss the underlined words.

Answers

b   one = a book/novel

c   It = a film

d She = an actress or film star
e them = their children
f It = a holiday
g They = pizzas
h It = a football match

As you go through the answers, ask students which words in the sentences helped them reach a decision.

2 Students remain in pairs to match the questions and opinions.

T 3.7 Play the recording so that students can check their answers. Ask them particularly to listen for stress and intonation, and practise it in pairs afterwards.

Answers and tapescript

2 a 3 g 4 b 5 e 6 f 7 d 8 h

T 3.7

1 **A** Did you like the film?
   B It was excellent. Have you seen it yet? It stars Julia Kershaw and Antonio Bellini.
2 **A** What did you think of the play?
   B It was really boring! I fell asleep during the first act.
3 **A** Did you like your pizzas?
   B They were delicious. John had tomato and mozzarella and I had tuna and sweetcorn.
4 **A** Do you like Malcolm Baker's novels?
   B I didn't like his first one, but I couldn't put his latest one down until the last page.
5 **A** What do you think of their children?
   B I think they spoil them. They always give them whatever they want.
6 **A** What was your holiday like?
   B It was a nice break, but the weather wasn't very good.
7 **A** What did you think of Sally Cotter?
   B She's usually good, but I don't think she was right for this part.
8 **A** What was the match like?
   B It was really exciting, especially when David Stuart scored in the closing minutes.

3 This is a freer, personalized activity to practise giving opinions.

Ask students to write down some things they did, places they went to, and people they met last week. When they are ready, put students in pairs and tell them they are going to ask for and give opinions about what they did. Do the examples in open pairs to illustrate the idea. Go around listening and monitoring as they talk. Finish the lesson by asking a few pairs to act out their conversations, or record some and play them back.

Don't forget!

Workbook Unit 3
Exercise 14 Vocabulary – Adverbs
Exercise 15 Pronunciation – Words that sound the same
Exercise 16 Vocabulary – *in, at, on* for time

Word list
Photocopy the Word list for Unit 3 (TB p155) for your students. Ask them to write in the translations, learn them at home, and/or write some of the words in their vocabulary notebooks.

EXTRA IDEAS UNITS 1–3

1 On p122 of the Teacher's Book, there is a questionnaire about living in the modern world, 'How up-to-date are you?', and suggested discussion questions to exploit it.
2 On p123 of the Teacher's Book, there is a song 'California Dreamin'' and suggested activities to exploit it. You will find the recording for the song after Unit 3 on the Class CD/cassette. There is also a short poem focusing on passive and active verb forms.

If you have time, and feel your students would benefit from these extra ideas, photocopy them to use in class as follow-up material to Units 1-3.

The answers to the activities are on p149 of the Teacher's Book.

Stop and check 1 (TB pp134–135)
A suggestion for approaching the *Stop and check* tests is in the introduction on TB p5.

Modal verbs 1 – obligation and permission
Nationality words • Requests and offers

Doing the right thing

Introduction to the unit

The theme of this unit is rules. Modal verbs of obligation and permission are presented in the context of family rules, school rules, and social rules.

The *Reading and speaking* section looks at how to behave when visiting different countries, and a listening passage looks at entertaining at home in different countries. There are many opportunities for students to learn about customs in other places, as well as share their own.

The *Writing* section at the back of the book practises expressing arguments for and against an opinion.

Language aims

Grammar – modal auxiliary verbs   In this unit the modal auxiliary verbs used to talk about obligation and permission are revised and practised. These include *can* and *could* to express permission; *must, should*, and the full verbs *have (got) to* to express different types of obligation; *don't have to* to express a lack of obligation; and *be allowed to* to express permission.

Many languages express obligation and permission with phrases that roughly translate as *you are obliged to* or *it is necessary that you*. It can seem very unnatural to some students to use modals here, and they will tend to avoid them. You need to provide a lot of practice of this language area.

Equally, students need a lot of practice in context to understand the subtle variations of use. In this unit, the following contrasts are highlighted and practised in simple, clear-cut contexts:

Have to to talk about rules in everyday life, and *don't have to* to talk about when those rules don't apply.

Can to say when you have permission, and *can't* to say when you don't.

Should and *must* to talk about mild and strong obligations.

It is a good idea to think about how these concepts are expressed in students' L1. If it is very different, students are likely to have problems.

> **POSSIBLE PROBLEMS**
> Key errors often come from applying rules for regular verbs to modals: **Do you can play baseball? *He musted. *I must to go.* Make sure that students realize these verbs work like auxiliaries. *Have to* is more difficult because it is modal in use but follows the form rules of a full verb.
>
> Making a modal past or negative is not always as easy as it looks, for example, the past of *must* is *had to*, and the negative forms of *must* and *have to* have very different meanings. Note that *mustn't* expresses prohibition, it does not mean the same as *don't have to*, and you may need to explain the difference:
>
> *You mustn't drive home.* = It is prohibited.
>
> *You don't have to drive home.* = You can if you want, but it isn't necessary. Exercise 7 in Unit 4 of the Workbook deals with this.

Don't expect students to have mastered the area by the end of the unit. They will probably continue to have problems, and will need more practice.

At some stage of the unit, refer students to the Grammar Reference on SB p139, the introduction to modal auxiliary verbs. It should help them begin to see a pattern in the form and use of these verbs.

Vocabulary   The vocabulary input is on nationality words. It focuses on the punctuation and stress rules.

Everyday English The functions of requests and offers are presented and practised. This is not only because they are high-frequency functional areas, but also because they offer the opportunity of furthering students' understanding of modal auxiliary verbs.

Notes on the unit

TEST YOUR GRAMMAR (SB p30)

The aim here is to raise students' awareness of a few of the form problems presented by modal auxiliary verbs.

Ask students to look at the sentences. Ask if they know what *can*, *should*, and *must* are called (*modal auxiliary verbs*).

Put students in pairs to write the negatives, questions, and third person singular.

This exercise highlights the fact that modal verbs don't use *do/does* to form the negative and the question, and that there is no *-s* in the third person singular; that *have to* also expresses obligation, but it is a full verb, not a modal verb.

Answers
1 I **can't** go.
   I **shouldn't** go.
   I **mustn't** go.
   I **don't have to** go.
2 **Can** I go?
   Should I go?
   Must I go?
   Do I **have to** go?
3 **He/She can** go.
   He/She should go.
   He/She must go.
   He/She has to go.
4 *Have to* is different. It behaves like a modal verb in meaning and use but like a full verb in form.

TEENAGERS AND PARENTS (SB p30)

have (got) to, can, and *be allowed to*

The aim of this section is to compare and contrast *have (got) to, can,* and *be allowed to.*

Can will be very familiar to students. It is a more informal way of expressing *be allowed to. Have to* in the positive is less of a problem than in the negative. The concept of absence of obligation as expressed by *don't have to* is quite difficult to convey, and many languages express this idea with a paraphrase, such as *it isn't necessary to.* Notice the pronunciation of *have to* /haef tə/.

1 If you have a teenage class, lead in by asking them what they like and don't like about being a teenager. Make a list on the board. If your students are older, ask them to say what is good or bad about being a teenager today.

Alternatively, you could divide the class into two. One half works in small groups to think of things teenagers can do, and the other half works in small groups to think of things teenagers can't do. Ask someone from each small group to briefly report back to the whole class, then decide as a class whether teenagers have it easy or not!

T 4.1 Play the recording. Ask students to listen to Sarah and Lindsay talking about being teenagers and to answer the question. Write some of their answers on the board. Point out that the girls use *you* to refer to all teenagers in general, not a specific *you.*

Answers and tapescript
They like the fact that they don't have to go to work or pay bills. They are free to go out with friends, go shopping, go to the cinema.

They don't like the fact that they don't have enough freedom or money. They can't wear make-up or chew gum, or bring mobile phones to class. There are too many rules.

T 4.1
I = Interviewer S = Sarah L = Lindsay
I Tell me, what are some good things about being a teenager and not an adult?
S Um ... well, for one thing, you don't have to go to work.
L Yeah. And you don't have to pay bills.
I OK ...
L And you can go out with your friends, and you can go shopping, and you can go to the cinema, and you can ...
S Oh, come on, Lindsay. Adults can do all that too! But what's different is how much freedom teenagers have.
L Don't have, you mean.
S Right. How much freedom we don't have. I mean, I always have to tell my mum and dad where I'm going and what time I'm coming home.
L Mmm.
I And what time do you have to get back home?
S Mmm – by 10 o'clock on a week-day, maybe 11 or 12 at the weekend.
L It doesn't matter because you never have enough money anyway!
S Definitely. You get pocket money from your parents, but it's never enough. And you aren't allowed to buy whatever you want.
I OK, OK. Life's tough for kids, but what do you think it's like being an adult? Lindsay?
L Well, adults have to worry about paying the bills and taking care of their family. They can't always do what they want when they want.
I They have responsibilities, you mean?
L Yeah. I feel more sorry for my mum than my dad. She's always rushing around and she has to go to work as well. She doesn't have to work on Thursdays and Fridays, but she still has loads of different things to do in a day, like shopping and cooking, and taking me to dance classes.
I So, do you think your dad has an easier life?
L Well, I don't know. He has to drive over 500 miles a week.
I Sarah, tell me about school. What are some of the rules at your school?

S Oh! There are so many! Let's see. We can't wear make-up. We aren't allowed to chew gum. We aren't allowed to bring mobile phones to class ...

L There are millions of rules – all of them stupid.

S And if you break one of the rules, you have to stay after school!

L Well, speaking of school, I've got to go. I've got to do my homework!

2 Ask students in pairs to complete the sentences.

T 4.2 Play the recording so that students can check their answers. Then ask them to practise saying the sentences.

> **Answers and tapescript**
> 1 You **don't have to** go to work.
> 2 You **don't have to** pay bills.
> 3 You **can** go out with your friends.
> 4 I always **have to** tell my mum and dad where I'm going.
> 5 What time **do you have to** get back home?
> 6 You **aren't allowed to** buy whatever you want.
> 7 Adults **have to** worry about paying the bills.
> 8 They **can't** always do what they want.
> 9 We **aren't allowed to** bring mobile phones to class.
> 10 I**'ve got to** go. I**'ve got to** do my homework.

3 The aim of this exercise is to provide practice of the third person singular of *have to*. Focus attention on form in the positive and negative *has to/ doesn't have to*. If you anticipate problems, do a couple of examples as a class. Then put students in pairs to prepare some sentences about the parents before reporting back to the class.

> **Answers**
> Her mother has to go to work, do shopping and cooking, and she has to take Lindsay to dance classes.
> She doesn't have to work on Thursdays and Fridays.
> Her father has to drive over 500 miles a week.

> **SUGGESTION**
> Personalize this stage by asking students to talk about their own families. They could do this in groups or as a class. Monitor and see how well they use *have/has to* and *don't/doesn't have to*.

GRAMMAR SPOT (SB p31)

1 Ask students in pairs to answer the questions, then discuss the answers with the whole class.

> **Answers**
> *I am allowed to/can* ... mean the same. They express permission.
> *I have to* ... expresses obligation.

2 Ask students in their pairs to complete the sentences.

> **Answers**
> Children **have to** go to school.
> Millionaires **don't have to** work.
> You **don't have to** go to England if you want to learn English.
> In England, you **have to** drive on the left.

3 Point out that *have got to* is an alternative in spoken informal English. For the negative we tend to say *We don't have to go* not *We haven't got to go*.

Refer students to Grammar Reference 4.1 on SB p140.

PRACTICE (SB p31)

Discussing grammar

This exercise aims to check whether students can manipulate the form of these modal auxiliary verbs.

1 Read through the example with the whole class, then ask students in pairs to complete the exercise. Monitor and correct carefully.

> **Answers**
> 2 I don't have to wear a uniform. Do I have to wear a uniform? I had to wear a uniform.
> 3 She doesn't have to work hard. Does she have to work hard? She didn't have to work hard.
> 4 He can't do what he likes. Can he do what he likes? He couldn't do what he liked.
> 5 We aren't allowed to wear jeans. Are we allowed to wear jeans? We weren't allowed to wear jeans.

Talking about you

This is personalized spoken accuracy practice that aims to get students manipulating the forms of *have to* in a meaningful context.

2 Focus attention on the chart. Ask students to write about themselves, then work in pairs to compare and discuss their sentences. Add *son* and *daughter* to the list of people if some of your students have children. Go around the room, helping as necessary.

> **Answers**
> Students' own answers.

3 This activity practises the *have got to* form. Do the first sentence with the class an an example, then put students in pairs to complete the exercise. Encourage students to use the contracted form *'s got to/ 've got to*.

T 4.3 Play the recording so that students can listen and check their answers. Then ask them to practise saying the sentences.

4 Students work in groups to discuss the questions. Then have a whole-class discussion.

Signs

The aim here is to get students to produce sentences using *have to/don't have to, can/can't, (not) be allowed to* from the signs. Make sure they know that they will need to use *you* meaning 'people in general'.

5 Focus attention on the signs. Ask students to say where they might see them. Students work in pairs to write sentences using modal verbs. In the feedback, write up any particularly good examples of using modals on the board.

What do you think?

The aim here is to provide some personalized fluency practice.

Ask students to read through the sentences and note whether these things are the same or different in their country. When they are ready, put them in groups of four or five to discuss laws in their country. Monitor and note errors, but don't interrupt too much. At the end, discuss the errors, especially those connected with the use of the language of permission and obligation. In a multilingual class, this can be an interesting exercise that develops rapport and understanding between students.

should and *must*

The aim here is to contrast the use of *should* and *must* for obligation. Students may well have come across these two items already, but they may not know them as compared and contrasted items. Stress that *must* expresses strong obligation and *should* expresses milder obligation – a suggestion or advice.

1 Ask students to look at the pictures, and ask them what the two young men are doing (*planning a trip*). Elicit and check key vocabulary: *rucksack, map, guidebook, traveller's cheques*. You could extend and personalize this lead-in by asking students if *they* have ever planned a backpacking trip. *Where did you go? What did you take? What was it like?*

T 4.4 Play the recording. Ask students to listen to Antony and George. What two decisions do they make?

2 Ask students in pairs to practise the conversation. Then ask them to look at the structures, *I think we should …* and *I don't think we should … .* Tell students that we use *should* here to ask for and make a suggestion.

3 Check difficult vocabulary: *suncream, valuable, vaccinations*. Then ask students in pairs to complete the suggestions in **A** and match them with the sentences in **B**. Check answers with the whole class. Make sure students are pronouncing *should* /ʃʊd/ correctly.

You can extend this activity by asking students to close their books, find a new partner, then work together to plan a trip. Ask them to decide where they are going, what they are going to do before they go, and what they are going to do when they get there. Encourage students to use some of the phrases in the exercise above. Monitor and listen for errors.

4 **T 4.5** Play the recording. Ask the students to listen to Antony and his grandmother.

Ask students to listen again and repeat what Antony's grandmother says. Make sure they are paying attention to the pronunciation of *must* /məs/ and *mustn't* /mʌsn/, /ˌju məs raɪt/ /ˌju mʌsn ˈluːz/

Check that students understand the vocabulary in the prompts, then ask them in pairs to make conversations using *must* and *mustn't*. Monitor and prompt. Check that all the students are trying to pronounce *must* and *mustn't* correctly. When they have finished, change roles so that both students get a chance to practise *must* and *mustn't*.

T 4.6 Play the recording so that the students can check their conversations.

Tapescript
G = Grandmother   A = Antony
G You must look after your money.
A Yes, Grandma! I will.
G You mustn't talk to strangers.
A No, Grandma! I won't.
G You mustn't go out when it's dark.
A No, Grandma! I won't.
G You mustn't drink too much beer.
A No, Grandma! I won't.
G You must make sure you eat well.
A Yes, Grandma! I will.
G You must have a bath regularly.
A Yes, Grandma! I will.
G You must phone us if you're in trouble.
A Yes, Grandma! I will.
G You mustn't go anywhere that's dangerous.
A No, Grandma! I won't.

GRAMMAR SPOT (SB p33)

1 Read and discuss as a class. The sentence with *should* expresses a suggestion. The sentence with *must* expresses strong obligation.

2 *Should* and *must* are modal auxiliary verbs.

Refer students to Grammar Reference 4.2 on SB p140.

PRACTICE (SB p33)

Suggestions and rules

1 This activity provides spoken accuracy practice of *should*. Read the instructions and the example as a class. Put students in threes. One student reads the problem aloud, and the other two have to think of suggestions. Students take turns reading the problems and making suggestions.

Sample answers
2 I think you should phone the bank and stop your cheques.
3 I don't think he should drive. I think he should fly.
4 I think you should buy her an alarm clock.
5 I don't think you should buy so many new clothes. I think you should get a job.
6 I think they should wait a few years.
7 I think you should try to find one you like.
8 I think they should join a club.

Extend and personalize the activity by asking students to think for one or two minutes and write down a problem that they have. For example, *I never have time to do homework. I can't understand modal verbs.* Nothing too personal! Then ask them to read out their problem and ask people in the class to suggest solutions. Alternatively, get students to write two problems on two separate slips of paper, then divide the class into groups of four or five. Ask students to put their slips of paper in a pile in the middle of the group. Students should turn over one of the slips and suggest solutions.

2 This activity provides written accuracy practice of *must*. Read through the example as a class, then put students into twos or threes to make a list of rules. A good way of making this relevant is to make it a usable list of class rules. For example, *you must speak only English in class, you must arrive on time, you must work with different partners in every lesson.* When students have prepared some ideas, write the best on the board, then transfer the sentences to a poster that you could pin up on the class notice board as a definitive set of class rules.

A new job

3 **T 4.7** This listening briefly models the language needed for the roleplay that follows.

Focus attention on the photo of Dave. Write *What's Dave's new job?* on the board to help focus the students' listening. Read through the introduction, then play the recording.

Answer and tapescript
Serving customers at Burger Heaven.

T 4.7

D = Dave   M = Manager
D So, um ... what time do I have to start?
M 11.00 in the morning or 4.00 in the afternoon.
D And do I have to wear a uniform?
M Definitely. You have to wear the same uniform as everyone else – a short-sleeved white shirt, black trousers, and a red hat. And a name tag.
D So ... what do I do exactly?
M You serve the customers. Remember – you must always be polite. You say 'Good morning' or whatever the time of day, and then 'Can I help you?' When they tell you what they want, you have to enter it into the computer, and when they're

finished, you should read back what they've ordered. Then you take their money, and you put together their food. That's it.

D Great. When can I start?

M You start at 4.00 tomorrow afternoon.

D Cool.

M Here's your hat. And your name tag. You're all set. Welcome to Burger Heaven, Dave.

4 This activity gives students an opportunity to practise the modal verbs introduced in the lesson in a fluency-based roleplay. Set it up carefully to maximize students' use of modals.

Focus attention on the instructions and the sample questions. Put students into pairs. Ask them to decide who is **A**, the new worker, and who is **B**, the boss. Give them a few minutes to prepare their roleplay, thinking of questions and answers about the topics suggested in the Student's Book. When students are ready, ask them to act out their roleplays. Go around the room monitoring and noting any errors involving the use of modals. At the end, ask one or two pairs to act out their roleplays for the class, or simply ask each boss whether their interviewee got the job. Do an error checklist on the board. Write any sentences you noted that had mistakes, and ask students to work in pairs to correct them.

SUGGESTION

A fun alternative way of doing this is to divide half the class into **A** pairs and half into **B** pairs. The **A** pairs must prepare questions for an interviewee to ask at a job interview. The **B** pairs must decide on a job – it could be an unusual job like traffic warden, lion tamer, or chocolate taster – and think about rules and suggestions to describe the job. When they are ready, mix students so that each new pair has one **A** student and one **B** student. **A** asks questions, and must guess which job **B** is describing.

Check it

5 Ask students in pairs to complete the exercise, then check answers with the whole class.

Answers
1 Can you help me?
2 What time do you have to start work?
3 We aren't allowed to wear jeans at school.
4 We can't do what we want.
5 My mother has to work very hard six days a week.
6 You shouldn't smoke. It's bad for your health.
7 Passengers must have a ticket.

ADDITIONAL MATERIAL

Workbook Unit 4
Exercises 1 and 2 *have to/don't have to*

Exercises 3 and 4 *can* and *be allowed to*
Exercise 5 *should*
Exercises 6–8 *must* and *have to*

WRITING (SB p108)

For and against

Lead in briefly by asking students: *Do you think childhood is the best time of your life? Why/Why not?*

1 Ask students to read the text. What is the opinion of the writer?

Answer
Although the writer presents both sides of the argument, he or she does not think childhood is the best time of your life, because children have no real choice, independence, or money.

Ask students in pairs to replace the underlined words and phrases with those in the box.

Answers
Childhood – the best time of your life
Some people say that childhood is the best time of your life. However, being a child has both pros and cons.
One advantage is that you have very few responsibilities. For instance, you don't have to go to work, pay bills, or do the shopping, cooking, or cleaning. This means you have plenty of free time to do whatever you want – watch TV; play on the computer; go out with friends; play sports, or pursue other hobbies. Another point is that/Moreover, public transport, cinema, and sports centres cost much less for children. All things considered, being a child is an exciting, action-packed time in life.
However, for every plus there is a minus. One disadvantage is that you have to spend all day, Monday to Friday, at school. Studying usually means you have to do homework, and you have to take exams. Another point is that/Moreover, you may have a lot of free time, but you are rarely allowed to do whatever you want. You usually have to ask your parents if you can do things, from going shopping in town to staying out late or going to a party. Finally, although there are often cheaper prices for children, things are still expensive – and parents are not always generous with pocket money. There's never enough to do everything you want. In fact, sometimes there's not enough to do anything at all!
In conclusion, although some people see childhood as the best time in life, in my opinion, children have no real choice, independence, or money. Nevertheless, it is true that choice, money, and independence all bring responsibilities and restrictions – which increase with age.

2 Ask students in pairs to look at the paragraphs and decide on their purpose.

3   Ask students in pairs to match the pros with the cons.

4   Take time to set this up carefully in class. A good way of doing it is to try to turn it into a class brainstorm of ideas with lots of interaction. Try the following:

1   Have a class vote to decide which of the three topics the class would like to prepare.

2   Put students in pairs. Ask half of the pairs to make a list of pros, and half the pairs to make a list of cons. Then write two lists on the board.

3   As a class, edit the two lists so that there are no more than six points in each. Then ask students in pairs to match a pro in one list to a contrasting con in the other list.

4   Ask students in pairs to plan the first three paragraphs of their essay. How are they going to introduce it? What order are they going to put their pros and their cons in the second and third paragraphs?

5   Ask students to use their notes to write four paragraphs. Tell them to express their own opinion in the last paragraph. Set this for homework.

READING AND SPEAKING (SB p34)

How to behave abroad

The aim here is to develop students' ability to read a text intensively. The text is about good manners in different countries and provides a context that encourages further use of modals to express obligation and permission.

> **SUGGESTION**
> A vocabulary exercise on nationality words follows the reading. However, you might like to do it as an extended lead-in before you do this reading text.

1   Begin by asking students two or three questions about manners in their countries. For example, *What do you do when you meet someone new/an old friend? When you go to a friend's home, what do you take as a gift?* You could elicit key vocabulary at this stage, for example, *kiss on both cheeks, shake hands, bow* /baʊ/, *point, nod,* and *shake your head.*

Put students in pairs to discuss the statements. If you have a multinational class, put students in mixed nationality groups to discuss the differences.

2   Focus attention on the photos on SB p34 and ask students to describe what the photos show.

Ask students to read the text and put the missing lines a–e in the correct place. Put students in pairs to check their answers. If this is the first time students have done this sort of exercise, then do the first item as an example. The answer to number 1 is *d*. Ask students what clues helped them to find this, e.g. *vocabulary* (repetition of the word *bow*), *grammar* (use of comparatives, *the more respect/the deeper*).

3   Ask students to read the text again and answer the questions. Let them check their answers in pairs before going over the answers with the whole class.

What do you think?

Give students a few minutes to prepare answers to the questions, then put them in small groups to discuss. Try to mix nationalities if you can. Monitor and note any interesting comments to bring up in the class feedback.

Nationality words

The aim of this activity is to introduce nationality words. It focuses on word stress.

1 If you have a mixed nationality class, ask each student where they are from and what their nationality is. Write them on the board, and mark the stress. Briefly drill any words that are difficult to pronounce.

Ask students in pairs to match the people in **A** and the phrases in **B**. You could follow up by asking students to write a sentence to describe their own nationality in a stereotypical way.

T 4.8 Play the recording so that students can listen and check. Ask students to listen and repeat.

Answers and tapescript
The Italians eat a lot of pasta.
The Chinese cook lots of noodles and rice.
The British invented football.
The Canadians often watch ice hockey on TV.
The French produce champagne.
The Japanese eat raw fish.
The Scots wear kilts on special occasions.

 Focus attention on the Caution Box. It reminds students that all nationality words have capital letters, and if the adjective ends in /s/, /z/, /ʃ/, or /tʃ/ it has no -s at the end. Some nationality words are different from the adjective.

2 Students remain in pairs to complete the chart. Be a little careful about national pride being hurt here. If any of your students come from the countries mentioned in the chart, you may wish to elicit from them what would be typical of their nationality before letting other students write sentences. Encourage the students to add their own nationality and that of others in the class.

Sample answers

Country	Adjective	A sentence about the people
'Italy	I'talian	The Italians love pasta.
'Germany	'German	The Germans make luxurious cars.
Au'stralia	Au'stralian	The Australians love sport.
'Scotland	'Scottish	The Scots make whisky.
'Russia	'Russian	The Russians wear fur hats.
'Mexico	'Mexican	The Mexicans eat spicy food.
The U'nited States	A'merican	The Americans drink cola.
Greece	Greek	The Greeks love to sing and dance.
'England	'English	The English love animals.
'Sweden	'Swedish	The Swedes like skiing.

Come round to my place!

The aim here is to encourage interaction and fluency as students discuss the social rules involved in going to somebody else's home. The *Listening* practises note-taking skills.

1 Focus attention on the questions. This may work best if you ask students to discuss them in groups of three or four before asking each group to report their answers briefly to the class.

2 Before you play the recording, you may wish to check some vocabulary: *spray with water, bring a small gift, be modest, show off, see (someone) out, have people over, a family gathering, a barbecue, sit around, a metal skewer.*

T 4.9 Play the recording. You will probably need to play it a second time, pausing to allow students time to make notes.

Answers and tapescript

	Sumie	Kate	Lucas
Formal/ informal?	formal	informal	informal
Day/Time	about 7 o'clock in the evening at the weekend	around noon	from about 8 p.m. till midnight or later on a Friday or Saturday night
Preparations	tidy the front garden, clean entrance hall and spray it all with water	make one dish; get cups, glasses, knives, forks and supply drinks	none mentioned
Gifts	a small but carefully-chosen gift	a bottle of wine or flowers	a bottle of wine or the dessert
Food/Drink	traditional Japanese meals: sushi, tempura, sukiyaki for foreign guests; spaghetti, Chinese food, steaks for Japanese guests	it's pot luck, so it could be anything	barbecued meat (beef, pork, chicken, or Brazilian sausage), potato salad or rice, coffee or espresso

T 4.9 **Sumie**

My name is Sumie. I come from Nagano, Japan. In my country, we usually invite guests home at the weekend for dinner, at about 7 o'clock in the evening. Before they come, we must tidy the front garden and clean the entrance hall. Then we must spray it all with water to show that we welcome our guests with cleanliness. The guests usually bring a gift, and when they give you the gift they say, 'I'm sorry this is such a small gift,' but in fact they have chosen it very carefully.

When the meal is ready the hostess says, 'We have nothing special for you today, but you are welcome to come this way'. You can see that in Japan you should try to be modest and you should not show off too much. If you don't understand our culture, you may think this is very strange. When we have foreign guests, we try to serve traditional Japanese meals like sushi, tempura, or sukiyaki, but when we have Japanese guests, we serve all kinds of food such as spaghetti, Chinese food, or steaks.

When guests leave, the host and hostess see them out of the house and wait until their car turns the corner of the street; they wait until they can't see them any more.

Kate

My name is Kate and I'm from Bristol in England. We like to have people over for lunch and they usually get here around noon. We often have people over to eat, but sometimes when we invite a lot of people over, for a family gathering for example, we have what's called a 'potluck lunch'.

A potluck is an informal occasion, so people dress casually. If the weather is nice we'll have it outside in the garden. What makes it fun is that everyone who comes has to bring a dish of food. They're given a choice: starter, main course, salad or vegetable, or dessert. As the host, I'll know how many of each kind of dish the guests will bring, but not exactly what the foods will be. That's why it's called 'potluck' – it's a surprise, having a dinner party and not knowing what you're going to feed the guests! All I have to do is make one dish myself and get cups, glasses, and knives and forks together, and supply the drinks.

As the guests arrive, they put their dish on the table, and people help themselves. Some guests might bring a bottle of wine or flowers as a gift but I don't expect anything. It's a fun, relaxed way of getting together with friends or family.

Lucas

My name is Lucas and I'm from Porto Alegre which is in the southern part of Brazil. We like to invite our friends over at weekends, on a Friday or a Saturday night for a 'Churrasco', or Brazilian barbecue. These are very popular in this part of Brazil.

People come about 8.00 in the evening and stay to midnight or even later – sometimes until 2.00 in the morning, whenever people start getting sleepy. People stay a long time; there is no set time for dinner to end. We'll sit around and play cards or just talk. It's very informal. If people want to bring something, I'll tell them to bring something for the meal like a bottle of wine or something for dessert.

Ah, but what about the food? At a 'Churrasco', we cook different kinds of meat on long metal skewers over an open flame. We have all kinds of meat: beef, pork, and maybe Brazilian sausage. Sometimes chicken too. Then we cut off slices of meat from the skewers to serve the guests. It's really delicious. We usually have potato salad or rice as side dishes. After the meal we drink coffee or espresso.

3 Put students in groups to compare information. Go round monitoring and helping.

> **SUGGESTION**
>
> If you have the facilities to have three groups, each working with a tape/CD player, this activity could easily and profitably be done as a jigsaw. Send each group off to listen to a different person, then split the class into groups of three, with one person from each of the original groups in one of the new groups. Students must ask each other questions to complete the chart.

4 Discuss the questions in small groups and then as a class.

EVERYDAY ENGLISH (SB p37)

Requests and offers

Like all the *Everyday English* activities, this one doesn't necessarily have to be done last. It is probably a good idea to break up the rest of the unit by doing this before the end of the unit.

Students will be familiar with a few basic ways of making requests and offers. These activities are aimed at increasing their range, both receptively and productively.

1 Ask students in pairs to match a line in **A** with a line in **B**, and then say who is talking and where the conversations are taking place.

2 **T 4.10** Play the recording so that students can check their answers. Ask students to decide which are offers and which requests, and then to practise the conversations in pairs, paying attention to intonation and stress.

Answers and tapescript
1 A Could you bring us the bill, please? (request)
  B Yes, sir. I'll bring it right away. (offer)
2 A Would you give me your work number, please? (request)
  B Of course. Oh, shall I give you my mobile number, too? (offer)
3 A Can I help you? (offer)
  B Just looking, thanks.
4 A Two large coffees, please. (request)
  B White or black?

5 A Can you tell me the code for Paris, please? (request)
 B One moment. I'll look it up. (offer)
6 A I'll give you a lift if you like. (offer)
 B That would be great! Could you drop me off at the library? (request)
7 A Would you mind opening the window? (request)
 B No problem. It's stuffy in here.
8 A Could I have extension 238, please? (request)
 B That line's engaged. Would you like to hold? (offer)

4 A Hi, Bob. Where are you going?
 B I have a meeting with the web designer and the programmer about our new website this afternoon.
 A Could you do me a favour? Would you mind asking the programmer to call me? I have a question for him about the budget.
 B Sure. No problem.

Roleplay

Put students in pairs to choose one of the situations and prepare a conversation. When they are ready, ask them to come to the front and act out their conversations, preferably without a script. It can be fun to record students with a camcorder, if possible, and give feedback and correction as you view.

Don't forget!

Workbook Unit 4
Exercise 9 Vocabulary – Word formation
Exercise 10 Pronunciation – Correcting wrong information
Exercise 11 Phrasal verbs – Separable or inseparable?

Word list
Photocopy the Word list for Unit 4 (TB p156) for your students. Ask them to write in the translations, learn them at home, and/or write some of the words in their vocabulary notebooks.

Now practise the conversations in open pairs across the room. Ask students to close their books. Indicate which two students you want to talk, and say a one-word prompt, for example, *shop, restaurant, phone, café*. Students must remember the conversation.

Refer students to Grammar Reference 4.3 and 4.4 on SB p141. This is short enough to do in class. Or you could set it for homework prior to the lesson.

3 **T 4.11** Play the recording. Students listen to the four conversations and complete the chart. Play the recording a second time. Ask students to write the words used to make each request.

Answers and tapescript

	Who are they?	What are they talking about?
1	Husband and wife	something that happened at work
2	Customer and shop assistant	a pair of shoes which are faulty
3	Parent and child	music which is being played too loud
4	A boss and employee	a meeting; a computer programmer

1 Could you ... ?
2 Can I ... ?
3 Will you ... ?
4 Could you ... ? Would you mind ... ?

T 4.11
1 **A** So, anyway, there I was, sitting in my boss's office. All of a sudden, the phone rings and my boss says ...
 B Sorry to interrupt, darling, but I think the baby's crying. Could you go and check?
2 **A** Can I help you?
 B Yes, I bought these shoes here two days ago, and the heel on this one is already broken. Can I change them for a new pair?
 A Of course. Let me see if we have another pair in your size.
3 **A** Will you turn down that awful music?
 B What?
 A Will you turn down that awful music? Or better still – turn it off!
 B Oh, all right.

5

Future forms
The weather
Travelling around

On the move

Introduction to the unit

The theme of this unit is travelling and going on holiday. It naturally contextualizes the various uses of future forms contrasted in this unit.

Sorting out the various future forms that exist in English is often difficult for both teacher and learner. The *Practice* sections provide practice with different ways of talking about the future.

In the *Reading and speaking* text, the owner of a travel agency describes her ideal holiday. In the *Listening and vocabulary* section, students listen to a weather forecast and complete four weather summaries.

The *Writing* section at the back of the book practises booking holiday accommodation by fax.

Language aims

Grammar – future forms   It is often said that English does not have a future tense. Instead, it has four or five main *forms* that refer to the future. What dictates the speaker's choice of form depends on aspect, that is, how the speaker views the event, not certainty or proximity to the present, which is what students often believe. It is the abstract nature of aspect that makes the area difficult and often makes more than one form possible – it depends how you see it!

Another factor which influences the choice of future form is *when* the decision is made – *before* the moment of speaking or actually *at* the moment of speaking.

In many languages, the spontaneous intention or offer is expressed by a present tense, but this is not possible in English.

*I'll give you a ride to the station. Not *I give you …*

This use was practised in the *Everyday English* section of Unit 4.

POSSIBLE PROBLEMS

This unit looks at three ways of referring to the future: *will*, *going to*, and the Present Continuous. Your students will probably have come across all three at some time, but it is unlikely that they are using them correctly. Students often overuse the Present Simple to refer to the future, and they use *will* where English would more naturally use *going to* or the Present Continuous.

Common mistakes

A *What do you do tonight? A Have you decided yet?
B *I watch TV. B *Yes. We'll go to Spain.

A The phone's ringing. A *When you go home?
B *OK. I answer it. B *I'm go home soon.

Try to stress the following:

• Use *will* for future facts and intentions or offers made at the moment of speaking.
• Use *going to* for intentions made before speaking.
• Use the Present Continuous for arrangements between people.

Vocabulary   The vocabulary input is the lexical set of the weather, looking at nouns *(sunshine)*, adjectives *(It's sunny)*, and verbs *(The sun's shining)*.

Everyday English   The *Everyday English* section deals with language used when travelling on different kinds of transport.

Notes on the unit

TEST YOUR GRAMMAR (SB p38)

This section aims to find out whether students can recognize the different future forms and how much they know about their use. Often students can identify the forms but are unable to say what is the difference between them. If students look worried, reassure them that learning this is the aim of Unit 5. Keep any explanations of use very short at this stage.

1 Ask students in pairs to match sentences in **A** with sentences in **B**. When they have finished, ask them to underline the future forms and discuss the difference in meaning. Monitor to see how much they know.

Answers

1 **A** The phone's ringing.
   B I**'ll get** it!
   (The *will* future or Future Simple for a decision – an offer – made at the moment of speaking.)

2 **A** Look at those black clouds!
   B I think it**'s going to rain**.
   (*Going to* for a prediction based on present evidence.)

3 **A** What **are** you **doing** tonight?
   B I**'m staying** at home. I**'m going to watch** a video.
   (The Present Continuous is used here to ask about and state a pre-planned arrangement. The last sentence is *going to* for an intention made before speaking.)

4 **A** I'm sick and tired of winter!
   B Don't worry! It**'ll be** spring soon.
   (The *will* future for a future fact.)

5 **A** Where **are** you **going** on your holiday?
   B We **might go** to Prague, or we **might go** to Budapest.
   (Modal verbs, like *might*, can be used to refer to the future. Here it expresses an intention, but it also expresses uncertainty.)

> **NOTE**
> The rules of use are explained more fully in Grammar Reference 5.1 on SB p141. However, at this stage, don't spend time with lengthy explanations. Just try to discover what students know.

Check answers with the whole class.

You may wish to extend this activity by asking students in pairs to improvise longer conversations based on these opening lines.

2 Students ask and answer the questions in pairs. Ask several students to share their answers with the whole class. Correct as necessary.

Future forms

1 Ask students to read the introduction and the examples. Point out the form *going to* + infinitive. Note that we don't usually say *going to go* or *going to come*. *He's going to go to the hairdresser's* sounds unnatural.

Drill the examples around the class, correcting any mistakes.

Focus attention on the handwritten list. Look at the second item on the list, and ask *Where's he going? What's he going to do?* to elicit *He's going to the petrol station* and *He's going to fill up the car with petrol*. Model the sentences a few times yourself, then drill them around the class to establish the form and pronunciation of going to /gəʊɪŋ tə/ and to reinforce that we don't usually say *going to go*.

Ask students in pairs to make other sentences that answer the questions, *Where's he going today?* and *What's he going to do?*

Answers

Places to go	Things to do
He's going to the hairdresser's.	He's going to get a haircut.
He's going to the petrol station.	He's going to fill up the car with petrol.
He's going to the bank.	He's going to pay the electricity bill.
He's going to the travel agent's.	He's going to get/pick up the plane tickets.
He's going to the library.	He's going to take some books back to/get some books out of the library.
He's going to visit Nick.	

Things to buy
He's going to buy some sugar.
He's going to buy some yoghurt.
He's going to buy some milk.
He's going to buy some tennis balls.

Ask individual students around the class to give you sentences. Correct carefully.

> **SUGGESTION**
> You could set up a question and answer drill across the class with different pairs, such as:
> **A** *What's he going to get from the travel agent's?*
> **B** *He's going to get the plane tickets.*
> **C** *What's he going to do at the library?*
> **D** *He's going to get out/borrow some books.*
> **E** *What's he going to buy at the supermarket?*
> **F** *He's going to buy some sugar and some milk.*

2 **T 5.1** Ask students to cover the conversation, but look at Ben's list on SB p38. Play the recording. Students listen to the conversation between Ben and Alice and tick all the things they mention that are on the list.

Ask students to work in pairs to complete the conversation with the correct future form. Then play the recording again so that they can check their answers.

Answers and tapescript

B = Ben   A = Alice

B I'm going shopping. Do we need anything?
A I don't think so. ... Oh, hang on. We haven't got any sugar.
B It's OK. It's on my list. **I'm going to buy** some.
A What about bread?
B Good idea! **I'll get** a loaf.
A Erm, what time will you be back?
B I don't know. I might stop at Nick's. It depends on how much time I've got.
A Don't forget we**'re playing** tennis with Dave and Donna this afternoon.
B Don't worry. I **won't** forget. **I'll be** back before then.
A OK.

Put students in pairs, then give them three or four minutes to memorize the conversation. Ask them to close their books and practise.

3 The aim of this exercise is controlled practice of *will* for spontaneous intentions. Focus attention on the list of things and ask students where you would go to buy them.

Model the conversation between Alice and Ben by asking a student *Can you get some stamps, please, honey?* and prompting the student to respond with the next line in the example conversation. Then say *And we need two steaks* and prompt another student to respond. Make sure they are using and pronouncing *I'll* /aɪl/ correctly. Put students in pairs to continue making conversations. Monitor closely, correcting pronunciation and intonation.

SUGGESTED CONVERSATION

A *Can you get some stamps, please?*
B *OK. I'll go to the post office.*
A *And we need two steaks.*
B *OK. I'll go to the butcher's and buy them.*
A *Don't forget some shampoo.*
B *OK. I'll go to the chemist's and buy some.*
A *Can you get some film for the camera?*
B *OK. I'll go to the photographer's and buy some.*
A *And don't forget a newspaper.*
B *OK. I'll go to the newsagent's and buy one.*
A *Can you get a tin of white paint?*
B *OK. I'll go to the hardware shop and buy one.*
A *Can you get a video?*
B *OK. I'll go to the video shop and rent one.*

A *And don't forget a CD.*
B *OK. I'll go to the music shop and get one.*

Discuss as a class: *Why does Ben use 'will' and not 'going to'?* Explain that Ben is deciding as he is speaking.

GRAMMAR SPOT (SB p39)

1 Put students in pairs to answer the questions, then discuss answers with the whole class.

Answers

I'm going to buy some = a decision made *before* speaking.
I'll get a loaf = a decision made *at the moment of* speaking.

Note that if students have problems here, you can ask questions to check their understanding. Ask students to look at the list, and ask the following:
Is sugar on the list? (Yes.)
Did Ben decide to buy the sugar before Alice reminded him to buy some? (Yes.)
So why does he use 'going to'?

Is a loaf of bread on the list? (No.)
Did Ben decide to buy the loaf before Alice reminded him to buy it? (No.)
So why does he use 'will'?

2 Ask students to answer the question in their pairs, then discuss answers with the whole class.

Answers

a future possibility = I might stop at Nick's.
a prediction = I'll be back before then.
a future arrangement = We're playing tennis this afternoon.

You can check the use of the Present Continuous here by asking, *Did Ben and Alice plan this tennis match before the conversation?* (Yes.)

Refer students to Grammar Reference 5.1 on SB p141.

PRACTICE (SB p40)

Discussing grammar

1 Ask students in pairs to underline the correct verb form in each sentence.

Answers

1 *I'm going to take* (decision made before speaking)
2 *I'll call* (spontaneous decision/promise)
3 *They're going to lose* (prediction based on present evidence)
4 *I'll send* (spontaneous decision)
5 *we're getting married* (future arrangement)
6 *We might go* (not certain)

What's going to happen?

The aim of this exercise is controlled practice of *going to* for planned intentions. Note that there are one or two examples where we avoid saying *going to go* or *going to come*.

2 Tell students they are going to hear three short conversations. Do the first conversation with the whole class to get them started. Focus students' attention on the example and the picture of the suitcase. Ask the class *What can you see in the suitcase?* to elicit useful vocabulary from the listening such as *passport, traveller's cheques, swimming costume, pack a suitcase.*

T 5.2 Play the recording for conversation 1. Elicit sentences with *going to* and write them on the board. (See answers below.) Play the recording again so students can listen and check.

Put students in pairs. Play the recording for conversations 2 and 3. In their pairs students write sentences about the other two conversations using *going to*. If necessary, students may refer to the tapescript on SB p124 for help.

> **Suggested answers and tapescript**
> **Conversation 1**
> They're going on holiday.
> They're going to get a taxi to the airport (in half an hour).
> They're going to stay at the Grand Hotel.
> They're going to take traveller's cheques, swimming costumes, tennis rackets, and books.
> They're going to play tennis and read on holiday.
>
> **Conversation 2**
> They're going to get married (in a church).
> They're going to have the reception at a hotel.
> They're going on honeymoon in Rome.
>
> **Conversation 3**
> They're going to move house/flat.
> The removal men are coming early at about 7.00 a.m.
> They're going to live in the country.
> They're going to get the baby's room ready.
> They're going to have a baby.
> They're going to call the baby Tom if it's a boy and Natalie if it's a girl.
>
> **T 5.2**
>
> 1 A Have you got the plane tickets?
>   B Yes. They're with the passports and traveller's cheques.
>   A What time is the taxi coming?
>   B In about thirty minutes. What's the name of the hotel we're staying at?
>   A The Grand Hotel.
>   B Have you remembered your swimming costume this year?
>   A Oh, yes, it's packed. What about tennis rackets?
>   B I put them in my case, with the fifteen books.
>   A Right. Let's get these cases closed.

> 2 A Well, darling, it's our big day soon.
>   B I know. I can't wait. I hope the weather's good.
>   A Yes, it makes such a difference, doesn't it?
>   B The church is looking beautiful.
>   A And the hotel's getting ready for the reception.
>   B And then there's our honeymoon in Rome.
>   A Ah!
>
> 3 A Have you packed the books and the pictures from the living room?
>   B Yes. And all the kitchen things are packed, too.
>   A That's it then. What time are the removal men coming?
>   B Early, I hope. About 7.00 in the morning.
>   A Good. It's a long drive, *and* it's right in the middle of the countryside.
>   B I can't wait to be there.
>   A And I can't wait to get the baby's room ready.
>   B Tom if it's a boy and Natalie if it's a girl. How exciting!

Check answers with the whole class. Encourage students to correct one another for content and linguistic correctness.

What do you think will happen?

3 The aim of this exercise is to practise *will* for a future fact or prediction. For many of the sentences in this exercise, it could be argued that *going to* is also possible, but for now stress that *will* in this exercise is used to express future facts, i.e. predictions, and not intentions or offers.

Read the instructions and example with the whole class, then get students started by asking for a sentence with *it/be a nice day tomorrow*. Elicit *I think it'll be a nice day tomorrow*, say it yourself, then ask students to repeat. Ask the class to match it with a sentence from column **B**.

Put students in pairs to complete the exercise. During feedback, help students with their pronunciation.

T 5.3 Play the recording so that students can check their answers. Play it again, this time pausing for students to repeat the sentences.

> **Answers and tapescript**
> 1 I think Jerry will win the tennis match. He's been playing really well lately.
> 2 I think it'll be a nice day tomorrow. The forecast is for warm and dry weather.
> 3 I think I'll pass my exam on Friday. I've been studying for weeks.
> 4 I think you'll like the film. It's a wonderful story, and the acting is excellent.
> 5 I think we'll get to the airport in time. But we'd better get going.
> 6 I think you'll get the job. You have the right qualifications and plenty of experience.

4 Read the instructions. Point out that we don't say **I think I won't …* Instead, we say *I don't think I will … .* (This is

called *transferred negation*, but students don't really need to know this.)

Read the example, and drill it around the room. Again, ask for a sentence with *it/be a nice day tomorrow*. Elicit *I don't think it'll be a nice day tomorrow*, say it yourself, then drill it. Ask students to complete the exercise in pairs. Correct any errors during feedback, paying particular attention to the form and pronunciation of *I don't think … will/'ll*.

T 5.4 Play the recording so that students can check their answers. Play it again, this time pausing for students to repeat the sentences.

Talking about you

5 Model the activity by producing one or two *I think I'll …* sentences of your own. They could be amusing: *I think I'll give you extra homework tonight. I think we'll have an exam next week.* Then put students in pairs or threes to make sentences about themselves from prompts 1–7. Go around the room, helping and correcting as necessary.

This activity can be easily personalized. List some prompts on the board that refer to pertinent events or activities that may be happening soon. It could be *Italy/win the World Cup*, or *it/be a white Christmas*, or *Maria/pass her driving test*. Ask students to make predictions about these things.

Arranging to meet

This section practises the Present Continuous for future arrangements. This is an area that students at this level are usually familiar with, but it is unlikely that they use it accurately and appropriately on the occasions a native

speaker would. Remind students of its rules of form and use before doing the activities which follow. Write some diary entries on the board, for example:

Monday	play tennis with Jill
Tuesday	visit Uncle Frank
Wednesday	go to the doctor
Thursday	go swimming
Friday	see friends

Tell students that this is your diary for next week. Model and drill each sentence: *I'm playing tennis with Jill on Monday*, etc. Elicit the question, *What are you doing on Monday?* Drill it, then get students to ask questions across the class. Finally, put students in pairs to ask and answer questions based on the diary or using their own information.

Ask students why we use the Present Continuous here (*we are making arrangements ahead of time*). Point out that we only use the Present Continuous with a limited number of verbs, all to do with moving, meeting, activities, and entertainment, for example *seeing friends, going swimming, having lunch, catching a train, playing tennis*.

6 **T 5.5** This listening provides a model for the simulation activity which follows. Read through the introduction and the questions as a class, then play the recording.

MY	I don't know. I might be free.
L	OK. Why don't we meet at the Internet Café at about 5 o'clock? We can have a coffee and do our work.
MY	Sounds good to me. Are you going out in the evening?
L	Yes. I'm going out for dinner with a couple of friends. Do you want to join us?
MY	That would be great! I'd love to.
L	OK. So we'll meet tomorrow at 5 o'clock at the Internet Café.
MY	Good.

Ask a volunteer to draw the chart on the board and fill in the information. Discuss any questions. Play the recording again if necessary.

7 Read the instructions as a class. Students work individually to fill in their diary for the weekend. Stress that they should leave one morning, one afternoon, and one evening free.

8 Put students in pairs to decide why they need to meet, then start the activity. The pairs must find a time and a place to meet. This will be done very quickly by some pairs, while others will take longer. Go round monitoring and helping.

Finish the activity by asking different pairs to tell the class why, when and where they're meeting.

ADDITIONAL MATERIAL

Workbook Unit 5
Exercises 1–6 Future forms

READING AND SPEAKING (SB p42)

Hotels with a difference

In the reading text, the owner of a travel agency describes some unusual holiday destinations. It involves a prediction task, a comprehension task, vocabulary in context, and finally, a personalized discussion.

1 Begin this activity and raise interest by personalizing it. If your class is reasonably well-travelled, ask them to think of the best hotel they have ever been to, then put them in groups of three to describe it. Write questions on the board to help them: *Where was it? When did you go there and why? What was special about it?* Alternatively, you could describe a hotel that you have stayed in. Bring in a picture if you have one.

Ask students in pairs to look at the pictures on SB p42 and answer the questions. You may want to pre-teach *an igloo, a sail, a helipad,* and *a safari.*

Answers
1 The Ice Hotel: Canada   2 The Burj al-Arab: Dubai
3 The Baobab Rivers Lodge: Tanzania

2 Students work in their pairs to think of another question to write about each hotel. Monitor and help.

3 Ask students to read the article and the brochure and try to answer the questions in exercise 2. Let them check their answers in pairs before discussing with the whole class.

Then ask students in their pairs to answer the questions in exercise 3. They should be able to remember most of the answers, or to find them quickly in the article. Encourage them to talk together, skimming and scanning the text, rather than reading through the whole article again.

Answers
• She has her own travel agency. She helps people plan holidays.
• She needs to know where she's sending people.
• A little bit of everything: lazing on a beach, reading, exploring new places, going around markets and food stores.
• Because she travels a lot, and she's not home very often.
• Deer – sleeping bags in the Ice Hotel are made of deer skins. Camels – you can visit camel races in Dubai.
  In Tanzania, you can see elephants, rhinos, lions, crocodiles, hippos, and rare birds.

4 Ask students to work in pairs to complete the chart.

Answers

	Canada	Dubai
Which hotel is she staying at?	The Ice Hotel	The Burj al-Arab
How long is she staying there?	Four nights	A few days
What's special about the hotel and her room?	The hotel is made of ice. The room has a sleeping bag made of deer skins.	It's shaped like a giant sail. Each room has sea views.
What's she going to do there?	Visit the art galleries and ice cinema, and have drinks in glasses made of ice.	Eat in the hotel restaurant, shop in the markets, and visit the camel races.

5 Ask students in pairs to look again at the brochure, then to take turns asking and answering similar questions to those in exercise 4, using the information in the brochure. You may wish to get additional reading material and photos about these hotels on the Internet to give to students.

Language work

Ask students to find synonyms in the text. Do the first as an example.

Encourage students to make guesses from the context of the sentence before checking in their dictionaries.

What do you think?

Depending on time, you could ask students to do this as a discussion in pairs, or you could give them a bit more preparation time, and organize a more extended discussion in groups around one of the questions.

For the second question ask students to think of five things that are important to an ideal holiday, for example, hot weather, good company, etc. Then put them in groups of four, and ask them to work together to agree on a list which represents all their interests. Alternatively, ask each student to think of their ideal holiday and four reasons why it would be special. Then, in groups of four, each student has to tell the others about their ideal holiday.

Rather than just asking where students are going for their next holiday, write a list of prompts on the board, and give them four or five minutes to prepare a short presentation for the class based on the prompts. When they are ready, listen to as many presentations as time allows. Prompts might include *Who are you going with? When are you going? What's special about the place? What are you going to do there?* If your class is large, ask students to do this in small groups.

WRITING (SB p109)

Making a reservation

This exercise introduces key phrases used to make and confirm a reservation at a bed and breakfast. It also practises writing a formal letter.

Note: *Bed and breakfast* accommodation is usually in private houses or small hotels and includes breakfast in the price of the room.

Lead in by asking students about faxes. *Have you ever sent a fax? Why? Who to? When you write a fax, what information do you need to provide?*

1 Read the introduction, and ask students to fill in the details on the fax form.

Answers

To: Anne Westcombe
Subject: accommodation enquiry
Date: today's date
To fax no. 01326 230579

2 Ask students in pairs to put the words in order and write them into the message part of Janet's fax.

Answers

a I would like to reserve two rooms at your bed and breakfast.
b We are arriving on 27 August.
c We hope to stay for six nights departing on 2 September.

d My husband and I would like a double room preferably with an en-suite bathroom.
e I would also like to reserve a room for our two teenage daughters.
f Both should be non-smoking rooms.
g Would it be possible to have rooms facing the sea?
h Do you have rooms available for these dates?
i Could you also tell me the price of each room?
j I look forward to hearing from you.

3 Ask students in pairs to look through the information and think about how they can express it. Ask them to write a reply letter or fax to Janet. You could set this for homework.

LISTENING AND VOCABULARY (SB p44)

A weather forecast

This section revises and extends weather vocabulary. It involves word-building around nouns, verbs, and adjectives. The listening is a weather forecast. It involves listening for specific information, and revises the use of *will* for prediction.

1 Ask students in pairs or small groups to complete the chart with words from the box.

POSSIBLE PROBLEM

Students will probably know one word to go with each symbol, but not all the parts of speech. They may get the different parts confused, for example, *It's sunshine today. *It was rain yesterday. *The weather was sun.*

Answers

Adjective	Noun	Verb
It's **sunny**.	**sunshine**	The sun's **shining**.
It's **rainy**.	**rain**	It's **raining**.
It's **snowy**.	**snow**	It's **snowing**.
It's **windy**.	**wind**	The wind's **blowing**.
It's **cloudy**.	**cloud**	
It's **stormy**.	**storm/thunderstorm**	
It's **foggy**.	**fog**	
It's **icy**.	**ice**	

You now need to practise these items. You could do a little sketch of the symbols on the board, and point to them one by one. Students have to give you all three items for each symbol. Correct all mistakes carefully.

2 Ask students to look at the map of Western Europe, and work in pairs to name the countries 1–10. Ask them which countries make up Scandinavia and to find them on the map.

Answers

1 Scotland	5 Holland	9 Switzerland
2 Northern Ireland	6 Belgium	10 Italy
3 Wales	7 France	
4 England	8 Spain	

Scandinavia is made up of Denmark, Sweden, Norway, Finland, and Iceland.

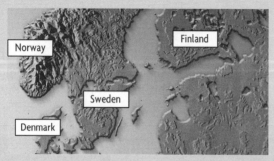

Note: Iceland does not appear on the map.

Ask students in pairs to choose two countries and prepare to talk about them. Make sure that between them the students describe all the countries. Ask two or three pairs to tell the class about their countries.

If your students are likely to know very little about these places, you could bring in pictures, and be prepared to describe them in feedback. To link with the rest of the unit, make sure you talk about the climate.

3 Ask students to look at the map, and ask them what they think the weather will be like in the different areas.

T 5.6 Put students into four groups **A–D**. Explain that they are going to listen to a weather forecast, and that they should make notes about their part. Play the recording. Let them check with the other members of their group before checking with the whole class. They will probably need to listen twice.

Answers and tapescript

A weather: rain, snow on mountains; temperatures: 5° or 6°, or lower

B weather: rain, sunshine, light winds from the south; temperatures: 8° – 15°

C weather: clear skies, lots of sun, some cloud, strong winds; temperatures: 24° in the far south, 18° or 19° elsewhere

D weather: stormy with thunder and lightning, 2 inches of rain, snow, early morning fog, strong winds; temperatures: 10°

T 5.6

And here's the weather for some popular destinations in Western Europe for the next twenty-four hours.

A Let's begin in the north. I'm afraid spring isn't here yet! Another major frontal system will move in from the Atlantic affecting Northern Ireland and Scotland, before moving on to Scandinavia. It's going to bring plenty of rain, which could fall as snow on Scottish mountains. So it will feel very chilly everywhere. Temperatures around five or six degrees at best in the rain but much lower in snowy areas, where they will stay around freezing all day, you'll be lucky to see two degrees.

B Moving south now, into England and Wales, most of northern France, and across through Belgium and Holland. Things look more springlike here and it will be a lot brighter than in recent weeks. Along Channel coasts especially, there may be a little rain at first, with temperatures reaching only eight degrees. Inland, however, there will be more sunshine than showers, with all areas becoming warmer and drier as the day goes on. Towards the end of the day temperatures could be as high as 15 degrees in these regions. The winds will be light, coming from the south but it will feel very pleasant.

C If you're lucky enough to be going to southern France or Spain you'll find the best of today's weather. In the far south of Spain, mainly clear skies, lots of sun with high temperatures for the time of year up to 24 degrees, and everywhere else 18 or 19 degrees with some cloud. But it's not all good news. Strong winds along the southern French coast could spoil your evening walk.

D Further east, across the Alps, from Switzerland into northern Italy, there are the remains of another weather system. There will be stormy weather during the day with thunder and lightening, bringing over two inches of rain to some lowland areas and heavy snow to the mountains. Strong winds and rain will continue most of the day. The winds will make it feel much cooler for the time of year with temperatures struggling to reach ten degrees. And watch out for early morning fog.

So that's it, a quick tour of Western Europe – not bad in central countries, warm and sunny in Spain; cool, wet and windy in parts of Italy, and Switzerland – oh, and stay away from those Scottish mountains unless you're wearing warm clothes.

4 Ask students in pairs to say what the weather is like where they are today. Then ask students what they think it will be like tomorrow – and ask them to write a forecast. This could take a while, so allow enough time. Go round monitoring and helping. Make sure they are using the vocabulary from the lesson, and *will* for prediction. When they are ready, ask one student from each pair to read out their forecast. A fun way of doing this is to put a large map of the country you are in on the board or wall, and ask the students to point to different parts as they deliver their forecast, just like on the TV. If your students are different nationalities, they could prepare a forecast for their own country.

EVERYDAY ENGLISH (SB p45)

Travelling around

This section introduces useful phrases connected with travelling and extends the use of future forms.

Begin by asking students questions about public transport in their country. *How do you travel around? How do you get to school? What's the cheapest form of transport? Are the buses/trains reliable? What's the traffic situation like?*

1   Read the introduction as a class. Ask students to match each line with a form of transport.

Answers		
1 ferry	4 taxi	7 plane
2 train	5 plane	8 car
3 bus	6 taxi	9 underground

2   Ask students to match a line from exercise 1 with a reply.

Answers				
a 8	c 5	e 7	g 3	i 6
b 4	d 2	f 1	h 9	

T 5.7   Play the recording so that students can listen and check their answers.

Tapescript
1   **A** Do you think it'll be a rough crossing?
    B Well, the forecast is good, so it should be pretty smooth.
2   **A** Excuse me, I think those seats facing the front are ours.
    B Oh, I'm sorry. We didn't know they were reserved.
3   **A** We're going to Market Street. Could you tell us when it's our stop?
    B Just sit near the front and I'll call it out.
4   **A** Can you take us to the airport?
    B Of course. Hop in!
5   **A** Can I take these bags on with me?
    B I'm sorry. Only one item of hand luggage per passenger.
6   **A** That's all right, you can keep the change.
    B Thanks a lot. Do you want a hand with those bags?
7   **A** Excuse me, are we landing on time?
    B Yes. We're beginning our descent soon.
8   **A** No, no! He said turn *left* at the lights, not right!
    B Look! *You* drive and *I'll* give directions from now on! Right?
9   **A** How do I get to Oxford Circus?
    B Take the Piccadilly Line, eastbound, and change at Green Park.

Ask students to practise some of the conversations in pairs. Insist on good pronunciation.

Roleplay

Read through the introduction and examples and answer any questions. Students prepare their roleplays. Notice that the roleplay should review the functional areas of requests and offers, which were practised in the *Everyday English* section of Unit 4.

Ask some of the pairs to act out their roleplays for the rest of the class. Encourage comments from the others.

Don't forget!

Workbook Unit 5
Exercise 7 *somebody, nobody, anybody, everybody*
Exercise 8 Vocabulary – *make* or *do*
Exercise 9 Pronunciation – Vowel sounds and spelling
Exercise 10 *in, at, on* for place

Word list
Photocopy the Word list for Unit 5 (TB p156) for your students. Ask them to write in the translations, learn them at home, and or write some of the words in their vocabulary notebooks.

6

like • Verb patterns
Describing food, towns, and people
Signs and sounds

I just love it!

Introduction to the unit

The theme of this unit is descriptions. Question forms with *like* as a verb and a preposition are introduced, and various verb patterns are examined.

The *Reading and speaking* section is about pizza, its history and popularity. The *Listening and speaking* is a jigsaw activity, comparing living in the United States and living in the United Kingdom.

The *Writing* section at the back of the book practises relative pronouns and participles in a description.

> **NOTE**
> There are many examples of comparative adjectives in the *Vocabulary* section and the two recordings. If you think your students would benefit, you could do some further revision on comparatives and superlatives; or, you might decide they have a reasonable grasp already.

After Units 4 and 5, where the language aims were quite challenging, students should find Unit 6 a bit easier.

Language aims

Grammar – *like*   Students will, of course, be familiar with *like* as a verb, although they might confuse *like* and *would like*.

Common mistakes

A **Do you like a coffee?*   B *Yes, please.*

A *Would you like a coffee?*   B **Sometimes.*

A *Do you like swimming?*   B **Yes, that's a good idea. Let's go.*

Another common mistake is with the short answer.

A *Do you like coffee?*   B **Yes, I like.*

There are more problems with *like* as a preposition, and more specifically with the question *What … like?* This is a very common question. Students will have come across it many times already, but may not be using it.

> **POSSIBLE PROBLEMS**
> On a superficial level, the question *What is X like?* asks for a comparison: *Compare X to something that I am familiar with.* The answer could be a comparison, but it is more likely to be a general description. So on a deeper level, the question means *Tell me some relevant features about X because I don't know anything about it.*
>
> **Common mistakes**
> Students confuse *What … like?* with *How …?* and *like* as a verb.
> A *How's your mother?*   B **She's very kind. She's taller than me.*
> A *What's your mother like?*   B **She's like cooking and reading.*
>
> Students usually appreciate that *What does he look like?* asks for a physical description, but they probably won't realize that *What's he like?* may be asking for a description of either his appearance or his character, or both.

Verb + *-ing* or infinitive?   Students will probably know that there are a lot of verbs followed by another verb. These simply have to be learnt. There is a list of Verb patterns on SB p158.

Vocabulary   The important area of collocation is practised with adjectives that commonly go with people, places, and food.

Everyday English   This activity focuses on examples of language, some spoken and some written, that students will encounter in an English-speaking environment, for example, *Pay and Display* in a car park and *Dry clean only* on clothes.

Notes on the unit

TEST YOUR GRAMMAR (SB p46)

This section's main aim is to check whether students know the difference between *like* when used as a verb and *like* when used as a preposition.

1   Do the first item as an example, then ask students to complete the sentences about themselves. Monitor and see whether students are correctly using the verbs presented and *like* as a preposition.

> **Sample answers**
> 1   I look just like my **mother**.
> 2   I like my coffee **black with one sugar**.
> 3   On Sundays, I like **staying in bed late**.
> 4   After this class, I'd like to **go for a coffee**.
> 5   When I'm on holiday, I enjoy **walking and sightseeing**.
> 6   Yesterday evening, I decided to **go to bed early**.

2   Ask a few students to read their sentences to the class.

Check the form during the feedback. Ask which sentences use *like* as a verb (2, 3, and 4) and which use *like* as a preposition (1). Ask which are followed by -*ing* (*like* and *enjoy*) and which are followed by an infinitive (*would like* and *decide*).

A STUDENT VISITOR (SB p46)

Questions with *like*

The aim here is to help students distinguish between the different uses of *like*, which are confusing in that they are of a similar form and often don't translate easily. Note that in many languages *How is she?* means *Describe her.* Consequently, students will choose this form instead of *What's she like?*

1   Introduce the idea of studying in a foreign country, and ask the question in the Student's Book. If your students are already abroad, you could ask some questions about their experience: *Where are you staying? What's it like? Have you made any friends? What are they like?*

2   Focus students' attention on the photos and read the instructions together to set the scene. Ask students to read the conversation without worrying about the gaps. Ask a simple comprehension question: *Do Sandy and Soon-hee have much in common?* (Yes.)

Put students in pairs to read the conversation again, putting one of the questions in the box into each gap. Don't give students an explanation of each question before they read the conversation. Let them see how much they know. There are plenty of exercises that explain and practise the questions in the next section.

> **Answers**
> 1   What's she like?

2   What does she like doing?
3   What does she look like?
4   What would she like to do?
5   How is she now?

T 6.1   Play the recording so that students can listen and check their answers. Ask students in pairs to practise the conversation.

Tapescript
S = Sandy   N = Nina
S   Our student from Seoul arrived on Monday.
N   What's her name?
S   Soon-hee.
N   That's a pretty name! What's she like?
S   She's really nice. I'm sure we'll get on well. We seem to have a lot in common.
N   How do you know that already? What does she like doing?
S   Well, she likes dancing, and so do I. And we both like listening to the same kind of music.
N   What does she look like?
S   Oh, she's really pretty. She has big, brown eyes and long, dark hair.
N   Why don't we do something with Soon-hee this weekend? What should we do? Get a pizza? Go clubbing? What would she like to do?
S   I'll ask her tonight. She was a bit homesick at first, so I'm pretty sure she'll want to go out and make some friends.
N   How is she now?
S   Oh, she's OK. She called her parents and she felt much better after she'd spoken to them.
N   Oh, that's good. I can't wait to meet her.

GRAMMAR SPOT (SB p47)

1–2   Do the first item as an example, then ask students in pairs to complete the rest.

> **Answers**
> a   What's she like? (preposition)
> b   What does she look like? (preposition)
> c   What does she like doing? (verb)
> d   What would she like to do? (verb)
> e   How is she now?

Refer students to Grammar Reference 6.1–6.3 on SB pp142–143.

PRACTICE (SB p47)

Talking about you

This activity provides controlled, personalized, spoken practice. Students might feel that they know all these questions already, although they continue to make mistakes with them. The personal nature of the questions will make the activity fun and interesting for students.

1 Ask students around the class three or four of the questions. Then nominate three or four students to ask you questions. Make sure they are asking the questions with good pronunciation and intonation. Then, put students in pairs to ask and answer the questions. Go round helping and correcting as necessary.

Listening and asking questions

2 **T 6.2** Play the recording. Students listen and tick the correct questions.

Answers and tapescript
1 What's Thai food like?
2 What's Bridget like?
3 How's your brother?
4 What does she like?
5 What's the weather like there?
6 What does he look like?
7 What was your holiday like?
8 What kind of books do you like?

T 6.2
1 Thai food? It's delicious. It can be spicy, but it doesn't have to be.
2 Oh, she's very nice. You'd really like her. She's the kind of person you can always go to with a problem.
3 Not very well. He still has a temperature and a bad cough.
4 Well, she's crazy about horses. I don't think she has any other hobbies. Oh, she plays golf sometimes.
5 It's not very nice at all. It's raining, it's cold, and it's pretty miserable. What about where you are?
6 Mmm ... a little like you, as a matter of fact. He's about the same height, tall with blond hair, but your hair's longer and straighter than his. Other than that, you two are quite similar.
7 It was great. Really relaxing. Lots of sunshine, good food. We did almost nothing but sit by the pool and read books for the whole two weeks.
8 I like all kinds, but I suppose I like biographies and detective stories best.

ADDITIONAL MATERIAL

Workbook Unit 6
Exercises 1–2 *like*
Exercise 3 *like* and *as*

A THANK-YOU LETTER (SB p48)

Verb patterns

The aim here is to introduce and practise a number of basic verb patterns in English. The approach is to find out how much students know by testing their ability in the first

exercise, then going through some basic rules, and providing some practice. There are no difficult grammatical rules to grasp here, but since the verb patterns are likely to be different from those in your students' first languages, they need a lot of practice and revision.

Ask students to read the letter through once. Write two or three simple questions on the board to provide a focus: *Was Soon-hee homesick during her stay?* (Yes.) *What was Australia like?* (Hot.) *Did she get on with Sandy?* (Yes.)

Put students in pairs to read the letter again, and choose the correct verb form.

T 6.3 Play the recording so that students can listen and check their answers.

SUGGESTION
To reinforce the point, go through the exercise again, asking students to say what pattern follows each verb. Say a verb, for example, *want, enjoy, manage,* and get students to reply *Plus infinitive,* or *Plus '-ing.'*

This should highlight some problems. For example, *stop* can be used with both patterns and has a different meaning in each one.

Answers and tapescript

1 to say	6 to call	11 to do
2 having	7 to visit	12 going
3 meeting	8 me to stay	13 hearing
4 feel	9 to see	14 know
5 feeling	10 to go	

T 6.3
Dear Sandy and family,
I just wanted to say thank you for having me as your guest in your beautiful home. I had a great time. I really enjoyed meeting your friends. You all made me feel so welcome. You know how much I missed my family at first, but you were so kind that I soon stopped feeling homesick. I can't find the words to tell you how grateful I am. I'd like to call you. What's a good time to call?
You know that on my way home I stopped to visit my aunt in Perth. It was so hot! It was over 35 degrees all the time but I absolutely loved it. My aunt wanted me to stay longer, but I wanted to see my parents and my brother Sang-chul. But she's invited me to go back and I'd love to do that. I'm thinking of going next year.
Anyway, I'm looking forward to hearing from you very soon. Let me know if you ever want to visit Seoul. My brother and I could take you to a 'norebang' (a singing room). It's a bit like karaoke!
Love to you all,
Soon-hee
P.S. Do you like the picture of Sang-chul and me?

Verb patterns

1 Ask students to complete the examples from Soon-hee's letter.

Answers
a I really enjoyed **meeting** your friends.
b I just wanted **to say** thank you.
c My aunt wanted **me to stay** longer.
d You all made **me feel** so welcome.
e Thank you **for having** me as your guest.

Note that students often find it frustrating that some verbs are followed by -ing and others by the infinitive, and there seems to be no way for them to know which. The best advice is simply to revise, practise, and learn them. However, you may wish to point out, when reading sentence **b**, that verbs are often followed by the infinitive when there is some future idea. For example, *I hope* (now) *to be rich one day* (in the future), *I decided* (first) *to start a business* (after taking the decision). It is, though, only a tendency, and there are exceptions.

2 Ask students in pairs to match the sentences with the pictures. In the feedback, ask them if they can explain why. Ask if they know any other verbs that follow this pattern (*start, try, remember, forget*).

Answers
a 1 *stopped* + infinitive means that they stopped (interrupted) the activity – i.e. shopping – in order to talk to each other. They stopped, then they talked.
b 2 *stopped* + -ing means that they stopped doing the activity. They were talking, then they stopped.

3 Ask students to complete the examples from the letter.

Answers

I soon stopped **feeling** homesick.	(I was homesick, then I felt better.)
I stopped **to visit** my aunt.	(I interrupted my journey to visit her.)

Refer students to the list of Verb patterns on SB p158.

PRACTICE (SB p49)

What's the pattern?

1 Ask students in pairs to put the verbs from the thank-you letter in the correct columns.

It is a good idea to copy the completed chart onto an overhead transparency (OHT) or wall chart so that students can refer to it when checking their answers.

Answers

verb + -ing	verb + to + infinitive	verb + sb + to + infinitive	verb + sb + infinitive (no to)	preposition + -ing
enjoyed meeting stopped feeling	wanted to say would like to call stopped to visit wanted to see	wanted me to stay invited me to go	made me feel let me know	(thank you) for having (thinking) of going (looking forward) to hearing

2 **T 6.4** Play the recording. Pause after each sentence, and ask students to add the verbs they hear to the correct column in the chart in exercise 1. Do the first as an example. Let students check their work in pairs. Refer them to the list of Verb patterns on SB p158 to check their answers.

Answers and tapescript

verb + -ing	verb + to + infinitive	verb + sb + to + infinitive	verb + sb + infinitive (no to)	preposition + -ing
finish don't mind hate	promise forget need	tell ask	let help	(succeed) in (look forward) to

T 6.4
1 They **promised to bring** the wine.
2 The teacher **told them to do** their homework.
3 I've just **finished answering** my emails.
4 Don't **forget to take** you passport.
5 He finally **succeeded in passing** his driving test.
6 We **asked him to move** his car.
7 I just **need to go** to the loo. I'll be back in a minute.
8 I **don't mind looking after** your cat.
9 Just **let me finish** what I'm saying.
10 Please can you **help me carry** this upstairs?
11 I **hate shopping** for clothes.
12 She's really **looking forward to working** with us.

Discussing grammar

3 Focus attention on the example, then put students in pairs to tick the correct verbs.

Answers

2 a, b	3 b, c	4 a, b	5 b, c	6 a, b

4   Ask students in pairs to make sentences using the other
    verbs. Ask different students to give you sentences during
    the feedback.

Answers
1 My father **couldn't mend** my bike.
2 She **made** her son **turn** down his music.
3 I **refuse to go** on long walks.
4 We **enjoy going** shopping.
5 She **wanted** me **to do** the cooking.
6 I **decided to work** for the bank 20 years ago.

ADDITIONAL MATERIAL

Workbook Unit 6
Exercises 4–7 Verb patterns

READING AND SPEAKING (SB p50)

The world's favourite food

The topic of the reading text is the history and popularity
of pizza. There is a scanning and specific information task,
vocabulary work on types of food, and a review of *like* and
verb patterns. Food is a topic guaranteed to generate interest
and discussion, so allow plenty of time for the activities.

1   Ask students in pairs to think of typical dishes from the
    countries listed. If they can't think of one from a
    particular country, tell them to move on. If you have a
    mixed nationality class, ask them to discuss typical
    dishes from their countries.

Sample answers
Spain: paella, tortillas
Italy: pasta, pizza, polenta, gnocchi
Germany: sauerkraut, sausage
Japan: sushi, rice, raw fish
Hungary: goulash, cherry soup
China: chow mein, sweet and sour pork, chop suey
Mexico: taco shells, chili con carne, peppers, beans, tortillas
the United States: burgers, fried chicken, steak, hot dogs
England: roast beef and Yorkshire pudding, roast lamb, pies,
    sausages, fish and chips, bacon
all countries: hamburgers, pizzas, fried chicken, chips, rice

2   These words are common pizza ingredients which
    appear in the text. Students may not know them all, but
    may be able to guess. You could start by eliciting typical
    pizza ingredients and writing them on the board. Then
    put students in pairs to say which are fish or seafood. Let
    students use dictionaries, or define them in simple ways:
    herring is a type of fish; sweetcorn is yellow.

Answers
anchovies, eel, squid, herring, salmon, shrimp, tuna

T 6.5 Play the recording. Students listen and repeat
the words in the box.

3   Begin this scanning task by establishing a time limit,
    e.g. four minutes. Ask students to scan through the text
    in that time and underline or write down all the foods
    they can find. Let them check their answers
    in groups of three or four. Then, in the feedback, check
    to see how many words they found.

Answers
bread, onions, herbs, cheese, ham, tomato, mozzarella cheese,
basil, pepperoni, crème fraîche

4   Ask students to read the text more carefully and answer
    the questions. Let them check their answers in pairs
    before discussing as a class.

Answers
1 The McDonald's sign is found worldwide.
2 They are both popular, universal fast foods. Pizza is easier to
   make and serve and is more varied.
3 Nobody knows. It evolved over the years.
4 *Plakuntos* came first. They were eaten with simple toppings,
   like oil and garlic.
5 Tomatoes came from Mexico and Peru.
6 They are the same colours – red, white, and green.
7 It became popular after World War II when soldiers
   returning from Italy raved about the dish.

5   Ask students to read *Pizza Trivia* again quickly.

    Then put students in pairs or small groups to make
    questions. You may want to do one or two as examples to
    remind students how to form questions correctly. When
    they have finished, mix students so that they are paired
    with a student from another group. Ask them to take
    turns asking and answering questions. You could ask
    them to close their books and see if they can remember
    the answers.

Suggested questions
1 How many slices of pizza do Americans eat per second?
2 How many pizzerias are there in the United States?
3 How much money does the pizza industry make per year?
4 Which month is national pizza month?
5 Where and when did the first pizzeria open?
6 How many restaurants and delivery/takeaway outlets does
   Pizza Hut have?
7 Which is the favourite/least favourite topping in the US?
8 Which toppings are the most popular/Which are the
   favourite toppings in Japan/Russia?
9 Which toppings do they like in Brazil/Australia?
10 Which toppings do the French/English like?/do they like in
   France/England?

What do you think?

This works best if you put students in small groups to discuss. Ask one student from each group to summarize the discussion for the whole class.

Language work

This reviews the main grammatical focus of the lesson. If you feel students have already done enough work in this area, you may wish to leave it out.

Ask students in pairs to find the examples in the reading text or in *Pizza Trivia*.

> **Answers:**
> - *like* as a verb: *In Brazil, they like ...* (*Pizza Trivia*)
> - *like* as a preposition: *like the Italian flag.* (paragraph 1)
> - *enjoyed eating* (paragraph 1)
> - *asked to try* (paragraph 1), *decided to make* (paragraph 2)
> - *easy to make/serve* (introduction), *silly to talk about* (paragraph 1)

VOCABULARY (SB p52)

Adjectives for food, towns, and people

The aim is to expand students' vocabulary about these topics, and develop their awareness of collocation.

> **SUGGESTION**
> If collocation is a new idea for your students, you could begin by eliciting many words that go together. Ask for words that go with *turn off*, for example, *a light, an oven, a stereo*; words that go with *egg*, for example, *fry, boil, break*; words that go with *happy*, for example, *New Year, birthday, ending.*

1   Ask students in pairs or small groups to decide which four words in each group cannot go with the noun in the middle. Encourage them to make guesses, then use their dictionaries to check. Allow plenty of time – there is a lot to explore, and many related questions may arise.

> **Answers**
> **Food:** disgusted, wealthy, tasteful, starving
> **Town:** young, antique, excited, capital
> **People:** expensive, antique, long, crowded

2   Ask students in pairs to complete the conversations.

> **NOTE**
> In this activity and the jigsaw listening next, there is a lot of built-in practice of comparatives and superlatives. There is no *Practice* section for these exercises because students should be familiar with them by now. If your students are having problems, however, you could do a revision lesson.

T 6.6   Play the recording so that students can listen and check their answers. Then students practise the conversations in pairs.

> **Answers and tapescript**
> 1 **A** Nick's really quiet and **shy**. He never says a word.
>   **B** Yeah, his brother is much **more outgoing**.
> 2 **A** What's Carrie's boyfriend like?
>   **B** Well, he's **tall**, dark, and handsome, but he's not very polite. In fact, he's even **ruder** than Carrie!
> 3 **A** How was your lunch?
>   **B** Ugh! It was awful. The pizza was **disgusting**. We were really **starving**, but we still couldn't eat it!
> 4 **A** Mmm! These tomatoes are really **delicious**. Did you grow them yourselves?
>   **B** Yes, we did. All our vegetables are **home-grown**.
> 5 **A** Did you have a good time in London?
>   **B** We had a great time. There's so much to do. It's a really **exciting** city. And there are so many people from all over the world. I think it's nearly as **cosmopolitan** as New York.

You could extend this activity by asking students to write their own sentences, using some of the new words from the collocation exercises.

Talking about you

3   Put students in pairs. Ask them to look at SB p153.

1   Ask each student to write information on the three things listed. Encourage them to use the adjectives studied so far in the unit. Tell them to choose places and people that their partner probably won't know.

2   Students exchange lists with their partners and ask and answer questions about the things on the lists.

3   Each student reports back to the class about one item on their partner's list.

LISTENING AND SPEAKING (SB p52)

New York and London

This is a jigsaw activity. You will need two tape recorders, and ideally two rooms, so that each group can listen to their recording separately.

1   Ask students to look at the pictures of New York and London and write down what they know about them. Elicit ideas from the class and list them on the board. Find out whether any students have visited either city.

2   Divide students into two groups, **A** and **B**. If possible, send one group to another room, or at least make sure that the groups are at opposite ends of the classroom. Draw a chart on the board like the one in the Answer Key. Ask students to copy it into their notebooks, leaving enough room to fill in the information they will hear. Ask students to read the introduction relevant to them.

T 6.7 **T 6.8** Students play the recording and then fill in the chart. Let them operate the equipment. They may need to listen more than once.

Answers and tapescripts

	Justin and Cinda	Alan
people	Not unfriendly, in a hurry, many nationalities	Londoners are more reserved and cynical than Americans.
places	Love architecture	Fantastic theatres, art galleries, museums, concerts, orchestras
work / holidays	People work later, longer hours, take fewer holidays	Leisure time is really important to the British. More holidays than in the US.
getting around	Taxi drivers are rude, don't know where they're going. Subway is cheaper. Cinda doesn't drive in NY – too scary	Taxis are great. Taxi drivers are friendly. Underground is expensive.
shops	Great. Fifth Avenue is too expensive. Shops are always open.	Shops stay open longer than they used to.
food	Everyone eats out or gets food delivered. People don't cook.	Much better now. Favourite food is Indian.

T 6.7 New York

I = Interviewer   J = Justin   C = Cinda

I How long have you been here in New York?
J Nearly three years.
I And are you enjoying it?
J We love it.
C It's great.
I So what do you like best?
C Oh, the atmosphere, the mixture of all kinds of people. The speed of everything – it's exciting.
J I love the architecture, it's so different from London. Walking the streets and looking up at all those skyscrapers.
I And what about the people?
C Well, New Yorkers have a reputation for being rude and unfriendly, but I don't think that's true. People are always in a hurry, but they're not unfriendly.
J What I love is the – the great mixture of nationalities and cultures. It's got to be the most cosmopolitan city in the world.
I More than London?
J Hmm ... well, I think so, but they're both very mixed.
C Life here seems much faster than in London. Everyone's in such a rush. Everything's done for speed. For example, I – I

don't think people cook at home much – everyone seems to eat out or get food delivered because it's quicker and easier.
I Have you made many friends here?
J I've made friends at work mostly. But it's – it's difficult to make friends outside of work – people are so busy. But mostly I find people pretty friendly.
C Except the taxi drivers! Some of the rudest people I've ever met are New York taxi drivers!
J And some of the worst drivers. Every time I sit in a taxi I say a prayer. They drive so fast and suddenly they change lanes. And worst of all they don't seem to know where anything is.
C Yeah – you spend the entire journey giving directions. Anyway, I like using the subway. It's cheap.
J Yeah, and easy to use and it seems safe to me. We walk a lot as well. It's a lot safer now than it was ten years ago. It's still not very clean but it's getting better.
I Do you have a car?
J No. No, we don't. Not many of our friends do, actually. You don't really need one.
C I'd hate to drive in the city, I'd be terrified. Anyway, you can get everything delivered to your door – not just food.
I Don't you go shopping?
J Oh yeah, of course we do. Not all of us can afford to shop on 5th Avenue, you know! But it's – it's fun to look.
C Actually, the shops – sorry, the stores – are great. Always open – well nearly always – til 9.00 or 10.00 at night.
J People work much later here. I wasn't expecting to work such long hours! And the holidays – sorry, vacation time – and the – the public holidays they're, they're much shorter. I only get ten days a year. It's difficult for people like us with families in other countries. It's difficult to find time to visit them.
I But generally you're happy?
J Fantastic!
C It's an amazing place, but in a few years I think I'll be exhausted and ready for a quieter life!

T 6.8 London

I = Interviewer   A = Alan

I Alan, how long have you lived in London?
A Fifteen years.
I And do you like it here?
A Sure I like it – but London is one of those cities that you love and hate at the same time.
I So first – what do you hate?
A Oh the usual big city things – the crowds, the dirt, the traffic, and of course the Underground – it's so expensive compared with the subway in New York.
I And what do you like?
A Oh, a lot: fantastic theatres – I'm an actor so that's important for me – great art galleries, museums, I love the Natural History Museum. Concerts, wonderful orchestras. The best of everything comes to London.
I And what's best for you?
A For me? Oh, I just love standing on Waterloo Bridge and looking down the river at the Houses of Parliament and now, of course there's the London Eye – I think it's just

wonderful. And – I like travelling in the black cabs. Taxi drivers here are great, so friendly! They tell you their life stories AND they know every street in London – not like in New York.

I And what about the people? What do you think of Londoners?

A Ah well – generally speaking, I think that they do live up to their reputation – they are reserved. It takes a while to get to know people. They won't tell you about themselves. You say to an American 'How are you?' and you get 'Oh man, I'm just great. I got the promotion and I love working here in Dallas, Denver, Detroit or Delaware etc. y' know'. Ask an Englishman 'How are you?' and you get 'Er – fine, thank you'.

I So the stereotype's true?

A Yeah, they're – they're pretty reserved. They don't like giving personal details, but they complain a lot about life generally. They seem much less positive about life – much more cynical than Americans. They grumble about transport and politicians and money, how much things cost, their work …

I So, we're a miserable lot then!

A Not really. Leisure time – sorry – *free* time – is really important to the British. I think for many Americans, work is the most important thing in their lives. Americans work much longer hours. In Britain they get more vacation time and time off …

I … and still they grumble!

A Yeah.

I You've been in London 15 years. Has it changed in that time?

A Oh yeah a lot – especially the shops, they stay open much longer now. They used to close every Wednesday afternoon. People in the States could never believe that. Oh and the food!

I Everyone says English food is terrible. Is it?

A Well, when I first came it was terrible. It was so hard to get good food. Nowadays it's not hard at all. London has some *great* restaurants – my favourite here is the Indian food, it's fantastic. I think we have one of the best right here on our street. Just the best!

I You live in south London. Do you like it there?

A Very much. I love the mix of cultures and nationalities in every street.

I How long do you think you'll stay here?

A Oh, I don't know. Maybe five more years. Maybe forever!

3 Ask students to find a partner from the other group and compare their information. There is probably no need for you to check understanding, but you might want to ask a few questions just to make sure.

WRITING (SB p110)

A description (1)

1 Ask students to think of their favourite room. Ask them to close their eyes, and picture it. Then ask them to draw a plan of it on a piece of paper.

Ask students to write down why they like it and some adjectives to describe it, for example *My favourite room is my kitchen. I like it because it is light and spacious.*

Ask students in pairs to show each other their plans and talk about why they like their rooms.

2 Ask students to read the description of a favourite room, and answer the gist question.

> **Answer**
> It's the place where family and friends come together.

You may need to check new words. *Gravitate*, here, means naturally move towards.

3 Ask students to complete the description using the relative clauses.

> **Answer**
> 1 like best
> 2 where we cook and eat
> 3 where family and friends come together
> 4 who are cross and sleepy
> 5 which is the focal point of the room
> 6 which tells the story
> 7 whose family have all emigrated
> 8 that we're going to next Saturday
> 9 we haven't seen
> 10 which means

GRAMMAR SPOT (SB p110)

1 Ask students to find and underline the relative pronouns in exercise 3. In the feedback, ask students to say what they refer to, and when we use them.

> **Answers**
> *which tells the story* refers to the huge noticeboard.
> *that we're going to* … refers to a wedding.
> *where we cook and eat* refers to the kitchen.
> *whose family have all emigrated* refers to Auntie Nancy.
> *which is the focal point* refers to the rectangular table.
> *which means* refers to the fact that they use the front door.
> *who are cross and sleepy* refers to children.
> *where family and friends* … refers to the kitchen.
> We use *which* (or *that*) to refer to things.
> We use *who* (or *that*) to refer to people.
> We use *where* to refer to places.
> We use *whose* to refer to someone's possessions.

2 Ask students to look at the sentences. Which relative pronouns can be omitted and why?

> **Answers**
> This is the room ~~which~~ I like best.
> He's a friend ~~who~~ we haven't seen for years.
> When *who, that,* or *which* is the object of a relative clause, it can be left out.

3 Ask students to look at the examples of participles, and rewrite them with relative pronouns.

> **Answers**
> I have so many happy memories   **that we spent** there.
> of times   **which we spent** there.
>   **we spent** there.
> There is a large window **that/which looks** out onto two apple trees in the garden.

Refer students to Grammar Reference 6.5 and 6.6 on SB p143.

4 Ask students in pairs to link the sentences with the correct relative pronoun. Do the first as an example.

> **Answers**
> 1 The blonde lady **who/that** is wearing a black dress is Pat.
> 2 There's the hospital **where** my sister works.
> 3 The postcard **which/that** arrived this morning is from Auntie Nancy.
> 4 I passed all my exams, **which** made my father very proud.
> 5 Did you meet the girl **whose** mother teaches French?

5 Ask students in pairs to complete the sentences with a word from the box in the present or past participle. Do the first as an example.
Remind students that we use -*ing* clauses to say what somebody or something *is* or *was doing* at a specific time, and we use -*ed* clauses when the clause has a passive meaning.

> **Answers**
> 1 I spend hours in my room **listening** to music.
> 2 I have lots of posters **stuck** on the walls.
> 3 My brother is in his bedroom, **playing** on his computer.
> 4 There are photos of my family **arranged** on my shelves.
> 5 I also have a colour TV **given** to me on my last birthday.

6 Ask students to write a similar description of their favourite room in about 250 words.
Encourage them to use relative pronouns and participles to link their sentences. Set this for homework.

EVERYDAY ENGLISH (SB p53)

Signs and sounds

There is no production task to this exercise, and no extension. It is simply for recognition of signs and pieces of conversation that students will come across if they are living in an English-speaking environment.

1 Ask students to work in pairs to think about where they might see the words. Feedback as a class.

> **Answers**
> 1 At a reception desk in an office building
> 2 On an article of clothing
> 3 In a car park
> 4 On a tube or bottle of cream or medicine that is to be applied to the skin
> 5 In a cloakroom/changing room
> 6 In a restaurant
> 7 On a label on a container of a harmful household product like bleach
> 8 On a packet of cigarettes
> 9 At an airport
> 10 On a garage door or private entrance on a street

2 Ask students to work in pairs to think about where they might hear the words. Then get feedback as a class.

> **Answers**
> *Coming up next ...* : on the radio
> *Please listen ...* : on a telephone booking line
> *Please place your tray ...* : on a plane
> *How would you ...* : in a bank
> *Just looking ...* : said in reply to a sales assistant asking *Can I help you?*
> *We apologize ...* : on a station announcement

Don't forget!

Workbook Unit 6
Exercise 8 Vocabulary – Antonyms and synonyms
Exercise 9 Pronunciation – Sentence stress
Exercise 10 Phrasal verbs

Word list
Photocopy the Word list for Unit 6 (TB p157) for your students. Ask them to write in the translations, learn them at home, and/or write some of the words in their vocabulary notebooks.

> **EXTRA IDEAS UNITS 4–6**
> On p124 of the Teacher's Book there is a song with suggested activities to exploit it.
> If you have the time and feel that your students would benefit from this, photocopy it and use it in class. You will find the song after Unit 6 on the Class Cassette/CD.
> The answers are on p149 of the Teacher's Book.

Stop and check 2 (TB pp136–137)
A suggestion for approaching the *Stop and check* tests is in the introduction on TB p5.

Progress test
There is a *Progress Tests* for Units 1–6 on TB pp142–144.

7

Present Perfect active and passive
Phrasal verbs
On the phone

The world of work

Introduction to the unit

This unit marks the beginning of the second half of *New Headway Intermediate – the NEW edition*. The first half included revision and extension of many of the basic tenses of English, but did not focus on the one tense which is often the most difficult for students to master – the Present Perfect. The second half of the course, therefore, begins with a comprehensive study of all the main uses of this tense. The Present Perfect and Past Simple are contrasted in the context of interviewing for a job and discussing past life experiences. The Present Perfect active and passive are contrasted in the context of news stories.

The *Reading and speaking* section includes interviews with people who have jobs that they love, and the *Listening and speaking* section focuses on one man's retirement lifestyle.

The *Writing* section at the back of the book focuses on letters of application for a job.

Language aims

Grammar – the Present Perfect   Perfect tenses in English bring together different times. These tenses all give the idea that one thing *happens before* another time or event. The Present Perfect relates past to present.

I've lived here for six years. (I lived here six years ago, and I still live here now.)

You've cut your hair. (I see evidence now of something you did in the past.)

Students at this level will undoubtedly be familiar with the form of the Present Perfect, although they probably do not completely understand its uses, all of which relate past time to present time. This unit brings together all of its uses.

In the first section of the unit, *The Job Interview*, two of the uses of the Present Perfect are covered: talking about unfinished past (an event or activity that began in the past and continues into the present) and talking about life experiences (an event that happened at an unspecified time in the past).

The second section, *It's in the News*, covers the third use of the Present Perfect: to focus on the current evidence or importance of past events. It also covers the Present Perfect passive. Throughout, the Present Perfect is compared and contrasted with the Past Simple. All of the exercises are geared towards helping students make the distinctions necessary to decide which tense to use in a particular situation. Time expressions used with the different tenses are also reviewed and contrasted, for example *for, since, in, ago*, etc.

POSSIBLE PROBLEMS

1 The same verb form (auxiliary *have* + past participle) exists in many other European languages where it is often interchangeable with other past tenses. However, its uses in English are very specific (see above), and it is *not* interchangeable with the Past Simple.

2 The Present Perfect joins past and present in a way other languages do not. These languages express the same ideas by using a past tense or a present tense. Students' mistakes are usually as a result of this.

3 *For* and *since* are often misused.

Common mistakes	Corrections
*I have seen him yesterday.	I saw him yesterday.
*He has been there last year.	He went there last year.
*She is a teacher since six years.	She's been a teacher for six years.
*I live here since 1998.	I've lived here since 1998.
*How long do you know Mary?	How long have you known Mary?

Note that this unit deals with the Present Perfect Simple only. The Present Perfect Continuous is covered in Unit 10.

Vocabulary   This section focuses on phrasal verbs. Students will be familiar with many of these. Aspects of both their form and use are practised.

Everyday English   This section introduces useful telephone phrases. Different types of formal phone conversations are practised.

Notes on the unit

TEST YOUR GRAMMAR (SB p54)

This section reviews the Present Simple and the Past Simple and contrasts their uses with the Present Perfect tense.

It is also a personalized activity where students interview partners and then report back to the class. It's a particularly useful activity if the class is new or has new members.

Do not go into detail over the tense usage. The students are asked simply to form and name tenses.

1   Ask one or two students a few of the questions, then give students three or four minutes to read through the questions and think of their answers.

> **Sample answers**
> 1   I'm a student.
> 2   For two years./Since 2001./I don't have a job; I'm a student.
> 3   I worked in a bank./I was at school.
> 4   I've been to Hungary and Canada.
> 5   I went in 1993./Ten years ago. I went there on business/holiday.

2   In pairs, students take turns asking and answering the questions. Monitor and correct any grammar mistakes, but show more interest in the personalized side of the activity than the grammar. Ask a few students to report back to the class. They will now be practising the third person, e.g., *Yuji is a student.*

3   Ask the class to name the tenses in exercise 1.

> **Answers**
> 1   Present Simple
> 3, 5   Past Simple
> 2, 4   Present Perfect Simple

THE JOB INTERVIEW (SB p54)

Present Perfect

This section illustrates two uses of the Present Perfect – the unfinished past and life experience. They are compared with the Present Simple and Past Simple.

1   Begin by asking students about their jobs: *What do you do? How long have you had the job? What qualifications do you have?* Elicit or pre-teach the meaning of key vocabulary: *journalist, seeking, based in, cover, requirements, experience, a plus, CV.*

Ask students to read the advertisement for the position of business journalist and answer the questions.

2   Ask students to look at the photograph of Nancy Mann being interviewed by David Benton for the job advertised on SB p55.

T 7.1   With books closed, play the recording of the first part of Nancy's interview and ask students if they think she will get the job and if so, why. Has she got the right experience?

3   Ask students to read the first part of the interview, and work with a partner to complete the sentences. This section compares the unfinished past use of the Present Perfect with the Present Simple and Past Simple.

> **Answers and tapescript**
> **D = David Benton   N = Nancy Mann**
> **D**   Who **do** you work for now, Nancy?
> **N**   I work for Intertec Publishing. We publish international business magazines.
> **D**   I see. And how long **have** you worked for them?
> **N**   I**'ve** worked there for nearly five years. No, *exactly* five years.
> **D**   And how long **have** you been in charge of Eastern Europe publications?
> **N**   For two years.
> **D**   And what **did** you do before you were at Intertec?
> **N**   I worked for the BBC World Service.

T 7.1   Play the first part of the interview again. Ask students to listen and check their answers.

> **GRAMMAR SPOT** (SB p55)
>
> **1–2** Ask students to answer the questions in pairs. Then go over them with the whole class.
>
> > **Answers**
> > 1   Yes, she does.
> >   No, she doesn't.
> > 2   Nancy says *I **work** for Intertec Publishing* because she works for them now. (Present Simple)
> >   She says *I**'ve worked** there for nearly five years* because she is talking about past time and present time. She began working for them five years ago and she still works for them now. (Present Perfect)
> >   She says *I **worked** for the BBC World Service* because she doesn't work there any more. It is a finished event in the past. (Past Simple)
>
> Refer students to Grammar Reference 7.1 and 7.2 on SB pp143–144.

4   Ask students to read the second part of the interview and work with a partner to complete the sentences. This section compares the life experience use of the Present Perfect (events happening at an unspecified past time) with the Past Simple.

T 7.2 Play the second part of the interview so that students can check their answers.

> **Answers and tapescript**
> **D = David Benton   N = Nancy Mann**
> **D** As you know, this job is based in Geneva. **Have** you **ever** lived abroad before?
> **N** Oh, yes. Yes, I **have**.
> **D** And when **did** you **live** abroad?
> **N** Well, in fact, I **was** born in Argentina and I **lived** there until I was eleven. Also, I lived in Berlin for one year, when I **was** working for the BBC.
> **D** That's interesting. **Have** you **travelled** a lot?
> **N** Oh, yes, yes, absolutely. I've **travelled** to most countries in South America and many countries in Europe. I've also **been** to Japan a few times.
> **D** Oh yes? And why **did** you **go** to Japan?
> **N** It was for Intertec. I **went** there to interview some Japanese business leaders.

WRITING (SB p112)

A letter of application

Lead in by asking about letters of application for a job. *Have you ever written a letter of application? What information do you include in a letter of application?*

1   Ask students to read Nancy's letter of application quickly for gist: *What sort of job is she applying for?*

> **Answer**
> A job in journalism.

Then ask students to complete the letter using the phrases and words in the box. Let them check in pairs before checking with the whole class.

> **Answers**
> **I am writing in response** to your **advertisement** ...
> **As you will see** from the enclosed **CV** ...
> **I consider myself** the ideal candidate ... all the relevant **experience**.
> I have travelled **widely** in South America ... frequently go to Japan **on business**.
> I speak French, German, and Spanish **fluently**.
> I am an enthusiastic and **hard-working** person.
> I ... can meet **deadlines**.
> **I look forward to hearing** from you ...

2   Ask students to answer the questions.

> **Answers**
> 1 A journalist based in Geneva.
> 2 In today's *Guardian*.
> 3 Her CV. (curriculum vitae = a form that provides details of her work experience and qualifications).

4   She has the right qualifications, all the relevant experience, and she is enthusiastic, hard-working, and good at organizing and meeting deadlines.

3   Ask students to read the job advertisement. Ask a few questions to focus them on the text and the task: *What personal qualities are needed? What qualifications or experience might be useful? Would you like this job? Would you be good at this job?*

4   Ask students to answer the questions in exercise 2, and make notes. Students could imagine they are the 'ideal' candidate for the job – that they fulfil all the requirements (and more!). Check that they know that they are writing to Martin Ruane, and that they should include phrases like *I am writing in response to* ... , *I look forward to hearing from you* ... , and that they should end their letter with *Yours sincerely*. Ask them to use their answers to write a letter of application. Set this for homework.

PRACTICE (SB p56)

Life stories

The aim here is to practise the form and use of the Present Perfect for unfinished past and for experience.

1   Do one or two examples with the whole class. Then ask students in pairs to complete the exercise. Point out that they will learn more about Nancy's life – this activity does not simply repeat what she said in the interview.

T 7.3 Play the recording so that students can listen and check their answers. Then check answers with the whole class. You may want to ask why the Present Perfect and Past Simple are used in each case.

> **Answers and tapescript**
> 1 She was born in Argentina in 1969.
> 2 She went to school in Buenos Aires until she was eleven.
> 3 She studied modern languages and journalism for three years at University College, London.
> 4 She's worked for Intertec for the last five years.
> 5 She left the BBC five years ago.
> 6 She lived in Berlin while she was working for the BBC.
> 7 She's been married twice.
> 8 She's visited Japan a few times.
> 9 She hasn't heard if she got the job at Worldwatch Europe yet.

Ask students to close their books and tell the story of Nancy's life to their partners. Go round listening for any errors made with the Present Perfect.

2   Model this activity by writing similar information about your life on the board. Break each sentence into two parts as in exercise 1, and ask students to match the events with the time expressions. This can be a lot of fun.

It may be difficult for students to write jumbled sentences about themselves right away. First, get them to write six true sentences about their lives. Then they can either rewrite them with the time phrases in a jumbled order, or cut the sentences into strips. In pairs, students rearrange each other's sentences. End by asking a few students to tell the class about their partners.

Talking about you

3 Do the first one as an example, then ask students to complete the sentences.

Go round helping as necessary. Make sure that students are using the Present Perfect correctly. As a whole class, ask for sentences from different students. Ask the class to correct any errors.

Answers
Students' own answers.

Have you ever ... ?

4 If you think students need to revise past participle forms before doing exercise 5, put them in pairs to write the Past Simple and past participle forms of the irregular verbs. Or you can do this orally with the whole class. Remind students that there is a list of irregular verbs on SB p157. They can use this to check their answers.

Answers

Verb	Past Simple	Past participle
go	went	gone
write	wrote	written
drive	drove	driven
lose	lost	lost
have	had	had
read /riːd/	read /red/	read /red/
ride	rode	ridden
sleep	slept	slept
be	was/were	been
eat	ate	eaten
win	won	won
meet	met	met

5 Ask students to read the instructions and the example conversation. Practise the conversation with several different students. Try to model the fall-rise intonation in the *Have you ever ... ?* question, and the falling intonation in the short answers and the *When?* question. (See Unit 1 teaching notes p7 and p10 for intonation patterns.)

In pairs, students use the prompts to make conversations. Make it clear that they don't have to do the whole list, but only those that interest them. Go round helping as necessary. You can further prompt the conversations of strong students with more questions.

Ask various students to tell the class about their partners,

thereby practising the third person.

Sample answer
Sandra has never had an operation and she's never been on TV, but she has won an award. She won an award for a science project at school.

ADDITIONAL MATERIAL

Workbook Unit 7
Exercises 1–7 Present Perfect Simple
Exercises 8 Tense review

IT'S IN THE NEWS (SB p56)

Present Perfect active and passive

This presentation section has a dual purpose. It illustrates the third use of the Present Perfect – the importance or evidence in the present of a past event, often used when giving news. It also introduces the Present Perfect passive.

1 Ask students to read the newspaper headlines. Some words might be new to them, e.g. *escapes*, *awarded*, *hits*, *laid off* and *knocked out*. Answer questions about meaning, but don't go into detail now about grammatical form. Ask students to predict what the stories are about.

2 **T 7.4** Pre-teach the meaning of *widespread damage* and *slowdown*. Play the recording while students listen. Were their predictions correct? Play the recording again while students complete the sentences. Let them check in pairs before going over the answers with the whole class.

Answers and tapescript
Here are today's news headlines.
Convicted murderer Charles Watkins (1) **has escaped** from Belmarsh Prison in South London. Two Spanish novelists (2) **have been awarded** the Nobel Prize for literature. Hurricane Jeffrey (3) **has hit** the Caribbean, causing widespread damage in Puerto Rico. Two thousand workers from a UK car factory (4) **have been laid off** due to a slowdown in the economy. Desmond Lewis (5) **has been knocked out** in the fifth round of his heavyweight championship fight in Las Vegas.

GRAMMAR SPOT (SB p57)

1–2 Students answer the questions in pairs. Go over the answers with the whole class.

Answers
1 Students can answer questions 1 and 3, but not 2, 4, and 5. Charles Watkins has escaped from jail. Hurricane Jeffrey has hit the Caribbean. But we don't know the answers to the other questions because they are in the Present Perfect passive. Who did the action is not mentioned because it is not as important as the action itself.

Refer students to Grammar Reference 7.3 on SB p144.

PRACTICE (SB p57)

Writing news stories

Note that newspaper headlines are often written in shortened form and in the Present Simple. This is the dramatic use of the Present Simple, it adds immediacy and colour to a story. If the passive is needed, only the past participle is used in the headline. In radio or TV news, when the news is spoken, the Present Perfect active and passive replaces these.

1 Ask students to read all the newspaper headlines. Point out that the first contains just a past participle, and the second is in the Present Simple. Illustrate how newspaper headlines translate into radio or TV news headlines by looking at the example.

Ask students to work in pairs on the other newspaper headlines and rewrite them as spoken headlines using the Present Perfect active and passive. Explain that they need to make up any extra information.

Students check their answers with their partner. Ask individual students to write their answers on the board. Correct any errors as a whole class.

T 7.5 Play the recording so that students can compare their answers.

2 Encourage a class discussion. If students are from different countries, you can ask them what the major news stories are in their countries this week.

> **SUGGESTION**
>
> If you have the time and the equipment, it can be worthwhile and a lot of fun for students to create a complete news programme with newsreaders and reporters.
>
> Divide students into groups of three. Write four headlines on the board, and ask students to decide which two they are going to present on their news programme. Or, alternatively, students can think up their own headlines.
>
> Students must decide who will be the newsreader and who is going to report on which story. All three students will participate in the writing, working together to turn the headlines into news stories. Go round helping as necessary. Explain that the newsreader will introduce the story using the Present Perfect, then hand it to the reporter who will give details of the time of the events using the Past Simple.
>
> When they are ready, ask students to present their news programmes to the class. Write some useful phrases on the board to help: *Here is the news, And now over to … in Bristol, Our reporter, … , in Oxford has the latest.* These programmes can either be recorded or videoed.

Discussing grammar

3 Write the first sentence, *I've washed my hair*, on the board. Ask students to tell you where they can put words from the box in the sentence, and what these words add to the meaning. (See answers below.)

Ask students in pairs to discuss where the words in the box go in the rest of the sentences. In the feedback, discuss what these words add to the meaning of the sentences.

3 He hasn't learned to drive **yet**. (= up to now – it could imply that you either expect it to have happened, or that you expect it to happen soon)
He hasn't **ever** learned to drive.

4 They've **just** finished ... (= recently)
They've **already** finished ... (= before now)

5 She's **just** learned ... (= recently)
She's **already** learned ... (= before now)
She's **never** learned ... (= not at any time)

6 We've **just** met ... (= recently)
We've **already** met ... (= before now)
We've **never** met ... (= not at any time)

7 Have they **just** finished ... ? (= recently)
Have they finished ... **yet**? (= up to now)
Have they **already** finished ... ? (= before now)

8 Has it **just** stopped raining? (= recently)
Has it stopped raining **yet**? (= up to now)
Has it **already** stopped raining? (= before now)

4 Ask students in pairs to underline the correct verb form. This exercise checks and practises students' understanding of when to use the Past Simple (with a time reference) and the Present Perfect (when giving news if there is no time reference mentioned), and the difference between the active and passive forms.

Answers
1 has resigned; has been elected
2 was announced
3 did you go
4 Has ... been
5 took off
6 has hit; has fallen; have been advised

ADDITIONAL MATERIAL

Workbook Unit 7
Exercises 9 and 10 Present Perfect passive

READING AND SPEAKING (SB p58)

Dream jobs

This is a jigsaw reading on the theme of dream jobs. The texts are about a meteorologist who chases hurricanes, a trapeze artist with a travelling circus, and an ironworker who works on skyscrapers. The students have to read for specific information, and there is some language work on phrasal verbs. There is also a lot of speaking in the opening activity, in doing the information exchange when comparing the texts, and in the roleplay at the end. The Present Perfect in all its uses is used in context in the texts.

1 Ask students to close their eyes and think about their ideal or dream job. You can describe yours to get them started. Then ask them to read the questions. Put the students in pairs to ask and answer the questions to try and guess each other's dream jobs.

A fun way of doing this is to make sure the students really do close their eyes, give them a few minutes to visualize their dream job, then, as they sit with closed eyes, read the questions aloud to encourage their imaginations.

SUGGESTED VOCABULARY LEAD-IN
One useful area of vocabulary to pre-teach is jobs. Write the following jobs on the board:
meteorologist, ironworker, hurricane hunter, trapeze artist, crane driver, lawyer, construction worker, scientist, gymnast (*gymnastics* appears in the text)

Ask students in pairs to divide the words into three groups of jobs that go together. Elicit or teach the meaning of each.

Suggested answers
1 meteorologist, hurricane hunter, scientist
2 ironworker, crane driver, construction worker
3 trapeze artist, gymnast

---

2 Divide the class into three groups. Tell Group **A** to read about Stanley Karras. Tell Group **B** to read about Linda Spelman. Tell Group **C** to read about Michael Doyle.

Make sure there are several dictionaries in each group. Ask students to read about their person. Go round helping with new words. Encourage students to ask one another for help before using a dictionary or asking you.

In their groups, students discuss the questions in exercise 1 about their person. Get them to make brief notes for use in the next step. Give the groups about 10 minutes to answer the questions.

Answers
Stanley Karras – meteorologist
1 Yes. You need to study maths and science and get a degree in meteorology.
2 Yes.
3 Yes. You work with top scientists.
4 Both indoors and outdoors.
5 No.
6 Yes. You could fly into a hurricane.
7 Yes.

Linda Spelman – trapeze artist
1 Yes. Courses in gymnastics and trapeze.
2 No. A lot less than a lawyer.
3 Yes. Circus people.
4 Indoors. In a circus tent.
5 Yes.
6 Yes (although Linda doesn't say this).
7 Yes.

Michael Doyle – ironworker
1 No. It's handed down from father to son, and you have to get used to it.
2 Yes.
3 Yes.
4 Outdoors.
5 Yes.
6 Yes.
7 No.

3 Ask students to find a partner from each of the other two groups. Tell them to go through the questions together, and compare information about the people they read about. Then students discuss the two personalized questions.

Answers
Students' own answers.

4 Students quickly read the two articles they haven't read yet and answer the questions. Let them check answers in their pairs before going over them with the whole class.

Answers
1 all of them	6 Stanley Karras/
2 Linda Spelman	Linda Spelman
3 Stanley Karras	7 Stanley Karras
4 Michael Doyle	8 Stanley Karras
5 Stanley Karras/	9 Linda Spelman
Linda Spelman	10 Linda Spelman

Language work

Ask students to stay in groups of three and match the phrasal verbs in exercise 4 with the verbs or expressions in the box. This is preliminary work on phrasal verbs, which are looked at in more detail in the *Vocabulary* section of this unit.

It would be useful to ask your students to read Grammar Reference 7.4 on phrasal verbs (SB p144) for homework before you proceed to the *Vocabulary* section.

Answers
1 have a good relationship with
2 start doing (a hobby)
3 think of
4 pass down
5 separated from
6 finally find yourself
7 leave the ground and fly
8 find by chance
9 continue
10 stop doing

Roleplay

1 Ask students in pairs to turn to p153. Give them time to read their roles and prepare the roleplays.

Go round helping students to develop their roleplays. Ask several pairs to perform their roleplays for the class. You can record and/or videotape them if you have the equipment.

2 Ask students to switch roles and do the roleplay again.

Phrasal verbs

The aim here is to introduce literal and idiomatic phrasal verbs, and to study some of the rules for using them.

In addition to asking students to read through Grammar Reference 7.4 on phrasal verbs (SB p144) for homework before this lesson, you may want to look at it yourself as a reminder of the different types of phrasal verb.

Note that phrasal verbs are covered systematically in the Workbook. The different types are practised in a variety of exercises in approximately every second unit.

 1 Read through the examples in the Caution Box with the students, then ask them in pairs to find other examples in the reading texts on pp58–59.

Answers
Stanley Karras: take off, cut off, come up with
Linda Spelman: took up, heard of, get on with, hand out, gave up, carry on, go for
Michael Doyle: handed down, came over, get on, back off

2 Read through the examples as a class. Mime the literal meaning of *look out*, and elicit a synonym for the idiomatic meaning (*be careful*). Ask students if they can think of other phrasal verbs that have literal and idiomatic meanings.

Refer students to Grammar Reference 7.4 on SB p144.

Literal or idiomatic?

1 Ask students in pairs to decide which meaning is literal and which is idiomatic.

Answers
1 a idiomatic b literal
2 a idiomatic b literal
3 a idiomatic b literal
4 a literal b idiomatic
5 a literal b idiomatic

Separable or inseparable?/Verbs with two particles

2–3 Students remain in pairs to complete the exercises. Check the answers to exercises 2–3 with the whole class.

Answers
Exercise 2
3 She's taken them off.
4 He took it up when he retired.
5 I get on well with them.
6 I came across it.
7 I looked them up in my dictionary.
8 The waiter took them away.

Exercise 3
1 put up with
2 come up with
3 run out of
4 get on with
5 looking forward to

The meaning is different in pairs 3 and 4.
1 *put up with* in both sentences means *tolerate*.
2 *come up with* in both sentences means *find*.
3 *run out of* in sentence 1 means *finish the supply of*. In sentence 2 it has a literal meaning.
4 *get on with* in sentence 1 means *have a good relationship with*. In sentence 2 it means *continue doing*.
5 *looking forward to* in both sentences means *anticipating with pleasure*.

LISTENING AND SPEAKING (SB p61)

The busy life of a retired man

The aim here is to improve students' ability to listen for gist as well as specific information. It also revises question forms in the Present Perfect, and includes discussion questions on the theme of retirement.

1 Discuss the first question with the whole class. Then put students in small groups to discuss the other questions. Ask them to report back to the class. This is a stimulating speaking activity for students as many seem to enjoy talking about older members of their families.

2 Focus attention on the photo of Thomas and Philippa. Explain that Thomas is retired now, and ask some questions to help students make predictions about what they will hear, e.g. *Do you think Thomas misses his job? Do you think Philippa is happy? How do you think her life is different from her grandfather's?*

T 7.6 Students listen to the recording and answer the questions.

Answers and tapescript
Thomas seems very active and happy. He doesn't complain, even though he misses his wife and his dog. Philippa seems less happy with her life. She complains about not going to interesting places and only having exams and work to look forward to.

T 7.6
P = Philippa   T = Thomas
P How long have you been retired now, Grandpa?
T Oh, let me see. Uh, it's four years. Yes, I've been retired nearly four years now. I suppose I'm used to it after all this time. But, you know, I worked for Courtaulds for over forty years. Can you believe that? Forty years.
P One job for forty years. Incredible! I remember when you retired and they gave you that gold watch. Do you like being retired? I'd get bored, I'm sure I would. Don't you get bored?
T Well, I'm lucky. I've got my health so I can do a lot. I can get out a lot. I've just taken up golf, you know. It's a wonderful sport for an old man like me 'cos it's not really a sport at all, at least not the way your Grandpa plays it! It's just a good excuse for a walk, and I need an excuse since Rover died. I – I miss good old Rover; he and I were great friends ... but I don't think I want another dog at my age. I go to the golf club twice a week. I've made some good friends there, you know. Have you met Ted and Marjorie? They're my age. They're a – oh, they're a lovely couple.
P Er, no ... I don't think I've met them, but didn't you go on holiday with them?
T Yes, that's right. We went to Wales together last Easter. Oh, and we had a lovely time, lovely time. I do appreciate company since your grandma died ... you know I really miss your grandma. 35 years we were married, 35 years and still as much in love as the day we met. She was a wonderful lady, your grandma.
P Oh, I know that, Grandpa. We all miss her so much. We all loved her so much.
T So I like to keep busy. I've been on all sorts of special holidays, y'know. Package holidays for senior citizens, and I've done a bit of ...
P Well, I know you went to visit Uncle Keith in Australia. *And* you've just come back from a cruise round the Caribbean. You're so brown.
T I know. My word, that was an experience. I loved every minute of it! When you're older I'll tell you about the American widow I met! ... Miriam, she was called. Oh, just a baby of fifty-five, but she seemed to like me.
P Grandpa!
T And yes, of course, Keith. I saw him two years ago. You've not met your Australian cousins yet, have you? Oh, you'd love the baby, Kylie, she's beautiful. Looks just like your grandma. But you know, I've also been to Spain, and Morocco, and Turkey. These package holidays are so good for people like me.
P Grandpa, next time, please think of me. Don't you want a companion? Can I come with you? I'd love a suntan like yours! We never go anywhere interesting.

T Oh, Philippa, you know your mum and dad wouldn't let me. Not until you've finished your exams. Helen says I'm a bad influence on you.

P Well, I think *you* have more fun than *I* do! All I have to look forward to is exams and more exams, and then years and years of work!

T Oh Philippa. Don't wish your life away. Just enjoy it all. You only get one go at it!

3 Ask students in pairs to underline the correct verb forms and answer the questions. Do the first one as a class.

Answers
1 How long **has he been** retired? Four years. (He is still retired, not dead.)
2 How long **did he work** for Courtaulds? Forty years. (He doesn't work there any more.)
3 When **did he go** to Wales? Last Easter. (He is not there now.)
4 How long **was he married**? Thirty-five years. (His wife died. He's a widower.)

T 7.6 Play the recording again for students to check their answers.

4 Put the students in pairs to answer the questions.

Answers
1 Because it's an excuse for a walk and he has made some good friends at the golf club.
2 He has visited Wales, the Caribbean, Spain, Morocco, and Turkey. He went to Australia two years ago.
3 **Rover:** his dog, who died; **Ted and Marjorie:** good friends from the golf club – he went to Wales with them; **Keith:** his brother in Australia; **Miriam:** an American widow he met on the cruise; **Kylie:** his niece; **Helen:** his daughter
4 The deaths of his wife and his dog.
5 She complains about not going to interesting places and about only having exams and work to look forward to.

What do you think?

Ask students to discuss the questions in small groups before having a whole-class discussion. This is a subject many students have a lot to say about – especially the subject of the kind of retirement they would like for themselves!

EVERYDAY ENGLISH (SB p61)

On the phone

The aim of this section is to give practice of formal telephone conversations.

1 Ask students in pairs to complete the conversations with phrases from the box.

T 7.7 Play the recording so that the students can listen and check their answers. Ask students in pairs to practise the conversations.

Answers and tapescript
1 A Hello. Could I **speak to** Sam Jackson, please?
   B **I'm afraid** Mr Jackson's in a meeting. It won't be over until 3.00. Can I **take a message**?
   A Yes, please. Could you ask him to phone me? I think he's got my number, but **I'll give it** to you again just in case. It's 743 219186.
2 A Can I **have extension** 2173, please?
   B The **line's busy** at the moment. Would you like **to hold**?
   A Yes, please.
   (Five seconds later)
   B I'm **putting you through** now.
   A Thank you.
3 A Could I speak to Alison Short?
   B I'm afraid she isn't **at her desk** at the moment. Do you want to hold?
   A No, don't worry. I'll **phone back later**.
4 A Can I speak to Terence Cameron, please?
   B **Speaking.**
   A Ah, Mr Cameron! **This is** Holly Lucas. **I'm phoning** about a letter I got this morning.
5 A Hello. This is Incom International. There's no one here to **take your call** at the moment. Please **leave a message** and **we'll get back to you** as soon as we can.

2 This is a roleplay which practises functional language commonly used in formal telephone conversations. You will need to photocopy the Student **A** and Student **B** information on TB p125. There are five role cards.

Put students in pairs, and hand out one role card to each pair. Ask students to decide which role they are going to play, then ask them to read their card carefully and plan what they are going to say.

When the students are ready, start the roleplays. Monitor but don't overcorrect, or the students might stop talking. You could note down common mistakes and deal with them when students have finished.

Get pairs, one for each situation, to do their roleplays again in front of the class. Encourage the others to comment and correct. Alternatively, you could extend the activity by getting students to exchange role cards or change roleplays.

Don't forget!

Workbook Unit 7
Exercise 11 Vocabulary – Words with more than one meaning
Exercise 12 Pronunciation – Word stress
Exercise 13 Noun + preposition

Word list
Photocopy the Word list for Unit 7 (TB p157) for your students. Ask them to write in the translations, learn them at home, and /or write some of the words in their vocabulary notebooks.

8

Conditionals • Time clauses
Base and strong adjectives
Making suggestions

Just imagine!

Introduction to the unit

The theme of this unit is imaginary situations, both possible and unlikely. This provides a useful context for presenting and practising the grammar for the unit – first and second conditionals.

The first conditional is introduced in the context of someone worrying about two friends who are moving to Spain to live. The second conditional is introduced in the context of winning the lottery. In the *Reading and speaking* section a magazine article takes a look at how lottery winners react to becoming millionaires. The *Listening* section contains three charity appeals, and students are asked to discuss how they would divide a donation of £10,000 between different charities.

The *Writing* section at the back of the book practises the use of adverbs in a narrative, in the context of a disastrous holiday.

Language aims

Grammar – conditionals   English language teachers often talk about the first, second, third, and zero conditionals. Various commentators disagree with this, saying that it is a gross over-simplification – that there aren't just four but many, many more. What they mean is that there are numerous permutations – imperatives, alternative modal verbs and tenses in the result clause, and the words *unless, should, provided,* as well as alternative tenses in the condition clause.

Nevertheless, for the intermediate student it is worth pointing out that beneath all the various permutations, there is a basis on which all the others are formed.

POSSIBLE PROBLEMS

Conditional sentences present students with all kinds of problems of both form and meaning. Rarely can a student begin a sentence with *if* and get all the ensuing parts right. This is perhaps because there are two clauses (result and condition) with different tense rules for each; the form probably differs from their own language; and the choice of first versus second conditional can depend on how the speaker views the likelihood of the event. First and second conditionals can refer to present or future time.

Common mistakes

- **If it will rain, I'll stay at home.*
  Many languages use a future tense in the condition clause to refer to a future condition, which is quite logical. However, English does not.
- **If I see Peter, I tell him the news.*
  This is an example of learners resorting to a ubiquitous Present Simple/ verb stem tense to refer to any time.
- **What you do if you win a lot of money?*
  *If he asks me, I not say anything.
  This is an assortment of form and meaning mistakes.
- **When Germany wins the World Cup, I'll be very happy.*
  German, for example, has only one word to express both *when* and *if,* so speakers of German may confuse the hypothetical nature of *if* and the certainty of *when.*
- *If I lose my job, I'll … / If I lost my job, I'd …*
  The choice of conditionals is sometimes dictated by how possible or impossible the condition seems to the speaker. They can seem confusingly interchangeable to language learners.
- In the zero conditional, *if* does not express hypothesis. It means *when* or *whenever.*
  If I can't get to sleep, I read a book.

As with so many areas at this level, students will have seen first and second conditionals before, but they still make mistakes, and will probably continue to do so. This is not a reason to stop trying to help them! One step back, two steps forward.

Time clauses

Problems here are similar to those in the first conditional. English does not use a future verb form in the time clause.

| I'll do it | when
as soon as
before
until | she leaves.
she's left. | (NOT *she will leave) |

Vocabulary Two related areas of lexis are examined. The first area includes base and strong adjectives, such as *big* and *huge*. The second area is the intensifying adverbs that go with the different base and extreme adjectives, for example, *very big* and *absolutely huge*.

Everyday English Making suggestions is a very broad functional area. In this section, ways of making, accepting, and rejecting suggestions are practised. Some suggestions include the speaker (*Why don't we … ?, Let's … , Shall we … ?*), others don't (*I think you should … , Why don't you … ?, If I were you, I'd …*). Some are relatively mild (*I think you should …*), and others imply the speaker knows best (*You'd better …*).

Notes on the unit

TEST YOUR GRAMMAR (SB p62)

This section checks students' ability to recognize the form of conditional sentences. It mixes a number of different possible conditional forms, thus introducing students to the idea that conditionals can be formed in many ways and used in a variety of functional contexts. Don't forget that *Test your grammar* sections find out what students know and focus their attention on the grammar to come – they are not designed to actually teach the grammar.

1 Ask students to match the clauses. Do the first one as an example. Let students check their answers in pairs before checking with the whole class.

> **Answers**
> 2 If you're going to the post office, could you post this letter for me?
> 3 If I see Anna, I'll tell her the news.
> 4 If you want to do well in life, you have to work hard.
> 5 If you don't feel well, go to bed and rest.

Ask the class to tell you what verb forms are used. Don't try to explain rules of use at this point.

> **Answers**
> 1 second conditional: past/*would* + infinitive
> 2 mixed conditional and a request: *going to*/*could* + infinitive
> 3 first conditional: present/*will* + infinitive
> 4 zero conditional: present/present
> 5 present/imperative

2 Give students a minute or two to think of what they are going to say in response to the questions. Then put them in threes or fours to ask each other the questions. Monitor and note whether the students are using the three conditional forms accurately and appropriately. End with whole-class feedback.

A PLACE IN THE SUN (SB p62)

First conditional and time clauses

The aim here is to introduce and practise the first conditional in the context of a friend worrying about a couple's decision to move from England to Spain.

1 Read the introduction as a class. Ask students what problems they think an English couple might have if they move to Spain: *can't speak the language, don't understand the culture, miss their friends and family, can't find a job.* Elicit a few ideas and write them on the board.

T 8.1 Play the recording. Do they talk about any of the problems the students predicted? Ask students in pairs to complete the conversation, using the words in the box, then play the recording again to check.

> **Answers and tapescript**
> D = David   J = Jack   A = Annie
> D You're both mad. I think you**'ll regret** it. You were earning good money here. You **won't earn** much growing lemons.
> J We know that, but we **won't need** a lot of money to live there.
> D But what **will you do** if you can't find anywhere to live?
> A There are lots of cheap, old farms. We**'ll have** no trouble finding somewhere.
> D But you don't even like gardening. What **will you do** if you **don't like** farming either?
> J We**'ll only know** if we **don't like** farming when we try it.
> D Well, OK. But what if you … ?

Ask students to practise the conversation. You could do this in threes, or in pairs where one student reads both Jack and Annie's lines.

2 Before students make more conversations, you need to do a controlled practice drill of the first conditional to reinforce structure, form, and pronunciation.

Drill the question *What will you do if you can't find anywhere to live?* around the class, then the answer *We'll have no trouble finding somewhere.* Practise this in open pairs across the class.

Do the same with the first two or three prompts in the practice exercise, for example *What will you do if you miss your family and friends? No problem! We'll phone or email./We'll go back for holidays.*

Correct mistakes of form and pronunciation very carefully. Put the students in threes, or in pairs to make similar conversations between the friends, using the rest of the prompts. Monitor and correct carefully. Get some feedback. There may be some funny suggestions for the couple's replies to the friend's concerns.

> **Some suggested answers**
> **A** What will you do if you have problems with the language?
> **B** We'll take lessons./We'll buy a phrasebook.
> **A** What will you do if you can't stand the heat?
> **B** We'll get air-conditioning./We'll stay in the shade.
> **A** What will you do if you want to move back to the UK?
> **B** We'll sell the farm and come home.
> **A** What will you do if you fall ill?
> **B** We'll see a doctor.
> **A** What will you do if you run out of money?
> **B** We'll find a job.
> **A** What will you do if you get bored?
> **B** We'll travel round the country.
> **A** What will you do if you don't like the food?
> **B** We'll cook at home./We'll take food from England.

3 Ask students to look at the second part of the conversation, and work in pairs to put the verbs in the correct form.

T 8.2 Play the recording so that the students can check their answers. Ask students to practise the conversation in either open or closed pairs. Make sure their intonation is good.

> **Answers and tapescript**
> **D = David   J = Jack   A = Annie**
> **D** Will you keep in touch with friends?
> **A** Of course we will. When we **get** there, we**'ll give** you a call.
> **D** And how will I contact you?
> **J** Well, as soon as we **find** a place to live, we**'ll send** you our address.
> **D** Hmmm, I can always email you.
> **J** Yes, email's brilliant for keeping in touch, but you**'ll have to** wait until we**'ve set up** our computers.
> **A** And David, I promise, you**'ll be** our first guest when we **move** into our new home.
> **D** Excellent. I'll look forward to that!

> **GRAMMAR SPOT** (SB p63)

1–3 Answer the questions as a class. The first question is aimed primarily at speakers who confuse *when* and *if*.

> **Answers**
> 1 Sentence 1 (*If…*) expresses a future possibility.
>   Sentence 2 (*When…*) expresses a future certainty.
> 2 **When** we get there, we'll give you a call.
>   **As soon as** we find a place to live, we'll send you our address.
>   You'll have to wait **until** we've set up our computers.
> 3 The Present Simple and the Present Perfect Simple tenses are used in the time clauses.

Refer students to Grammar Reference 8.1 and 8.2 on SB pp145–146.

> **PRACTICE** (SB p63)

Another busy day

1 Ask students in pairs or small groups to complete the conversation. This is a difficult exercise, so go round helping as necessary.

T 8.3 Play the recording so that students can check their answers.

Ask students in pairs to practise the conversation.

> **Answers and tapescript**
> **D = David   S = Sue**
> **D** Bye, darling! Good luck with the interview!
> **S** Thanks. I'll need it. I hope the trains are running on time. If I**'m** late for the interview, I**'ll be** furious with myself!
> **D** Just stay calm! Call me when you can.
> **S** I will. I**'ll call** you on my mobile as soon as I **get** out of the interview.
> **D** When **will** you **know** if you've got the job?
> **S** They**'ll tell** me in the next few days. If they **offer** me the job, I**'m going to accept** it. You know that, don't you?
> **D** Of course. But we'll worry about that later.
> **S** OK. Are you going to work now?
> **D** Well, I**'m going to take** the children to school before I **go** to work.
> **S** Don't forget to pick them up as soon as you **finish**.
> **D** Don't worry, I won't forget. You'd better get going. If you **don't hurry**, you**'ll miss** the train.
> **S** OK. I**'ll see** you this evening. Bye!

2 Students remain in pairs to ask and answer questions using the prompts. Focus students' attention on the example; then give the pairs a few minutes to think about how to form the questions before they start. This is a challenging exercise, especially in forming the questions and changing the sentences from first and second person to third person. Go round monitoring and helping. Correct any errors in the feedback.

> **Answers**
> When will she call David? She'll call him as soon as she gets out of the interview.
> When will she know if she's got the job? In the next few days.
> What will she do if they offer her the job? She'll accept it.
> What will David do before he goes to work? He'll take the children to school.
> When will he pick up the children? As soon as he finishes work.

Workbook Unit 8
Exercises 1–4 Conditionals and time clauses

WINNING THE LOTTERY (SB p64)

Second conditional

The aim here is to introduce and practise the second conditional in the context of five people saying what they would do if they won the lottery.

1 Begin by writing the word *lottery* on the board, and asking some questions: *Do you have a lottery in your country? How much can you win? Do you buy lottery tickets? Have you ever won anything?*

Before you play the recording, focus attention on the photos of the five people and ask students in pairs to say what *they* think the people in the photos would do if they won the lottery. Monitor to see if they use *would* as they talk.

T 8.4 Ask students to listen to the recording and complete the task.

Sample answers and tapescript

1 He'd give some to friends and family/buy an island/give a lot to charity.
2 She'd give up her job/travel. She wouldn't move away.
3 He'd buy a house/some land.
4 He'd be a space tourist/fly to Mars.
5 She wouldn't give any away./She'd spend it all.

T 8.4

1 What would *I* do if *I* won £5 million? Well, I'd make sure my family had enough money, and my friends, and then I'd buy my own island in the Caribbean. And I'd give loads of money to charity.
2 Oh, that's easy! I'd give up my job and travel. Anywhere. Everywhere. Oh, but it wouldn't change me. I'd still live in the same area because I like it so much.
3 What would I do? I'd buy a nice house in the country. I'd make it the best place I could. And I'd have lots of land so I could have peace and quiet!
4 I'd be a space tourist and fly to Mars on the space shuttle.
5 I wouldn't give away a penny. I'd spend it all on myself.

2 Ask students in pairs to complete the sentences. You may need to play the recording again so that they can check their answers. Or students can read the tapescript on SB pp127–128.

Answers

1 I'd **buy** my own island in the Caribbean. I**'d give** loads of money to charity.
2 I**'d give up** my job and travel. But it **wouldn't change** me.
3 I**'d have** lots of land, so I **could have** peace and quiet.
4 I**'d be** a space tourist and fly to Mars on the space shuttle.
5 I **wouldn't give** away a penny. I**'d spend** it all on myself.

SUGGESTION

To consolidate form and pronunciation, you could practise some of the sentences, drilling them around the class and correcting mistakes very carefully. Alternatively, you could elicit other ideas from the students and write them on the board, then do a quick drill using them. Ask *What would you do?*, then point to one of the phrases on the board, and ask a student to respond. Make sure students are pronouncing *I'd* /aɪd/ correctly.

You could then practise a two-line conversation in open pairs across the class:

S1 *What would you do if you won a million pounds?*
S2 *I'd give up my job.*

GRAMMAR SPOT (SB p64)

This exercise contrasts the two conditional forms. Students need to understand the concept of a real condition (it could happen, it's possible), versus an unreal condition (it's unlikely or impossible, a dream, wishful thinking).

1 Ask students in pairs to look at the sentences and answer the questions. As a class, you can revise the correct form (present/future for first conditional, past/*would* + infinitive for second conditional). Point out that *had* looks like a past form, but in fact is referring to an unlikely event now or in the future.

Answers

The first sentence expresses a possible situation. It is possible that he/she will have time.

The second sentence expresses an unlikely or unreal situation. From the point of view of the speaker, the likelihood/reality of suddenly having £5 million is just a dream.

2 Read the instructions and example as a class. Students remain in pairs to complete the sentences.

Answers

If I had a car ... (But unfortunately, **I don't have a car.**)
If I didn't have to work ... (But unfortunately, **I do have to work.**)

Refer students to Grammar Reference 8.3–8.5 on SB p146.

What would you do?

1 This can be a time-consuming activity, so you should decide how long you want it to last.

Pre-teach *go on a spending spree* (going out and spending a lot of money), then put students in small groups of three or four to ask and answer the questions. This activity will also work as a mingle.

> **Answers**
> Students' own answers.

Conversations with *will* and *would*

2 Focus attention on the examples, then ask students in pairs to complete the exercise. This can be difficult, because students have to decide how probable the future situations are for themselves. Be prepared for some disagreement. Remember that it is the point of view of the speaker that matters. This exercise will help students create a context for exercise 3.

> **Possible answers**
> 3 unlikely   4 possible   5 unlikely   6 possible
> 7 possible

3 Read through the examples as a class, then put students in pairs to ask and answer questions using the situations from exercise 2. Go round helping and correcting as necessary.

Ask some pairs to model their conversations for the class. Encourage the others to comment and correct.

Conditional forms

4 This exercise shows some of the variations that can occur in both condition and result clauses.

Ask students in pairs to match a line in **A** with a line in **B** and a sentence in **C**.

T 8.5 Play the recording so that students can check their answers.

> **Answers and tapescript**
> 1 If Tony calls, tell him I'm at Alex's. He can reach me there.
> 2 If you've finished your work, you can take a break. Just be back in 15 minutes.
> 3 If I'm not back by 8 o'clock, don't wait for me. Go without me and I'll meet you at the party.
> 4 If you have the flu, you should go to bed. Keep warm and drink plenty of fluids.
> 5 If you're ever in London, please let me know. I'd love to show you around.
> 6 If you go to Russia, you have to have a visa. You can get one at the embassy.
> 7 I'd buy a computer if I could afford it. It would be really useful for work.

> 8 If I had more time, I might take up an evening class. I'd love to learn more about photography.

You could ask students to identify some of the different verb forms and other words used.

> **Answers**
> **In the condition clause**
> | Present Simple | (*If Tony calls ...*) |
> | Present Perfect | (*If you've finished ...*) |
> | Past Simple | (*If I had more time ...*) |
> | could | (*... if I could afford it*) |
>
> **In the result clause**
> | Imperative | (*don't wait ... , tell him ...*) |
> | have to | (*you have to have a visa*) |
>
> Notice the different pronunciations of *have*:
> You have /hæf/ to have /hæv/ a visa.
>
> | can | (*you can take a break*) |
> | should | (*you should go to bed*) |
> | might | (*I might take up ...*) |

Ask students in pairs to practise the sentences. Also practise the pronunciation of the modal verbs.

5 Read through the questions as a class focusing students' attention on the different verb forms. Then put students in groups of three or four to discuss the situations. This is a free personalized discussion to round off the lesson.

ADDITIONAL MATERIAL

Workbook Unit 8
Exercises 5–7 conditionals 2
Exercises 8 *I'd rather ...*

Who wants to be a millionaire?

The aim here is to improve students' ability to scan a text for specific information and to read more intensively in order to insert missing phrases back into the text.

1 The song has been included to introduce the theme of the reading text, and for fun. Don't spend too long on it – no more than a few minutes.

Ask students to read the pre-listening question.

Pre-teach *a flashy flunky* (a well-dressed servant), *bother* (trouble), *wallow* (spend time enjoying yourself in water or mud, so here it means bathing luxuriously in champagne), *uranium to spare* (a large quantity of uranium), *tire of* (get bored with).

T 8.6 Play the song. Students probably won't be able to understand everything after just one listening. Find out what students understood and discuss the questions; then play the song again while they read the words on

SB p128. Point out that *'cos* is a short form of *because* and is used when speaking.

Answers and tapescript
They want to be with each other.

They don't want to be millionaires with flunkies, a country estate, champagne, a plane, a landing field, uranium, a yacht, a fancy foreign car, caviar, and a swimming pool.

T 8.6

'Who Wants To Be a Millionaire?'
Who wants to be a millionaire?
I don't.
Have flashy flunkies everywhere?
I don't.
Who wants the bother of a country estate?
A country estate is something I'd hate.

Who wants to wallow in champagne?
I don't.
Who wants a supersonic plane?
I don't.
Who wants a private landing field too?
I don't.
And I don't 'cos all I want is you.

Who wants to be a millionaire?
I don't.
Who wants uranium to spare?
I don't.
Who wants to journey on a gigantic yacht?
Do I want a yacht? Oh, how I do not!

Who wants a fancy foreign car?
I don't.
Who wants to tire of caviar?
I don't.
Who wants a marble swimming pool, too?
I don't.
And I don't 'cos all I want is you.

Ask students if they would like to be millionaires. Do they think that being in love is more important than being very rich?

2 Focus attention on the chart. Ask students to decide which they think are good or bad suggestions and mark each item accordingly.

Note that at the top of the chart, the first conditional (*If you win a lot of money, …*) is used and not the second. This is because the article is about people who have actually won huge amounts of money, so in this context the condition is not viewed as improbable but as possible.

Answers
Students' own answers.

3 Ask students to read the article quickly, then complete the chart, this time marking the items according to the opinions expressed in the article. Let them check in pairs before going over the answers with the whole class.

Answers
The article's opinion:
1 ✗   2 ✗   3 ✓   4 ✗   5 ✗   6 ✓

4 Read through the phrases and make sure the students understand them all. Do the first one as an example with the whole class.

Ask students in pairs to complete the text. Go round helping as necessary. If students want to use dictionaries, let them, but encourage them not to look up every word they don't know.

Ask individual students to come up and write their answers on the board. As you go through each answer, ask *Why do you think that?* and encourage other students to comment.

Answers
1 e   2 c   3 b   4 g   5 h   6 a   7 f   8 d

5 Ask students in pairs or small groups to answer the questions. Teach the meaning of the question *How does a windfall* (sudden gift of money) *smash* (destroy) *the jigsaw* (the plan of our lives)?

Answers
1 A bad thing.
2 **Work:** there seems no purpose to day or reason to get up
   Home: we buy expensive houses but need guards to protect them.
   Friends: we leave them behind.
   Relatives: they demand money.
3 The different parts of our life, like work and friends, fit together like a jigsaw, and a windfall dramatically changes everything – so the pieces won't fit together any more.
4 On solicitors' fees, security guards, psychiatrists.
5 Abby Wilson spent all her money, had five marriages, and is now penniless and alone.
   William Church dropped dead because of ceaseless hounding from the press, the public, and relatives.
6 He gave his money away.
7 Support from her family. She has divided her fortune among her family.

What do you think?

These questions are probably best discussed with the whole class to save time as students may be getting a bit tired of the article by now. For the second question, ask students to look back to exercise 2 and see what they ticked in the *Your opinion* column. Have they changed their minds about what advice they would give?

Answers
Students' own answers.

Language work

Ask students in pairs to match the words in **A** with their definitions in **B**.

Answers
fantasized = dreamed
linked = connected
windfall = an unexpected sum of money you receive
smash = break violently
tempting = attractive, inviting
begging = asking for something very strongly
penniless = having no money
withdrew = took out (money from the bank)

EXTRA IDEA

There is a maze in the Extra ideas section on TB p126, which aims to create discussion and spoken interaction as students work together in groups to make decisions and speculate about outcomes. Hopefully, it is an opportunity for students to use conditional forms naturally.

Photocopy and cut out the instructions and a set of cards for each group. Divide students into groups of four or five. Give a set of instructions to each group and card number 1.

Students read the instructions, then proceed with the maze. Monitor groups carefully. Don't let them have the next card until they have fully discussed their decision. Make sure everybody contributes by handing the next card to a different student in each group each time.

You will need to make a decision about correcting. You probably won't want to interrupt the flow of the conversation as mistakes occur, so you could make a note of them and correct them later. There will no doubt be lots of mistakes with conditionals as students speculate about what will or would happen if they make a certain decision.

Different groups will finish at different times. If students seemed interested in the activity, they could go back and start again whenever they like – at the beginning, or at a point where they made an interesting decision. There are about 16 different outcomes, so it is possible for groups to go down a completely different route and make completely different decisions.

In the feedback, ask groups to report where their decisions took them, and how the maze ended.

Base and strong adjectives

The aim of this section is to introduce and practise base and strong adjectives and the intensifying adverbs used with them.

Students rarely use intensifying adverbs when they speak English. They tend to use just a single adjective. A native speaker's language, however, is full of such items. A feature of spoken language is exaggeration. We don't just say 'I'm hungry'; we say 'I'm absolutely starving' or 'I could eat a horse.' We don't say 'She was angry'; we say 'She went completely mad,' 'She went bananas,' or 'She hit the roof.' It is questionable whether such idiomatic language should be taught to foreign learners, but it will make their language richer if students know how to use intensifying adverbs.

POSSIBLE PROBLEMS

1 Students need to understand the difference between base and strong adjectives.

2 There are problems with collocation. Few intensifying adverbs go with all adjectives. *Very* and *really* seem to go with all base adjectives, and *absolutely* and *really* go with all strong adjectives. But there are many other adverbs that seem to go with certain adjectives only, for example:

deeply disappointed   *totally blind*
completely insane   *utterly useless*

It is best if students can begin to recognize and produce *very* and *really* with base adjectives, and *absolutely* and *really* with strong adjectives.

---

1 Focus attention on the examples and answer any questions. If you have a monolingual class, you can point out a few examples in their language. This is a feature of many languages, not just English.

2 Ask students to match the base adjectives in **A** with the strong adjectives in **B**. Notice that, not surprisingly, there are many words to express *good* and *bad*.

Answers

Base adjectives	Strong adjectives
tired	ex'hausted
'frightened	'terrified
good	great, 'wonderful, fan'tastic, su'perb
'tasty	de'licious
bad	'horrible, 'awful, 'terrible, dis'gusting
'pretty, a'ttractive	'beautiful, 'gorgeous
'hungry	'starving
'angry	'furious
'dirty	'filthy
sur'prised	as'tonished, a'mazed
'happy	thrilled, de'lighted
'funny	hi'larious

In the feedback, point out the stress on the long words (stressed syllables are marked in the answer key above), and make sure that the students' voices sound enthusiastic, especially with the strong adjectives.

 Read the Caution Box as a class. Encourage students to try using *very* and *really* with base adjectives, and *absolutely* and *really* with strong adjectives.

3 **T 8.7** Focus attention on the example and play the first conversation. Play the rest of the recording, pausing between each conversation to allow students time to write what they are about and the adjectives and adverbs they hear.

Answers and tapescript
1 a film – good, absolutely superb
2 someone who won the lottery – happy, absolutely thrilled
3 failing an exam – cross, really furious
4 a meal at a restaurant – really tasty, absolutely delicious
5 a weekend at the beach – wonderful weather – hot, absolutely gorgeous
6 a long plane journey – tired, absolutely exhausted

T 8.7
1 'What did you do last night?'
 'We went to the cinema.'
 'What did you see?'
 'Murder in the Park.'
 'Was it good?'
 'It was absolutely superb!'
2 'Is it true that Liz won the lottery?'
 'Yes! She won £2,000!'
 'I bet she was really happy.'
 'Happy? She was absolutely thrilled!'
3 'When I got home, I had to tell my parents that I'd failed the exam.'
 'Oh, no! What did they say?'
 'My mum was cross, but my dad was really furious.'
4 'We went out for dinner at that new restaurant last night.'
 'Oh! What was the food like?'
 'Well, the main course was really tasty, and as for the dessert, it was absolutely delicious.'
5 'We had a wonderful time at the beach last weekend.'
 'Oh, yeah? Was the weather hot?'
 'It was absolutely gorgeous!'
6 'How long was your flight?'
 '14 hours.'
 '14 hours! You must be really tired.'
 'You bet! I'm absolutely exhausted!'

As a follow-up activity, ask students in pairs to make up conversations based on what they heard on the recording. The situations all suggest the use of one of the strong adjectives. Strong pairs of students might be able to produce a conversation with several examples.

WRITING (SB p114)

A narrative (2)

1 Ask students to think about the worst holiday they have ever had. Ask some questions: *Where did you go? When was it? Who did you go with? What happened?* If they don't have much to say, get them started by telling a story of your own, either real or imaginary.

Ask students to take three or four minutes to write some notes about their worst holiday, then swap information with a partner.

2 Ask students to read the beginning of the story about Jack and Liza's holiday. Ask *What do you think is going to happen next in the story?* Ask students in pairs to put the words on the right into the correct place, and make any necessary changes. Sometimes there is more than one correct place.

Answers
A holiday horror story
Just after Christmas two years ago Jack and Liza **suddenly** decided to go away **somewhere** for New Year. They didn't want to stay in a hotel with crowds of people and so they were **really** delighted when they saw an advertisement in the *Sunday Times* for a holiday flat in a village near Oxford. **However**, it was no ordinary flat. It was on the top floor of an old Elizabethan mansion. They **immediately** booked it **(immediately)** and on New Year's Eve they set off in the car. **Although** it was raining **heavily** and freezing cold, they were happy and excited. They had been driving for **nearly** three hours when they **finally** saw the house in the distance. It looked magnificent with **incredibly** tall chimneys and a long, **(incredibly)** wide drive. They drove up to the house, went up the steps to the huge front door and knocked **loudly**. Nothing happened. They knocked again **more loudly**. **Eventually**, the door opened **slowly**, and a small, wild-looking old lady stood there.

3 Ask students in pairs to look at the pictures and complete the next part of the story using the prompts.

Suggested answers
The old lady was wearing old torn clothes. In one hand she was carrying a large glass of whisky, and she was carrying a cat in the other. The house was absolutely horrible and filthy. The old lady led Jack and Liza slowly up a huge staircase. There were two huge dogs growling menacingly at the top of the stairs. When they saw the rooms they couldn't believe their eyes because they were cold, dirty and bare with cobwebs, cracked plaster and no lampshades. They hurriedly raced down the stairs past the dogs and out of the front door.

4 Ask students to read their story out to the class. Alternatively, seat the students in a circle, and ask them to pass their stories round the class in a clockwise direction. Ask students to read the stories and write comments at the bottom before passing them on.

5 Ask students to read the end of the story, and put the words on the right into the correct place. Again, sometimes there is more than one correct place.

Answers

When they got outside again the rain had turned to snow. They ran to the car, laughing **hysterically**. They felt that they had been released from a prison and now they **desperately** wanted (**desperately**) to be with lots of people. They drove **quickly** to the next village (**quickly**) and, **fortunately**, **just** as midnight was striking they found a hotel with a room for the night. 'Happy New Year!' cried Jack, as he (**warmly**) kissed the surprised receptionist **warmly** on both cheeks (**warmly**). 'You have no idea how beautiful your hotel is!'

6 Ask students to write the story of their worst holiday in about 250 words. Ask them to make lots of notes in answer to the questions first, then think about how they can use adverbs in their story. Set this for homework.

LISTENING (SB p68)

Charity appeals

In this section, students listen for gist as well as specific information. In the discussion which follows the listening, second conditionals are revised.

1 Begin by asking students a few questions about charities, for example, *Do you regularly give to charity? What kind of charities do you support?*

Ask students to read through the list of charities. Check that they understand all the words. Then put them in groups of two or three to decide which three charities they think are the most worthy. Ask each pair or group to join another to discuss their answers. In the feedback, ask different groups to explain their choices.

2 Ask students to look at the charities in the chart. Ask them if they know or can predict what these charities do.

T 8.8 Focus students on the statements in the chart, then play the recording. Ask students in pairs to compare information before checking the answers as a class.

Answers and tapescript

Who or what the charity tries to help	How the charity helps
1 Amnesty International	
prisoners of conscience	publicizes the cases of prisoners of conscience; puts pressure on governments to practise human rights

Who or what the charity tries to help	How the charity helps
2 WWF	
wild animals around the world and the places where these animals live	works to save endangered species like the black rhino or the giant panda; works to establish and manage national parks and wildlife reserves around the world; works to address global threats to our environment, such as pollution and climate change
Crisis Now!	
3 refugees in Africa	supplies towns and camps with food and medical supplies, as well as doctors, nurses, blankets, tents, and clothes

T 8.8

1 Amnesty International

Amnesty International is a Nobel Prize-winning organization that works to support human rights around the world. It is independent of any government or political party and has over a million members in 162 countries. Amnesty International works to free all prisoners of conscience anywhere in the world. These are people who are in prison because of their beliefs, colour, ethnic origin, language, or religion. Amnesty International tries to help these prisoners in two ways: first, by publicizing their cases and, second, by putting pressure on governments to practise human rights.

2 WWF

WWF is the world's largest and most effecive conservation organization. It is dedicated to protecting wild animals around the world and the places where these animals live. WWF directs its conservation efforts towards three global goals. Firstly, it works to save endangered species like the black rhino or the giant panda. Secondly, it works to establish and manage national parks and wildlife reserves around the world. Thirdly, it works to address global threats to our environment, such as pollution and climate change.
(**Note:** When WWF was first set up in 1961, WWF stood for World Wildlife Fund. In 1986, it changed to World Wide Fund for Nature. Since July 2000, WWF has been known simply by its initials.)

3 Crisis Now!

Drought and famine have come to Africa again this year, just as they have every year for the past fifteen years. In some parts of Africa it hasn't rained for three years. There have been no crops, and the animals on which many people depend died long ago. Refugees are pouring from the countryside into the towns in their desperate search for food, and it has been estimated that over 1,000 people are dying every day. We are supplying towns and camps with food and medical supplies, but our efforts are drops in the ocean. We need a hundred times more food and medical supplies, as well as doctors, nurses, blankets, tents, and clothes. Your help is needed now before it is too late. Please give all you can. No pound or penny will ever be better spent or more appreciated.

What do you think?

Read the question as a class. Give students a little time to think about the question on their own, then discuss their thoughts in pairs. End with some class discussion.

In this speaking activity, students should use some second conditional sentences. Monitor and make a note of errors, but don't interrupt as this will stop the flow of ideas and conversation. In the feedback, write errors on the board and correct them as a class.

EVERYDAY ENGLISH (SB p69)

Making suggestions

Students will, of course, be using some of this language already to make, accept, and reject suggestions. This activity will widen their knowledge base in this high-frequency functional area.

1 Ask the students to look at the photo of Maria and Paul. Elicit or teach that *being broke* is colloquial for *having no money*. It is not as strong as *penniless*, which students met in the reading text.

Ask students in pairs to decide which of the suggestions are for Maria and which are for Paul. Ask them to underline the words used to make suggestions, and to decide which suggestions include the speaker.

Answers
Suggestions for Maria
Let's go shopping! (+ speaker)
Why don't we go for a walk? (+ speaker)
Shall we see what's on TV? (+ speaker)

Suggestions for Paul
If I were you, I'd get a better job.
Why don't you ask your parents?
You ought to ask your boss for a pay-rise!
I don't think you should go out so much.
You'd better get a loan from the bank.

2 **T 8.9** Ask students to listen to the conversations and read the tapescript on SB p128 at the same time. Ask them to identify ways of accepting and rejecting suggestions, and then practise the conversations in pairs.

Answers and tapescript
Accepting suggestions
That's a good idea.
Why didn't I think of that?
That would be great.

Rejecting suggestions
I don't feel like …
Oh, no! I'd rather do anything but that!
I'd rather/rather not …
No, I can't.
Good idea, but I've already tried that.

M = Maria   A = Anna
M I'm bored!
A Well, it's a beautiful day. **Why don't we** go for a walk?
M No, I don't feel like it. I'm too tired.
A You need to get out. **Let's** go shopping!
M Oh, no! I'd rather do anything but that.
A OK, **shall we** see what's on television?
M That's a good idea.
A Do you want to watch the news?
M Mmm, I'd rather watch *The Simpsons*.

P = Paul   M = Mike
P I'm broke, and I don't get paid for two weeks. What am I going to do?
M If I were you, I'd get a better job.
P Oh, why didn't I think of that? Thanks, Mike. That's a big help.
M Well, **you'd better** get a loan from the bank, then.
P No, I can't. I owe them too much already.
M Why don't you ask your parents? They'd help you out.
P No, I'd rather not. I'd rather work out my problems for myself.
M You ought to ask your boss for a pay-rise!
P Good idea, but I've tried that and it didn't work.
M Oh well, I suppose I could lend you some money.
P Really? Oh, that would be great! Thanks, Mike. You're a real mate.
M Yeah, well, OK then, but really, **I don't think you should** go out so much. That way, you won't be broke all the time.
P Yeah, yeah. I know. You're right.

Roleplay

Ask students to read the example conversation, and the situations. Answer any questions, then ask them in pairs to make up conversations for one or two of the situations using different ways of making suggestions. When they are ready, ask volunteers to perform their conversations for the class.

Don't forget!

Workbook Unit 8
Exercise 9 Vocabulary – Money
Exercise 10 and 11 Pronunciation – Ways of pronouncing *oo* and *ou*
Exercise 12 Phrasal verbs

Word list
Photocopy the Word list for Unit 8 (TB p158) for your students. Ask them to write in the translations, learn them at home, and/or write some of the words in their vocabulary notebooks.

9 Modal verbs 2 – probability
Character adjectives
So do I! Neither do I!

Introduction to the unit

This is the second unit on modal verbs. Unit 4 dealt with modals of obligation and permission, and their use in requests and offers.

Remind students of the introduction to modal verbs in the Grammar Reference section of Unit 4, SB p139, and ask them to reread this prior to starting Unit 9.

In this unit the focus is on present and past modals of probability. This is one of the main uses of modal verbs because *all* modals can be used to express different degrees of certainty or probability. However, at this intermediate level, the range of modals covered is limited so as not to overwhelm students.

The theme of this unit is relationships. In the *Reading and speaking* section, a father and daughter describe their relationship, and in the *Listening and speaking* section, two women talk about their families.

In the *Writing* section at the back of the book, students describe a relative.

You will need a couple of magazines or newspapers with advice columns to introduce the *I need help!* presentation section. Later in the unit both you and the students will need to bring to class some photographs of various family members. Ask students to look for these now, before you start the unit.

Language aims

Grammar – modal verbs of probability The first presentation section, *I need help!*, covers modal verbs of probability in the present with *must, could, might, can't* + the infinitive.

The second presentation section, *A holiday with friends*, covers the same modal verbs but in the past with *must, could, might, can't + have +* past participle.

POSSIBLE PROBLEMS

The use of *must* and *can't* to express strong possibility/probability does not usually cause problems of concept as similar forms exist in many languages. However, it is more difficult to get students to use *might* and *could* to express weaker probability as there are no comparable forms in other languages. They often use the words *perhaps* or *maybe* in direct translation from L1, but this can sound very *un*-English!

Common mistakes	**Corrections**
*Maybe they'll come.	They might come.
*Maybe she failed her test.	She might/could have failed her test.
*Perhaps he takes a break.	He could/might be taking a break.
*Perhaps I left my bag on the train.	I might have left my bag on the train.

Vocabulary The vocabulary section takes the form of a personality quiz. This not only enlarges the students' repertoire of adjectives used to describe character, such as *moody* and *ambitious*, but also does some work on the negative prefixes *in-* and *un-*.

Everyday English This section continues with the theme of relationships in its focus on ways of agreeing and disagreeing.

Notes on the unit

TEST YOUR GRAMMAR (SB p70)

This is a recognition exercise. It assumes that the students have some awareness of modal verbs of probability.

1 Ask students to read the question. Do the first item as a class. Write the two sentences on the board. Ask *Which sentence is a fact – definite/absolutely 100% sure? Which is fairly sure but not 100%?* Mark them with a ✓ for sure and a *?* for not so sure so that the students understand exactly what to do.

2 Ask students to read the sentences again and answer the question quickly. Don't be tempted to go over this in depth at this time. Students will practise it later.

I NEED HELP! (SB p70)

must, could, might, can't

The aim here is to introduce and practise modal verbs to express degrees of probability in the present in the context of discussing problems in advice columns.

1 Bring in several magazines or newspapers that have advice columns. Ask how many students read (or admit to reading) these pages. Ask *What are some typical problems people write about in these columns?*

2 Elicit or pre-teach the meaning of: *daydreams, encourage, hide your feelings, resentment.*

   Ask students to read Susie's advice to Lucy and Pam. What do they think the problems might be?

> **SUGGESTION**
> Discuss this question as a whole class to elicit the target language of the unit. Ask questions like those below, creating contexts from which the students can produce sentences with *must, could, might,* and *can't.* Once you have elicited a sentence, write it on the board. Then say it and ask students to repeat chorally and individually.
>
> **Sample questions and answers**
>
> *How old do you think   She must be a teenager.*
> *Lucy is?*
>
> *Why do you think that?   Because she lives with her parents.*
>
> *How old do you think   She can't be a teenager. She*
> *Pam is?   must be older. She might be in her late twenties or thirties.*
>
> *Why do you think that?   Because she's married …*
> *What do you think Lucy's   She might be … , etc.*
> *problem is?*

3–4 Ask students in pairs to discuss who they think the sentences refer to and give reasons. Students are being asked to recognize the target language here, before they produce it in practice. Go round helping as necessary. Then have a whole-class discussion.

5 Ask students to read Lucy and Pam's letters on SB p154, and check their answers.

GRAMMAR SPOT (SB p71)

1 This is a quick check of the form and use of these modal verbs. Remind students that *must, could,* and *might* are followed by the infinitive without *to.* Then, elicit which sentence is the most sure and which sentences are less sure.

2 Ask the second question.

You could ask students to look back at exercise 3 and find examples of the different modals.

Refer students to Grammar Reference 9.1 on SB p147.

Grammar and speaking

The aim here is to give students some controlled speaking practise with the new language. It is a chance for students to concentrate on correct form and pronunciation.

1 Focus attention on the example, then ask students in pairs to take turns reading the statements or questions and responding. You can give students time to prepare responses first if you think this might be difficult. Go round helping and correcting as necessary.

T 9.1 Play the recording so that the students can check their answers. Focus students' attention on stress and intonation. Then practise the sentences with the whole class: you or a student say a sentence and another student responds as naturally as possible with good stress and intonation.

> **Answers and tapescript**
> 2 He can't have much free time.
> 3 It might be Jane.
> 4 It must be raining.
> 5 There must be a fire somewhere.
> 6 He could be in his bedroom.
> 7 She can't be cooking dinner.
> 8 It might be John's.
>
> **T 9.1**
> 1 'I haven't eaten anything since breakfast.'
>   'You must be hungry.'
> 2 'Steve has three jobs.'
>   'He can't have much free time.'
> 3 'The phone's ringing.'
>   'It might be Jane.'
> 4 'The cat's soaking wet!'
>   'Oh, it must be raining.'
> 5 'Listen to all those fire engines!'
>   'Ooh, there must be a fire somewhere.'
> 6 'I don't know where Sam is.'
>   'He could be in his bedroom.'
> 7 'Marta isn't in the kitchen.'
>   'She can't be cooking dinner.'
> 8 'Whose coat is this?'
>   'It might be John's.'

What are they talking about?

This activity provides freer, more creative practice of the new language.

2 **T 9.2** Put students in pairs or small groups. Read through the example with the whole class, then play the recording, pausing after each conversation, so the groups can discuss the answers. Go over each item and encourage students to give reasons for their decisions. You may have to push students into using modals in their replies and not just *perhaps* or *maybe*.

> **Sample answers and tapescript**
> 2 They must be in a pub. They could be in a café or a hotel restaurant. They can't be at home.
> 3 He must be a taxi driver. He can't be a lorry driver because he has customers. He can't be an actor.
> 4 She must be talking about an interview for a job. She might be talking about taking a test but she can't be talking about meeting her boyfriend's parents because she says they'd let her know if she got it.
> 5 They must be talking about a dog. They could be talking about a cat. They can't be talking about a baby.
>
> **T 9.2**
> 1 'It's Father's Day next Sunday.'
>   'I know. Should we buy Dad a present or just send him a card?'
> 2 'A half of lager and a fizzy mineral water, please.'
>   'Ice and lemon with the water?'
>   'Yes, please. And do you do bar meals?'
>   'Yes, we do.'
> 3 I don't work normal hours and I like that. I'd hate one of those nine-to-five office jobs. Also I meet a lot of really interesting people. Of course, every now and then there's a difficult customer, but usually people are really nice. I took that really famous film star to the airport last week, now what was her name? Anyway, she was lovely. Gave me a big tip!
> 4 'So how did it go?'
>   'I'm not sure. I think it was OK.'
>   'Were you nervous?'
>   'Yeah, very, but I tried not to show it.'
>   'Could you answer all their questions?'
>   'Most of them.'
>   'And what happens now?'
>   'They said they'd phone me in a couple of days and let me know if I got it.'
> 5 'We've never had one before.'
>   'Really? We've always had them in our family. We're all crazy about them.'
>   'Well, we are now. The kids love her. And she's so good with them, very good-natured. But it wasn't fair to have one when we lived in the flat.'
>   'It's OK if they're small and you live near a park, but I know what you mean. What's her name?'
>   'Poppy.'

Who's who in the family?

3 Put the students in groups to do this. Ask them to look at the photographs on SB pp154–155, decide who is who, and give reasons for their answers. Go round encouraging the use of modals, and note down errors to go over in the feedback.

> **Answers**
> **Picture 1** Simon, granddaughter
> **Picture 2** older brother, Simon, younger brother, sister
> **Picture 3** wife, older son, younger son (or Simon's lap), Simon

Picture 4 *(back row)* nieces
(middle row) younger brother, older brother, brother-in-law (sister's husband), sister, Simon, brother-in-law (wife's brother), wife
(front row) younger son, older son

Picture 5 *(back row)* Simon, sister
(front row) older brother, younger brother

SUGGESTION

It would be interesting and fun for students to bring in photos of their families and to do a mingle activity with students commenting on who they think the people are in other students' photos. You could bring in photos of your own relatives to show the students. Elicit *That must be …, He could be …,* etc.

ADDITIONAL MATERIAL

Workbook Unit 9
Exercises 1 and 2 Modal verbs of probability in the present
Exercise 3 Continuous infinitives

A HOLIDAY WITH FRIENDS (SB p72)

must have been/can't have been

This section introduces and practises modal verbs to express probability in the past, in the context of two friends talking about a holiday. Because students hear only one side of the telephone conversation, they have to work out what is being talked about. This gives practice of the past modals because Andy and Carl are talking about a past event (a recent holiday). Students will hear both sides of the conversation at the end of the activity.

1 Set the scene by asking students to look at the photos of Andy and Carl. Ask a few questions about them. *Are they friends? What do you think they are talking about?* Elicit or teach the meaning of *crutches* and *plaster*.

   T 9.3 Play the recording. Ask students to read and listen then discuss with a partner what they think Andy and Carl are talking about.

   Answer
   They're talking about a holiday in the mountains with friends. It was probably a skiing holiday.

2 This is a recognition exercise to check that students know the use of the modal verbs. Do the first one as an example with the whole class. Explain that in each item, one statement about the conversation is possible and one is not. Ask students in pairs to look back at the conversation and decide on the answers. Go round helping as necessary. Give students about ten minutes to complete the activity. Check answers with the whole class, asking students to give reasons for all their deductions.

Answers
1 What is the relationship between Andy and Carl?
   ✓ They must be friends.
   ✗ They could be business colleagues.
2 Where have they been?
   ✓ They could have been on a skiing holiday.
   ✗ They can't have been on a skiing holiday.
3 What happened to Carl?
   ✓ He must have broken his leg.
   ✗ He might have broken his arm.
4 How many people went on holiday?
   ✗ There must have been four.
   ✓ There might have been five or more.
5 Where did they stay?
   ✗ They could have stayed with friends.
   ✓ They must have stayed at a hotel.
6 What did they do on holiday?
   ✓ They must have taken a lot of photos.
   ✗ They can't have taken any photos.
7 Why did Andy and Julie send an email to the manager?
   ✗ They could have written to thank him.
   ✓ They might have written to complain about their room.
8 What did Marcia lose?
   ✗ It might have been her skis.
   ✓ It could have been her suitcase.

3 Students can do this in pairs, but it is best to do it as a class, inviting members of the class to continue the story, beginning with the example. You and the students can correct the grammar and the story until a final version is decided upon. Don't expect students to produce as full a version as the following, but stretch their stories out as much as you can.

Sample answer
Andy and Carl must be friends and they could have been on holiday together. They might have gone to Switzerland. Carl must have had an accident and broken his leg and come home early. There can't have been just three friends because they talk about five people, so there must have been at least five. They must have stayed at a hotel because they are trying to get their money back. They must have been skiing and taken a lot of photos. Andy can't have written to the manager to thank him; he might have written to him to complain about the view from his room. The airline must have lost Marcia's suitcase.

4 **T 9.4** Play the recording of both sides of the telephone conversation. Students should be interested to find out if all their deductions were correct. Ask how much they learned. Were there any surprises?

Tapescript

A = Andy   C = Carl

A Hi! Carl? It's Andy. How are you? Feeling better?

C Er – not really. I have to sit down most of the time. It's too tiring – walking with these crutches.

A Really? Still on crutches, eh? So you're not back to work yet?

C No. And I'm bored to death. I don't go back to the hospital for another week.

A Another week! Is that when the plaster comes off?

C I hope so. I can't wait to have two legs again! Anyway, how are you? Still missing the snow and the mountains?

A No, I'm fine. We're both fine. Julie sends her love, by the way.

C Thanks. Send her my love, too. I miss you all. By the way, have you got any of your photos back yet?

A Yes, yes, we have. Julie picked them up today. They're good. I didn't realize we'd taken so many of us all.

C What about that one with the amazing sunset behind the hotel?

A Yes, the sunset. It's a good one. All of us together on Bob and Marcia's balcony, with the mountains and the snow in the background. Brings back memories, doesn't it?

C Yeah. The memory of me skiing into a tree!

A Yes, I know. I'm sorry. But at least it happened at the end; it could have been the first day. You only missed the last two days.

C OK, OK. Oh, Andy, have you written to the hotel yet to complain about your room? That view you had over the car park was awful!

A Yeah, and it was noisy too! We didn't have any views of the mountains. Yeah, we've written. We emailed the manager yesterday, but I don't know if we'll get any money back.

C And Marcia's suitcase, did she find it?

A Yeah. The airline found it and put it on the next flight. Marcia was very relieved.

C I bet she was! All in all I suppose it was a pretty good two weeks, wasn't it?

A Absolutely. It was a great holiday. Some ups and downs, but we all had fun, didn't we? Shall we go again next year?

C I'd like to. All six of us again. Lisa wants to go again, too. It was her first time skiing and she loved it, but she says she'll only come if I don't break a leg!

A Great! It's a date. And next time go around the trees! I'll call again soon, Carl. Take care!

C You too, Andy. Bye now.

A Bye.

GRAMMAR SPOT (SB p73)

These grammar questions not only ask about modal verbs of probability, they also remind students of the uses and past forms of other modal verbs which they studied in Unit 4.

1–2 Read the questions as a class and ask students what the past tense of each sentence is.

Answers

1 She must/can't/could/might **have been** on holiday.

2 I **had to** buy some sunglasses. (Explain that *must* here is a modal verb of obligation, not of probability.)
   I **had to** go home early.
   I **could** see the mountains from my room.

Refer students to Grammar Reference 9.2 on SB p147.

PRACTICE (SB p73)

Grammar and speaking

This controlled oral practice is to help students gain confidence in producing the correct form of past modals of probability with good stress and intonation.

1   Do the example as a class, then ask students in pairs to take turns reading the statements and responding. Alternatively, if they find this difficult, give them time to prepare responses before practising. Go round helping and correcting as necessary.

Answers

2   He must have been ill.

3   She might have overslept.

4   You must have dropped it.

5   She can't have finished already.

6   He must have cheated.

T 9.5   Play the recording so that students can check their answers. If you think the students still need more practice, you can ask them to repeat or write the sentences on the recording.

Tapescript

1   **A** I can't find my homework.
    B You must have forgotten it.

2   **A** Mark didn't come to school last week.
    B He must have been ill.

3   **A** Why is Isabel late for class?
    B She might have overslept.

4   **A** I can't find my notebook.
    B You must have dropped it.

5   **A** The teacher's checking Maria's work.
    B She can't have finished already!

6   **A** How did Bob get such good marks in that test?
    B He must have cheated!

Discussing grammar

This exercise reviews the modals of obligation and ability (Unit 4) and compares them with those of probability studied in this unit. If you lack time, you can set the exercises for homework. The discussion could then follow in the next lesson and will take less time.

2 Ask students to complete the activity individually. Discuss the answers as a class.

> **Answers**
> 1 He **can't/could/must/might** have been born during World War II.
> 2 **Can/Could** you help me with the dishes, please?
> 3 You **can/can't/must/should** see the doctor immediately. (*Could* is only possible if part of a conditional sentence such as *You could see the doctor immediately, if you left now.*)
> 4 It **can't/could/must/might** be raining.
> 5 **Can/Can't/Could/Must/Should/Shall** we go out for dinner tonight? (*Might we ...* sounds very formal and old-fashioned. *Can't we ...* expresses the speaker's strong desire to go out for dinner, whereas *Must we ...* expresses that the speaker does not want to go.)
> 6 I **can/can't/must/might/should/shall** stop smoking. (*Could* is only possible if it is part of a conditional sentence, such as *I could stop smoking, if I wanted to.*)
> 7 It **can't/could/must/might** have been Bill that you met at the party.
> 8 I **can/can't/must/might/should/shall** learn to speak English. (*Could* is only possible if part of a conditional sentence, such as *I could learn to speak English if I really wanted to.*)

ADDITIONAL MATERIAL

Workbook Unit 9
Exercises 4–6 Modal verbs of probability in the past

READING AND SPEAKING (SB p74)

A father and daughter

This is a jigsaw reading. The aim is to improve students' ability to read for specific information and to infer facts about a text. The nature of the jigsaw task provides a lot of opportunity for speaking practice. There is also some follow-up work on using modal verbs. The texts are quite long, so leave plenty of time, or think about adapting the material.

1 A fun way to begin is to bring in some pictures of your close relatives. Ask students to tell you which family members you resemble and to ask you who you are like (personality). You can also ask the students to bring in photos of their families.

Ask students in pairs to ask and answer the questions.

> **SUGGESTION**
> The level of vocabulary in the text is not too demanding, and you can check it briefly after the reading. However, another way of pre-teaching key new words is to combine them with the personalized introductory activity above. For example, write the following questions on the board:

> *Are you <u>close to</u> people in your family?*
> *Do you <u>get on with</u> your parents?*
> *Are they <u>proud of</u> you?*
> *Are you <u>moody</u>?*
> *Are you <u>obsessed with/crazy about</u> pets/computers/ learning English?*
> *Do you <u>have things in common</u> with anyone in your family?*
> Elicit or teach the meaning of the underlined words, then get the students to ask each other these questions as well as those in the Student's Book.

2 Divide the class into two groups, Group **A** and Group **B**. Write question 1 in exercise 3 on the board as a general comprehension question to focus the students' reading. Ask Group **A** to read what Oliver says, and Group **B** to read what Carmen says. Briefly discuss the answers to the question as a class (see answers in exercise 3 below).

> **SUGGESTION**
> If you have a large class, divide students into groups of four, with an equal number of **A** and **B** groups. So, if you have 24 students, that makes three **A** groups and three **B**s. If possible, get each group to sit together around a table or in a circle. It's worth planning the logistics of a jigsaw, or any activity where students have to change partners, in advance.

3 Ask the students to work in groups to answer the other questions about their person, and make brief notes of their answers.

> **Answers**
> 1 a and c
> 2 b and c
> 3 a and c
> 4 He used to show Carmen's friends his film awards.
> 5 She didn't do well and had no friends.
> 6 Yes. She says *I was miserable until I met my husband.*
> 7 She wasn't interested in following the same career. She probably resents it because her father was always more interested in his career than in his family.
> 8 Carmen doesn't like his new wife. She feels her father doesn't like her husband, George.

4 Now put the students in **A/B** pairs. Ask them to compare their answers, and then quickly read the other text.

What do you think?

Ask students to discuss this question in their pairs, then discuss it as a class.

Language work

The aim here is to provide further practice of past modals of deduction. If you think the students have had enough practice, you can omit this exercise.

Ask students in pairs to rewrite the sentences.

> **Sample answers**
> 2 Oliver can't be a famous actor because I've never heard of him.
> 3 He might have won an Oscar® because Carmen says he was proud of his awards and showed them to her friends.
> 4 She must have had a lot of friends when she was a teenager because there was an endless stream of young men coming to the house.
> 5 She can't have worked hard at school because she was unhappy there and left early.

VOCABULARY AND SPEAKING (SB p76)

Character adjectives

This exercise contains a quiz that introduces adjectives to describe people's characters.

1 Begin by eliciting character adjectives from the students. Bring in pictures of two very different people that you think your students will be familiar with. Ask *What are they like?* or *What type of person are they?* See how many words the students can come up with.

   Then ask the students to do the quiz. Tell them to look up any new words in a dictionary.

2 Put students in pairs to do the quiz again, but this time about their partner, then students compare their answers with their partner's. This can be great fun! End with whole-class feedback.

3 Ask students in their pairs to match the adjectives. Check answers with the whole class. Ask students which adjectives according to the quiz describe them. Do they agree?

> **Answers**
> reliable 8   reserved 13   lazy 11   easygoing 16
> optimistic 7   shy 3   generous 14   untidy 9
> sociable 2   impatient 10   moody 5   cheerful 1
> talkative 15   ambitious 4   hardworking 12   sensitive 6

4 Now ask them to categorize the adjectives. There will inevitably be some debate about which are positive and negative qualities.

> **Possible answers**
> **positive:** reliable, optimistic, sociable, generous, hardworking, easygoing, cheerful
> **negative:** impatient, lazy, moody, untidy
> **both:** talkative, reserved, shy, ambitious, sensitive

5 Do one or two as examples, then ask students, still in their pairs, to write the opposites. If you are short of time, you could do this with the whole class and go through it quite quickly.

> **Answers**
> reliable: unreliable   lazy: hardworking
> optimistic: pessimistic   generous: selfish
> sociable: unsociable   moody: easygoing, even-tempered
> talkative: quiet/reserved hardworking: lazy
> reserved: outgoing/sociable easygoing: moody/temperamental
> shy: outgoing/sociable   untidy: tidy
> impatient: patient   cheerful: depressed/miserable/sad
> ambitious: unambitious   sensitive: insensitive
>
> *reliable, sociable, ambitious, tidy,* and *sensitive* can use *in-* and *un-* to make negatives.

6 Begin by describing someone yourself. Make it fun! Alternatively, if you are concerned that some students might find this too personal, you could write the names of seven or eight famous people on the board and ask students to describe them. The rest of the class must decide which one is being described.

WRITING (SB p116)

A description (2)

Lead in by putting a picture of a person on the board and asking students to ask you questions about him/her.

1 Ask students to think of someone in their family; then to write sentences to answer questions 1–6 about him/her. Ask some students to read their sentences to the class.

2 Ask students to look at the photo of Emily Morgan. Ask *What do you think she is like?* Ask students to read the description and write the parts that describe physical appearance, character, and habits on the chart.

physical appearance	a fair complexion; curly grey hair; deep blue eyes; her face is a little lined; rather attractive
character	young in spirit; the kind of person you can always go to if you have a problem; generous; not very tolerant; contented
habits	likes reading and gardening; likes to take her dog, Buster, for long walks; either she's making something, mending something, doing something to help others; she does the shopping for some of the old people

3 Ask students to find 'She's … not very tolerant' (line 16) and read out the explanation. Do the first adjective with the class to give them the idea and then ask them to complete the rest in pairs. The adjectives should be familiar to them.

Answers

1 rude: not very polite
2 boring: not very interesting
3 cheap: not very expensive
4 ugly: not very pretty/handsome/beautiful/attractive/good-looking
5 cruel: not very kind
6 stupid: not very clever/intelligent

4 Ask students to write a description of a relative for homework. Ask them to use sentences from exercise 1, and to use polite ways of expressing negative things.

ADDITIONAL MATERIAL

Workbook Unit 9
Exercise 7   Vocabulary – Word formation

LISTENING AND SPEAKING (SB p77)

Brothers and sisters

The aim here is to improve students' ability to listen for specific information. It is followed by a personalized discussion on families.

1 This is a mingle activity to set the scene for the topic of the listening, rather than a serious class survey.

Set it up by telling students about your family. Then ask them to walk round the room, asking as many people as possible about their brothers and sisters. Continue for about five minutes before whole-class feedback.

2 The first part of the listening contains some difficult vocabulary that needs pre-teaching. A good way of doing this is to use the vocabulary to create a prediction task. For this part, write on the board: *a nun, hand-me-down clothes* (passed from one sister/brother to another), *keep in touch*. Tell the students that these are words and expressions they will hear Louisa use when she describes her childhood. Elicit or teach the meanings of the words. Then ask *Do you think Louisa came from a rich family? Why not? Do you think one of her sisters has an unusual job? Do you think she often speaks to her family?*

T 9.6 Focus attention on the questions in the chart. Play the part about Louisa. Ask students to listen and write notes in the chart, then compare answers in pairs. Play the recording again so that students can check their answers. Answer any questions as a whole class.

Now elicit or teach *only child* (no brothers or sisters), then follow the same procedure for the second part of the recording about Rose.

Possible answers and tapescript

Louisa

- She is the youngest of seven. She had four sisters and two brothers.
- She was happy for many reasons: she got along well with her brothers and sisters and her parents. They had little money but lots of freedom. The only things she didn't like were hand-me-down clothes and not going away on holiday.
- Yes, she's happy now. They are still a close and happy family. They have a family reunion each year. She is very close to her sister, Julia. But only six out of the seven are still alive.
- When they were children, the older ones looked after the younger ones. Now the three youngest look after the oldest. When Louisa's husband died, her sister Julia and she became very close.
  She had rich cousins who envied her freedom because they had to dress formally all the time. She has twin great-grandchildren now.

Rose

- She has none. She's an only child.
- She was quite happy when very young because she had lots of cousins to play with. Also, she had a best friend who lived next door. But then the friend moved. Being a teenager was very difficult because she had no one to talk to about her parents, and she got too much attention.
- Now it is difficult – her father has died and there is nobody to share the responsibility of looking after her mother.
- Now, she's married with two children. She didn't want an only child.

T 9.6

I = Interviewer   L = Louisa

L I'm the youngest of seven children. My oldest sister is still alive, age ninety-three, and there are sixteen years between us. There were four girls, two boys, and then me.

I Seven children! Wow! How did you all get on together when you were children?

L Amazingly well. Being the youngest, my two brothers and I called our sisters 'the others', because they were either married or working by the time we were born. But the seven of us all got along very well. But it's different now, of course.

I Really? How?

L Well, when we were small, my older sisters often took care of us. Now my brothers and I are busy taking care of them.

I Tell me about your big sister Julia. How has your relationship with her changed over the years?

L Julia was the sister who used to … on her holidays … used to take me for walks and so on. But then she became a nun and went to Africa for twenty-three years. We wrote to one another and I was still her little sister. When she came back, it was shortly after my husband died. We became very close and our whole relationship changed and we became great friends.

I What do you see as the main advantage and disadvantage of coming from such a large family?

L Hmm. I think the main advantage was that we learned how to enjoy life without having a lot of money. I think our other relatives, my rich cousins in the city, envied us. We had old bikes, old clothes, but we had lots of freedom. In the city, they had to wear nice suits and behave correctly.

I Disadvantages?

L I think it was very difficult sometimes to have hand-me-down clothes, especially for a little girl like me. And I was sad that we didn't go away on holiday like some other children. But the advantages outweighed the disadvantages enormously, there's no doubt about that.

I Six out of the seven of you are still alive. How closely have you kept in touch over the years?

L Very closely. Of course we still phone each other all the time and see each other whenever we can. And we have a big family reunion every year. My granddaughter's just had twins. That means we'll have four generations there this year. How marvellous!

I = Interviewer   R = Rose

I So, Rose, do you have any brothers or sisters?

R No, I don't. I'm an only child.

I So what was it like growing up as an only child? Were you happy?

R When I was little, I liked it. I had lots of cousins and most of them lived in the same town, so we all played together all the time. And I had a best friend who lived next door to me. She was the same age as me and so she was a bit like a sister I suppose. But she moved away and that was sad. It was hard when I was a teenager.

I Why was that?

R Well, you know what it's like being a teenager. You're kind of unsure of how to deal with things and how to deal with people, especially parents. It would have been nice to have a brother or sister to talk to.

I Some people who come from large families might envy you because you had all of your parents' attention.

R Yes. But I think it has its negative side as well as its positive side. I think you don't want all your parents' attention, especially as a teenager. It was hard to find myself and my place in the world, I suppose.

I What about now that you're an adult?

R Again, I think it's difficult really. My father died about ten years ago, so of course I'm the one who's left totally responsible for my mother. I'm the one who has to look after her if she has a problem and help her if she needs help in any way. There's nobody else to help at all.

I You're married now with two children of your own. Was that a conscious decision to have more than one child?

R Yes, definitely. And they seem very happy and they get along very well with one another. Usually.

What do you think?

Students discuss the questions in small groups. Then conduct a whole-class feedback. This can be a very interesting topic, especially when you get diverse opinions.

EVERYDAY ENGLISH (SB p77)

So do I! Neither do I!

1 Begin by expressing a few opinions, and inviting the students to agree or disagree, for example *I hate football. I love Indian food. I don't want to go out this evening.* It's fine if they just say something like *Me too!*

T 9.7 Ask students to read the statements in the chart. Answer any questions. Then play the recording. Ask the students to listen and complete Sue's column. Ask them to check their answers in pairs.

2 Read through the list of phrases with the students. Ask which ones are used to agree with the speaker and which ones are used to disagree.

T 9.7 Play the recording again and ask students to listen carefully, this time to Sue's exact words. You may need to pause the recording to give them time to write the words in the 'Sue's words' column. Let them compare answers in pairs, then go through the answers with the whole class, pointing out the differences.

Answers and tapescript

Sue's friends	Sue	Sue's words
1 I want to travel the world.	✓	So do I.
2 I don't want to have lots of children.	✓	Neither do I.
3 I can speak four languages.	✗	I can't.
4 I can't drive.	✓	Neither can I.
5 I'm not going to get married until I'm 35.	✓	Neither am I.
6 I went to London last year.	✓	So did I.
7 I've never been to Australia.	✗	I have.
8 I don't like politicians.	✓	Neither do I.
9 I'm bored with Hollywood actors.	✓	So am I.
10 I love going to parties.	✓	So do I.

When it's the same for her, Sue says *So ... I./Neither ... I.* When it's different, she says *I am/do/can ...* or *I'm not/don't/can't ....*

T 9.7

S = Sue   A–J = Sue's friends

1 **A** I want to travel the world.
  S So do I.

2 **B** I don't want to have lots of children.
  S Neither do I.

3 **C** I can speak four languages.
  S I can't.

4 **D** I can't drive.
  S Neither can I.

5 **E** I'm not going to get married until I'm 35.
  S Neither am I.

6 **F** I went to London last year.
   S So did I.
7 **G** I've never been to Australia.
   S I have.
8 **H** I don't like politicians.
   S Neither do I.
9 **I** I'm bored with Hollywood actors.
   S So am I.
10 **J** I love going to parties.
   S So do I.

Make sure that students understand these forms. Refer them to Grammar Reference 9.4 and 9.5 on SB p147.

3 Ask students in pairs to take turns reading out the statements from exercise 1, and giving a true response from the list in exercise 2. Go round the room monitoring and correcting as necessary. End with some open pairwork across the class, paying attention to correct stress and intonation.

4 Ask everyone to write down a few statements about themselves. Call upon individuals to read examples, to which other members of the class must respond with their opinions. Alternatively, get students to write three statements on three different pieces of paper. Divide the class into groups of four, and ask each group to collect the pieces of paper from everyone in their group, mix them up, and place them face down on the table. The students take turns picking up a piece of paper and reading it out. The other students must agree or disagree.

Don't forget!

Workbook Unit 9
Exercise 8 Connected speech
Exercise 9 Pronunciation – Shifting stress
Exercise 10 Adjective + preposition

Word List
Photocopy the Word list for Unit 9 (TB p159) for your students. Ask them to write in the translations, learn them at home, and/or write some of the words in their vocabulary notebooks.

EXTRA IDEAS UNITS 7–9
On pp125–132 of the Teacher's Book, there are two additional activities: a roleplay (to use with Unit 7), and a maze (to use with Unit 8). When to use each activity is signposted from the teaching notes at the recommended point in the units.

If you have the time and feel that your students would benefit from these, photocopy them and use them in class.

Stop and check 3
(TB pp138–139). A suggestion for approaching the *Stop and check* tests is in the introduction on TB p5.

10

Present Perfect Continuous
Time expressions
Compound nouns • Quantity

Obsessions

Introduction to the unit

The theme of this unit is people who have obsessions – about texting on a mobile phone, about becoming famous, and about collecting things. This theme provides a context for contrasting and practising the Present Perfect Simple and Continuous.

The reading text is about a man who has spent most of his life trying (unsuccessfully) to become famous as a Hollywood film star. The *Listening and speaking* section is about two people who collect things as a hobby.

The *Writing* section at the back of the book practises using relative clauses, participle clauses and other linking devices to transform isolated facts about a person into a biography.

Language aims

Grammar – the Present Perfect Continuous   Although they have probably come across this tense, it is unlikely that your students are using the Present Perfect Continuous correctly, if at all. This tense is one of the hardest for learners to grasp, made more difficult because there are two aspects to understand, the perfect aspect and the continuous aspect.

We saw in Unit 7 why students make so many mistakes with the Present Perfect. The form of auxiliary verb *have* + past participle exists in many other European languages, but its use is different. To refer to definite time, English uses the Past Simple, not the Present Perfect, and English has a way of expressing past-joined-to-present that other languages don't have. We say, *I live here, I have lived here for ten years*, and not the more logical **I live here, I live here for ten years.*

The Present Perfect Continuous presents another difficult element for students to grasp, because the continuous aspect probably doesn't exist in their language either. They will probably choose to apply a tense that translates directly from their own language(s), for example **I'm living here for six years,* instead of *I have been living here for six years.*

The approach in the Student's Book is to keep the rules simple and lead students to an understanding by asking them to contrast sentences and complete many controlled tasks.

You may want to read through *Continuous forms* in the grammar reference on SB p148 with the class to refresh students' memories about continuous forms in general before starting the unit.

Time expressions   Ways of referring to points in time and periods of time are introduced and practised. *How long are you here for?* and *How long have you been here?* are examined. Students often confuse these because, often, the direct translation of the second question takes the form of the first question in their language.

Vocabulary   The focus is on compound nouns, an area which students generally like. Perhaps this is due to the fun of putting two known elements together to make a third meaning.

Everyday English   This section introduces and revises some expressions of quantity.

Notes on the unit

TEST YOUR GRAMMAR (SB p78)

This section will start students thinking about the continuous aspect. In order to understand the way the Present Perfect Continuous works, they need to understand the idea of continuous as an aspect in other tenses.

1 Ask students in pairs or small groups to match a line in **A** with a line or picture in **B**. Students will probably find this fairly easy.

Check answers with the whole class, encouraging students to comment and correct.

Answers
1 What do you do for a living?
  What are you doing on the floor?
2 He speaks three languages.
  He's speaking to the teacher.
3 She has a house by the sea.
  She's having a baby next month.
4 What have you done with my pen? I can't find it.
  What have you been doing since I last saw you?
5 Who drank my beer? (picture of empty glass)
  Who's been drinking my beer? (picture of half-empty glass)
6 I read that book. It was really good.
  I was reading that book when you called.

2 Ask students what the verb in the second sentence of each pair has in common. (They are all continuous in form, that is, they all use a form of *be* followed by *-ing*.)

TONY'S PHONE BILL (SB p78)

Present Perfect Continuous

The aim here is to introduce the Present Perfect Continuous to talk about an activity which started in the past and continues to now. The context – a newspaper article about a teenager who has received a huge telephone bill as a result of sending thousands of text messages – contrasts the Present Perfect Continuous with uses of the Present Perfect Simple.

1 Lead in briefly by asking students about their mobile phone use. *Do they send lots of text messages? Who pays their bill? Have they ever received a very large bill?* Pre-teach key vocabulary: *text (someone), make a phone call, receive/pay a phone bill, clear a debt.* You may also want to explain that the phrase 'state of the art' is often used adjectivally to describe something which has all the very latest technology, and that 'textitis' is a word made up by the writer to imply that texting has become like an illness, like appendic**itis** or bronch**itis**.

T 10.1 Ask students to read and listen to the newspaper article, and answer the questions.

Answers
1 £450
2 He has been doing well at school.
3 His father has taken it away.
4 He has been working in a shoe shop.

2 Ask students in pairs to write the questions. Do the first two as an example. They will need to refer back to the text. Remember, students often have problems forming questions, so monitor carefully.

Get feedback, and encourage the others to comment. You could practise questions and answers in open pairs across the room.

T 10.2 Play the recording so that students can listen and check their answers. You could ask them to look at the tapescript on SB p130 and tell you which verbs are simple and which are continuous.

Answers and tapescript
1 How long has he had his mobile phone?
2 How long has he been asking his father for a phone?
3 Why did he want one?
4 Who has he been texting?
5 What time has he been going to bed?
6 Has his father forgiven him?
7 How much has he paid back?
8 How long will it take him to clear the debt?

GRAMMAR SPOT (SB p79)

The aim here is to get students to recognize the two different forms, and to introduce a very simple rule to show how they are used.

1 Ask students in pairs to find examples quickly in the text and underline them.

Answers
Present Perfect Simple: has received, has had, has taken, have forgiven, has made, has found, has paid.

Present Perfect Continuous: 's been asking, 's been doing, 've been texting, 've been going, has been working.

2 As a class, match the rules to the examples.

Answers
How long have you been learning English? asks about an activity.
How many teachers have you had? asks about a quantity.

Refer students to Grammar Reference 10.1 and 10.2 on SB p148.

Conversations

These exercises provide controlled accuracy practice of the Present Perfect Simple and Continuous.

1 Read through the example, then ask students to write questions with *How long … ?* Let them check in pairs before going over the answers as a class. The purpose of this exercise is to show students that in cases where either the Present Perfect Simple or the Present Perfect Continuous can be used to express an idea, the Present Perfect Continuous should be chosen. The exercise also highlights the verbs that aren't usually used in the continuous form.

Answers
2 How long have you been playing tennis?
3 How long have you known Jack?
4 How long have you been working in Hong Kong?
5 How long have you had a Japanese car?

2 In pairs, students write, then ask and answer, similar questions about themselves.

3 Ask students in their pairs to look back at exercise 1 and write follow-up questions in the Past Simple. Again, this is to reinforce the point that when definite time is talked about, we use the Past Simple, not the Present Perfect.

Answers
1 When **did you** move there?
2 How old **were you** when **you** started **playing**?
3 Where **did you** meet **him**?
4 Why **did you** decide **to work in Hong Kong/there**?
5 How much **did you** pay **for it**?

4 **T 10.3** Play the recording while students read the conversation. You could say each line and get students to repeat after you to practise pronunciation.

Ask students to read the prompts. Put them in pairs to prepare and practise similar conversations. Go round monitoring and helping as necessary. Ask some pairs to model their conversations for the class. Encourage students to correct each other.

T 10.4 Play the recording so that students can compare their conversations. Ask them to practise the conversations again with a partner.

Answers and tapescript
1 A You're covered in paint! What have you been doing?
  B I've been redecorating the bathroom.
  A Have you finished yet?
  B Well, I've painted the door and the ceiling, but I haven't put up the wallpaper yet.

2 A Your hands are dirty. What have you been doing?
  B They're filthy. I've been working in the garden.
  A Have you finished yet?
  B Well, I've cut the grass, but I haven't watered the flowers yet.

3 A Your eyes are red! What have you been doing?
  B I'm exhausted. I've been revising for my exams.
  A Have you finished them yet?
  B Well, I've done my chemistry and history, but I haven't done English yet.

Discussing grammar

5 In pairs, students discuss what is wrong with the sentences and try to correct them. Check answers with the whole class.

Answers
1 With the continuous form, it sounds as though the person cut their finger again and again. In the simple form, the suggestion is that it was accidentally cut once.
2 It would be unusual to expect students to understand why this is wrong. *I've swum* is an unlikely sentence in any situation. Swimming by definition takes time. We need the continuous form to express that this is an activity taking place over a period of time.
3 This is an activity over a period of time up to now, not a completed action.
4 The continuous form suggests that the action took place again and again, not just once.
5 This suggests that the speaker wrote their entire autobiography in one afternoon. We need the continuous form to suggest that the activity is taking place over a period of time, and is not yet completed.

ADDITIONAL MATERIAL

Workbook Unit 10
Exercises 1 and 2 Present Perfect Continuous
Exercises 3 and 4 Simple and Continuous revision

A LIFELONG PASSION (SB p80)

Time expressions

The aim here is not only to present and practise various ways of referring to time in the past, but also to reinforce the Present Perfect Simple and Continuous to refer to the indefinite past, and Past Simple and Past Continuous to refer to definite past.

1 A good way to lead in here is to elicit some of the key vocabulary around the topic of musicians. Ask students to look at the picture of Astrid Johnsson, and elicit the key words, *cello, cellist,* and *musician.* Write *Music* on the board. Then ask *What musical instruments do you know?* and elicit *piano, violin, guitar,* etc. Then ask *What do you*

call people who play these instruments? and elicit *pianist, violinist,* etc. Ask *What do musicians do?* and elicit *play an instrument, play in an orchestra, perform classical music, play in concerts and festivals, compose concertos/soundtracks, conduct an orchestra.*

Ask students to read the chart about Astrid Johnsson quickly and answer the gist question.

> **Answer**
> She has won awards and scholarships, toured, performed in concerts and festivals, appeared on TV, composed concertos and soundtracks, and taught music. She has also been married twice and has had a daughter.

2 Ask students in pairs to answer the questions. The aim of questions 1–8 is to practise the Present Perfect Simple and Continuous. Get whole-class feedback and encourage correct use of Present Perfect forms.

> **Answers**
> 1 She has been playing the cello since she was 3.
> 2 She has played with the Swedish Youth Orchestra, the London Symphony Orchestra, and the Chamber Orchestra of Great Britain.
> 3 She has composed concertos and film soundtracks.
> 4 She has won an award for *Young Musician of the Year,* a scholarship to the Royal Academy of Music, and Best European Film Soundtrack 1999.
> 5 She's been married to Georges since 1998.
> 6 She's been married twice.
> 7 She was married to him for eight years.
> 8 She has been teaching and lecturing since she was 42.

3 The aim of this exercise is to practise various time expressions.

Ask students in their pairs to complete the sentences. As always, get whole-class feedback and encourage comment and correction before you give the answers.

> **Answers**
> 1 at the age of three
> 2 After winning the award
> 3 between 1978 and 1982
> 4 while she was at music school
> 5 two years after she got married
> 6 while she was composing
> 7 until she married Georges
> 8 since she married Georges

Refer students to Grammar Reference 10.3 on SB p148.

> **SUGGESTION**
> There is an extra exercise on prepositions of time on TB p133 that you might want to photocopy and use before moving on to the *Writing* section at the back of the book, or the *Practice* section.

Writing a biography

1 Ask students in pairs to compare the sentences in **A** with the paragraphs in **B**. They must note all the ways the sentences combine, and underline the words in **A** that are not used again in **B**.

> **Answers**
> The sentences combine in the following ways: relative clauses, reduced participle clauses, and by means of linking words like *whilst* and *since.*
> The words in **A** that are not used again tend to be the pronouns *she* and *he,* and the auxiliaries *is* and *has.* In **B**, key words like *famous* and *lives* are not repeated.

2 Find out what students know about Alfred Nobel. (He is famous for inventing dynamite and leaving money to set up the Nobel Prizes.)

Then ask students in pairs to rewrite the sentences about him to form a natural-sounding paragraph. They should base their paragraph on the one about Astrid. Before conducting feedback, you could get pairs to compare their answers with another pair, or exchange their work so that they can correct each other. Copy the answer below on to an OHT or a handout.

> **Sample answer**
> Alfred Bernhard Nobel, the man behind the Nobel Prizes, was an engineer, an inventor, and a poet. Born in Stockholm in 1833, he left there at the age of nine when his family moved to Russia. Whilst there, he was educated by private tutors. He not only studied chemical engineering, he also studied languages and literature in both the United States and France.

3 Ask students to continue rewriting the biography of Alfred Nobel. Before conducting feedback, you could get pairs to compare their answers with another pair, or exchange their work so that they can correct each other. Copy the answer below on to an OHT or a handout.

> **Answer**
> Returning to Sweden with his brother Emil in 1852, he and his brother started work in their father's explosives factory. Deeply affected by an explosion in the factory which killed Emil in 1864, Alfred wanted to invent a safer explosive. In 1867, he invented 'dynamite' and started to set up factories in many parts of the world to make it. When he died in 1896, Alfred left a fortune of $9 million, which was used to set up yearly Nobel Prizes for science, literature, and world peace.

4 Ask students to research some facts about a famous man and a famous woman, dead or alive, that they admire. Ask them to write a short profile for homework.

Questions and answers

This exercise practises question formation and time expressions. There are several ways of expressing the time reference in the answers, so encourage students to explore these. Don't just settle for one answer, try to get several.

This is a tricky exercise if you want students to get everything right.

POSSIBLE PROBLEMS

Students always have problems with dates. They make mistakes such as *on third June* or *on three June*.

Don't leave such mistakes uncorrected. This is one of the main aims of this activity. Students must remember to use *the* and *of*, and get the ordinal numbers correct: *on the third of June* or *on June the third*.

---

1 Ask students in pairs to ask and answer questions. Get whole-class feedback. Be very careful with correction.

T 10.5 Play the recording so that students can compare their answers.

Answers and tapescript
1 'When was she born?'
  'In 1960.'
2 'When was she given the award of Young Musician of the Year?'
  'In 1968, when she was 8 years old.'
3 'When did she go to the Royal Academy of Music?'
  'In 1978. She won a scholarship.'
4 'What year was her daughter born?'
  'In 1983.'
5 'Which countries has she lived in?'
  'Sweden, England, the US and France.'
6 'When did she appear on British TV?'
  'When she was 22.'
7 'How many children has she got?'
  'One daughter.'
8 'How long has she been living in Paris?'
  'Since 1998.'

---

2 Ask students to write a chart of their life. Give them a few minutes to prepare, and ask them to include at least six pieces of information. You could write some prompts on the board to help:

Born … Went to … Visited … Met … Got married to … Graduated from … Bought …

Students work in pairs to ask and answer questions about their charts.

A lecture tour

3–4 Ask students to look at Astrid's schedule. Then ask them in their pairs to answer the questions.

T 10.6 Play the recording so that the students can listen and check their answers. In the feedback, explain the difference between the first two questions. *How long are you here in Britain for?* means how many days from the day you arrived (in the past) to the day you leave (in the future). *How long have you been in Britain?* means how many days from when you arrived to now.

Answers and tapescript
I = Interviewer   A = Astrid
1 I How long are you here in Britain for?
  A Just two weeks.
2 I How long have you been in Britain?
  A Eight days.
3 I Where were you the day before yesterday?
  A In Birmingham.
4 I Where were you this time last week?
  A In London.
5 I Where will you be the day after tomorrow?
  A I'll be in Edinburgh.
6 I Where will you be a week today?
  A Back in Paris.

You might want to refer students again to Grammar Reference 10.3 on SB p148. You could follow up by asking students to imagine and write their own itinerary. In pairs, they ask and answer questions. Monitor this very carefully.

Discussing grammar

5 Ask students to work individually to correct the mistakes. Let them compare with a partner before checking with the whole class.

Answers
1 What time did you go to bed last night?
2 What did you do last weekend?
3 What are you doing tonight?
4 Are you going to study English next month?
5 Have you been studying English for three years?
6 How long have you lived in this town?
7 When was your mother born?
8 How long have you known your teacher?

---

6 In pairs, students ask and answer the questions in exercise 5.

ADDITIONAL MATERIAL

Workbook Unit 10
Exercise 5 Time expressions

A big name in Hollywood

The aim of this reading is to improve students' ability to read for specific information. It also reviews Present Perfect forms and expands the students' vocabulary, particularly in the area of films.

1 Begin by eliciting the names of some popular film stars, their best films, and most famous roles. If possible, bring in two or three pictures of well-known actors / actresses.

Ask students in pairs to discuss the questions about their favourite film star. Go round monitoring and helping, then have a class discussion.

2 This activity pre-teaches some key vocabulary that will come up in the text that follows. Most of the words are connected with films.

Ask students to work individually to complete the exercise, then check answers with a partner. Definitions of the more difficult words are given in the answers below. You could brainstorm other words around the topic of films: *Academy Award, director, producer, horror, comedy, drama, science fiction, special effects.*

Answers
I was once an <u>extra</u> in a film. (a minor part, for example, standing in a crowd)
In films he is always <u>cast as</u> the bad guy. (given the part/role of)
She <u>auditioned</u> for the part of Mary. (she went to a sort of interview for actors where you read lines from the play, and they decide if they want you)
He's going to <u>make the big time</u>. (become very famous)
She was <u>turned down</u> for the part of Mary. (she didn't get the part)
Give her a <u>break</u>! (chance) She has real <u>talent</u>. (ability – she's very good at it)
He <u>set up a production company</u>. (he started a company which produces films)

3 Ask students to look at the headline. Ask *Do you think Dennis is a famous film star? Why/why not?* Get some ideas (teach *sort of*), then ask students to read the text and answer the questions in exercise 1. Students discuss their answers in pairs, then as a class.

Answers
1 *Dennis Woodruff the Movie, Parts I and II* and *Double Feature.* They're not really films though, they're documentaries.
2 Autobiographical documentaries.
3 Himself.
4 He is self-centred, always talking about himself, talkative, confident, and optimistic. He looks like a hippie with a long blond ponytail. He has rugged, unconventional looks but seems tired.

5 In a mobile home in East Hollywood.
6 He has a brother.
7 He is most famous for trying to be a film star, but failing.

4 Ask students in pairs to answer the questions.

Answers
1 Your favourite film star.
2 No.
3 He hands out videotapes of his films, wears a T-shirt with his name on it.
4 Probably not.
5 In front of the security cameras at local restaurants. They ignore him.
6 Because he's constantly failing.
7 When a casting director told him he wasn't a big name in Hollywood.
8 Yes. He feels success is just around the corner.

Language work

5 Ask students in pairs to write the questions. They will need to look back at the text. Go round checking that they are using the Present Perfect Continuous correctly. Conduct whole-class feedback.

Answers
1 How long has he been looking for work?
2 How many times has he been on television?
3 When did he first have the idea of promoting himself?
4 How long has he been living in a mobile home?
5 How many copies of his video has he sold?

6 Ask students in pairs to match the words in **A** with their meanings in **B**. Ask students to find the words in the text first, and make guesses as to the meaning from the context. They should be able to do this without looking in a dictionary.

Answers

trendy	fashionable
unlikely	improbable
fake	not real
trapped	caught so you can't move
ignore	pay no attention to
unconventional	different from what is considered usual
tales	stories
huge	enormous

Compound nouns

In this exercise, students do word-building exercises with compound nouns.

1 Ask students to read the examples of compound nouns from the article. Point out that there are no rules as to why compounds should be one word or two, or hyphenated. The stress tends to be on the first syllable of a compound noun.

2 Students write a word in each box that can be used to make the three compound nouns, then check with a partner. Ask volunteers to write the words on the board. The illogical spelling frustrates students. Tell them not to worry too much if they get it wrong; English speakers often can't remember the correct spelling, and even dictionaries don't always agree!

Answers

1 toothache	7 hairbrush
toothbrush	hairdresser
toothpaste	haircut
2 dining room	8 airmail
changing room	airport
waiting room	air-conditioning
3 traffic lights	9 tea cup
traffic warden	tea spoon
traffic jam	tea pot
4 newsagent	10 sunset
travel agent	sunglasses
estate agent	suntan
5 fireplace	11 wrapping paper
fire engine	writing paper
fireworks	toilet paper
6 credit card	12 shopping centre
birthday card	shopping spree
business card	shopping list

Model each word and ask students to repeat. For all words in exercise 2 the stress is on the first part of the compound. Students are often reluctant to stress the first part, as many languages are not as dependent on stress as English, so really push them to get the stress right.

3 Ask the students in pairs to match the definitions to the compounds.

Answers
- toothache
- airport
- hairdresser
- sunset
- shopping centre

4 Ask students in their pairs to write definitions of other words in exercise 2. Then get them to change partners so that they can test their new partners with their definitions.

LISTENING AND SPEAKING (SB p84)

Collectors

This is a jigsaw listening. The aim is to improve students' ability to listen for specific information. Students will also practise taking notes. Because it is a jigsaw task, students have ample speaking practice. The follow-up task involves question formation using Present Perfect forms. If possible, put the groups next to separate tape recorders/CD players in different parts of the classroom or in different rooms to do the listening simultaneously.

1 Ask students to read the questions. Discuss them with the whole class.

2 Divide students into two groups. Tell Group **A** that they are going to listen to Andrea Levitt. Tell Group **B** that they are going to listen to Jeff Parker. Ask them to look at the pictures connected with their person and say what they can see. Elicit *dolls*, *rag dolls* (for Andrea), and *Star Wars memorabilia, action figures, posters* (for Jeff). Ask them to discuss the other two questions.

3–4 **T 10.7** **T 10.8** Make sure that each group has a recorder and a cassette or CD. Ask each group to play their recording and answer the questions. It's a good idea to put one student in charge of playing the recording while you move back and forth between the groups. Let each group play the recording twice while students listen and take notes. Then ask them to compare answers with a partner. Let them play the recordings once or twice more to confirm their answers and fill in any missing bits of information.

5 When students are ready, ask them to choose a partner from the other group, and compare and exchange information. This will generate a lot of discussion.

At the end, let each group hear the other's recording.

Answers and tapescripts
Andrea Levitt
1 She lives alone in New York.
2 She works in the fashion industry.
3 She's been collecting for 25 years.
4 She has collected about 300 dolls.
5 There are dolls in every room.
6 A doll with an elephant mask.
7 All over. Doll shows. Doll artists contact her on her website.
8 Yes.

Jeff Parker

1 He lives alone in New York.
2 He works in a bank.
3 He's been collecting since he was four years old.
4 Not sure. About 700.
5 He doesn't say. Some of his collection is in New York, but most is at his parents' house in Philadelphia.
6 A Han Solo action figure.
7 He doesn't say. He collected a lot and his mother gave him a lot.
8 No.

T 10.7
Andrea Levitt
I = Interviewer   A = Andrea

I First of all, a little bit about you. Are you originally from New York City?
A I'm from Wilmington, Delaware, but I've been living in New York a long time, 36 years. I came to New York to work in the fashion industry. I still work in the world of fashion. I love it.
I So, how long have you been collecting dolls?
A Hmmm ... it must be about 25 years. Yeah, 25 years.
I So what led you to having such a love of dolls? Have you always loved them?
A Well, no. I didn't play with dolls much when I was a girl, but uh these aren't children's dolls that I collect.
I No?
A No, they're really works of art. When you say the word 'doll' people think of a toy for little girls, but these are not. When I opened my business, *Dolls-at-Home*, two years ago, that was the message I wanted to get across to all art lovers – that dolls are another art form.
I I can see that these are not dolls for little girls. Some of them are really quite amazing. How many dolls do you have in your collection?
A Oh, I would say – um I think maybe three hundred.
I Wow! And where are they all?
A Well, I had to buy a new apartment ...
I You bought an apartment for the dolls?!
A Yeah, I really did. My son, he's thirty-three now, he went off to college and I filled his room with dolls in two minutes so I realized that I needed a different apartment. I wanted to show off my dolls.
I So, you have what, maybe four or five rooms, all with dolls ...
A Actually there are dolls in *every* room, even the bathroom and the kitchen.
I I was going to ask, is there one room where you don't allow dolls?
A No! Oh no, they're part of my life. I mean sometimes when people visit there's nowhere to sit. It's a problem.
I So, what about keeping them clean? Dusting them?
A Erm, yeah, that's a problem too. New York is dirty. Erm, I suppose they should be under glass but I don't want them under glass, I want to enjoy them. I dust them occasionally.
I Well, they look immaculate.

A Thanks.
I That's a very unusual doll. Is it valuable?
A No, not really. But that doll over there ... It has an elephant mask. That's my favourite.
I Really?
A You see the mask goes up and it's a little boy's face and it goes down and it's an elephant's face. It's made by one of the best doll makers in the US, Akira Blount.
I And how do you find your dolls?
A I travel all over. I go to doll shows, and now that I have a website and I've started my own business, doll artists find me. As I said, it's been going on for two years now, and I have a mailing list of nine hundred people.
I Wow! What does your son think of all this?
A You know, he thinks I'm sort of ... crazy. He loves this apartment but he can't understand ...
I Why you fill it with dolls!
A Yeah, but two weeks ago he came to one of my doll shows, it was his first time, and I think he was impressed. Yeah, I think so.
I So, do you think you'll ever stop collecting them?
A No, there's always room for another doll. If you're a real collector you always find room.
I I'm sure you're right. Well, that's great Andrea. Thank you very much.

T 10.8
Jeff Parker
I = Interviewer   J = Jeff

I First of all, erm, just a little bit about you, Jeff. Are you originally from New York City?
J No, I'm originally from the Philadelphia area. But I moved to New York about five years ago when I got a job working for a bank on Wall Street.
I Oh? And do you mind talking about your *Star Wars* collection?
J No, not at all.
I So, how did you get interested in *Star Wars*?
J Well, *Star Wars* was one of the first movies I ever saw. I think I was four years old. My dad took me to see it and I just loved it. Loved the story, loved the idea of being in space. I think I saw it ten times.
I Wow! You sure did love *Star Wars*!
J Yeah, I guess so. Then all the toys came out, so I started collecting the action figures.
I Action figures?
J They're these little metallic figures. Models of the characters in the movie.
I I see. And which character did you like best?
J Oh, I was a Han Solo fan. I think he was my favourite. You know, I still have that Han Solo action figure. It's worth a lot of money now, but I like it because it was the first *Star Wars* thing I ever owned.
I So, did you just collect the figures?
J Oh, no. I collected the figures first – Darth Vader, Luke, Obi-Wan Kenobi, R2-D2, and of course Princess Leia. Then I

started collecting everything *Star Wars* – space ships, space stations, posters, videos …

I Well, you seem to have a lot of pieces in your collection. About how many pieces do you have all together?

J I'm not sure because most of my collection is at my parents' house in Philadelphia. I don't have the room for all of it here in New York … but I'd say I probably have about seven hundred pieces in all.

I Seven hundred pieces!? How did you get so many?

J Well, you know, I'd ask my mom for the newest toys, – every holiday, every birthday, and the collection just grew and grew. I think they really liked *Star Wars*, too. When I was a kid my mom gave me *Star Wars* birthday parties, and bought me *Star Wars* cereal for breakfast … I even had *Star Wars* pyjamas and *Star Wars* underwear.

I A real *Star Wars* family then?

J You could say that. They even called our family dog Princess Leia.

I And did you play with other kids who collected *Star Wars* stuff?

J No, not really. I liked to play with all the things by myself. I loved making up all these *Star Wars* stories about the characters … and uh …

I And – and now? Are you in touch with other *Star Wars* collectors?

J No. I – I don't have the time really.

I So what are you going to do with your collection?

J I don't know. I'm not sure. Sometimes I think I might sell it. Other times I think I might just keep it and give it to my kids some day.

I Oh, that would be something, wouldn't it? Thanks, Jeff.

EVERYDAY ENGLISH (SB p85)

Expressing quantity

This section revises and practises expressions of quantity. Students often make mistakes with the words in the box. Remind them of the following:

How many, too many, a few, as many as, all, and *any* are used with count nouns, for example *How many dolls … ?*

How much, too much, a little, as much as, all, and *any* are used with uncount nouns, for example *How much money … ?*

Enough comes before a noun and after an adjective, for example *enough money, hot enough.*

1 Students work individually to complete the sentences with words from the box. Let them compare their answers with a partner.

T 10.9 Play the recording so that students can check their answers. Ask students to practise the conversations with a partner.

Answers and tapescript

1 **A How much** coffee do you drink?
  B At least six cups a day.
  A That's **too much**. You shouldn't drink **as much as** that.

2 **A How many** aspirins do you usually take when you have a headache?
  B About four or five.
  A That's **too many**. You shouldn't take **as many as** that!

3 **A How much** do you earn?
  B Not **enough** to pay all my bills!

4 **A How many** people are there in your class?
  B Forty.
  A I think that's **too many**.

5 **A** Have you got **any** homework tonight?
  B Far **too much**. I'll never be able to do it **all**.

6 **A** How old are you?
  B Seventeen. I'm old **enough** to get married, but not old **enough** to vote!

7 **A** When did you last go to the dentist?
  B Very recently. Just **a few** days ago.

8 **A** Do you take milk in your tea?
  B Just **a little**.

2 Students remain in pairs to ask each other the questions in exercise 1, and answer with true information about themselves. Go round monitoring and helping as necessary. Ask two or three pairs to say their conversations in front of the class. Ask for comments and corrections.

Don't forget!

Workbook Unit 10
Exercise 6 Vocabulary – Suffixes and prefixes
Exercise 7 Pronunciation – Dipthongs
Exercise 8 Prepositions of time

Word list
Photocopy the Word list for Unit 10 (TB p159) for your students. Ask them to write in the translations, learn them at home, and/or write some of the words in their vocabulary notebooks.

Indirect questions
Question tags
The body • Informal English

Tell me about it!

Introduction to the unit

The theme of this unit is asking for and giving information. Indirect questions are presented in the context of a woman asking questions about an unfamiliar city. Question tags are introduced in a conversation between a little girl and her mother.

The reading text has questions and answers about our world. The *Listening and speaking* section is a radio programme about people who suffer from forgetfulness.

The *Writing* section at the back of the book practises different ways of joining ideas and sentences, using words like *however, in fact, actually, of course.*

Language aims

Grammar – indirect questions   These are similar in form to reported questions, which will be covered in Unit 12. The problems students encounter with indirect questions usually have to do with form, not meaning.

Common mistakes

*I don't know where does she live.   *I don't know what's the time?

It is difficult to get students to use *do/does/did* in direct questions. Now they have to learn that in indirect questions they shouldn't use *do/does/did.*

Question tags   Question tags are extremely common in spoken English. For students they present the same problem as short answers – the learner needs to work out which auxiliary verb to use, whether it should be positive or negative, and whether the intonation should go up or down, by which time it is often too late to use them! Interestingly, English-speaking children acquire question tags relatively early and easily, perhaps because they are a way of engaging people around them in conversation.

Your students will probably not be using question tags accurately and appropriately by the end of this unit. They will need a lot of exposure to them in order to produce them spontaneously. The aim of this work on question tags is, therefore, recognition more than production. Students need to become aware of them as a system, and as a part of spoken English.

Vocabulary   Vocabulary work in this unit focuses on the human body. Parts of the body are brainstormed, then verb-noun collocations are explored (*kick/feet; point/finger*). There is also work on idioms with these words, for example, *to kick the habit.*

Everyday English   Learners are often very interested in informal language, slang, colloquial English, and idioms. This is perhaps because they feel that this language represents real English as used by real English speakers, but it is probably safer to steer students away from trying to produce informal English at this level. There are too many potential problems. The slightest mistake of pronunciation, stress, or word order can make the foreign learner incomprehensible. It is almost as though native speakers don't expect idiomatic usage from a low-level speaker. It is also difficult for students to learn in which situations informal language is appropriate, and when it is safer to keep to neutral forms. Nevertheless, it is worth pointing out some informal language for recognition purposes.

Notes on the unit

TEST YOUR GRAMMAR (SB p86)

This section checks whether the students can recognize the forms of indirect questions and question tags.

1 Ask students in pairs to look at the sentences and answer the question.

> **Answer**
>
> In sentence 2, *where* introduces a *wh-* clause. This is common after *know*, *see* (*I see what you mean*), *wonder* (*I wonder who she is*), and *remember* (*I remember what she said*). Sentence 3 is an indirect question.

2 Still in pairs, students choose the correct question tags. Check answers with the whole class.

> **Answers**
>
> 1 It's a beautiful day, isn't it?
> 2 You like learning English, don't you?
> 3 You've been to Australia, haven't you?
> 4 Henry didn't say that, did he?
> 5 They had a good time, didn't they?

A STRANGER IN TOWN (SB p86)

Indirect questions

1 Ask students to look at the photos. Ask *Where is the woman? Is she in her own city? Is she on holiday? What does she want?*

Read the introduction as a class. Then ask the students to read *What Flavia wants to know.*

T 11.1 Play the recording. Students listen and complete *What Flavia says.*

> **Answers and tapescript**
>
> 1 I wonder if **you could** help me.
> 2 I'm not sure **if we're near** the CN Tower.
> 3 Can you tell me **if there are** any good restaurants nearby?
> 4 I don't know what time **the banks close**.
> 5 I'm sorry, but I can't remember which resturant **you suggested**.

> **T 11.1**
>
> **F = Flavia   R = Hotel Receptionist**
> **F** Hi. I've just checked in and I wonder if you could help me.
> **R** I'll be happy to try.
> **F** Well, first, I'm not sure if we're near the CN Tower.
> **R** The CN Tower? It's very close. It's only about a ten-minute walk.
> **F** Oh, good. Can you tell me if there are any good restaurants nearby?
> **R** Lots. Erm, one good one is the Café Giovanni. It's casual but they have very good food and live music in the evenings.
> **F** Sounds wonderful. Oh, and I need to cash some traveller's cheques, but I don't know what time the banks close.
> **R** Most banks don't close until 5.30 on weekdays, but some have extended hours.
> **F** Thank you very much. Oh ... I'm sorry, but I can't remember which restaurant you suggested.
> **R** The Café Giovanni.
> **F** Café Giovanni. Got it. Thanks for your help.
> **R** My pleasure.

GRAMMAR SPOT (SB p87)

The aim here is to check the rules for forming indirect questions.

1–3 Discuss the questions as a class.

> **Answers**
>
> 1 In indirect questions we use the same word order (subject + verb) as statements, for example, *I wonder if you could help me*.
> 2 *Do/does/did* are not used in indirect questions.
> 3 We use *if* when we make a *Yes/No* question indirect.

Go back to the direct and indirect questions in exercise 1 and ask students to compare them.

Refer students to Grammar Reference 11.1 on SB p149.

2 Ask students to check their answers by reading tapescript 11.1 on SB p131.

Ask students in pairs to practise the conversation with books open. Then ask them to close their books and practise it again.

3 This is a controlled accuracy practice exercise to check that students can form indirect questions. It can be done as either a written or a spoken exercise.

Do the first one as an example. Ask students in pairs to do the exercise, then check answers with the whole class, encouraging students to comment and correct.

> **Answers**
>
> 1 Do you know what the population of the city is?
> 2 Could you tell me if there's an underground?
> 3 Can you tell me where the best shops are?
> 4 Do you happen to know where I can go for a run in the mornings?
> 5 Do you have any idea if there's an art gallery near here?
> 6 I wonder what people do in the evening.

4 Ask students in their pairs to ask and answer indirect questions about a city or town they know well.

PRACTICE (SB p87)

Asking polite questions

In this section, students first practise making direct questions, using a wide variety of question words. They then practise the same questions but using the more polite, indirect form.

1   This first exercise practises *what* and *which* + noun, and *how* + adjective/adverb, *many* and *much*.

Ask students in pairs to make direct questions from the chart. Check answers with the whole class by telling different pairs to ask you a question, which you then answer, as long as it's correct.

2   Ask students in their pairs to prepare polite indirect questions from the ideas in exercise 1. When they are ready, put them in new pairs to ask and answer the questions, or do some open pair practice across the room. Remember that intonation is important here – correct students if their intonation sounds flat.

Finding out about Madonna

3   Lead in by asking students what they know about Madonna. Elicit ideas and write them on the board. It is a good idea to bring in a picture of Madonna to put on the board; you could even start the lesson by briefly playing part of one of her songs.

4   Students in pairs ask each other about Madonna using the phrases and the prompts. Read through the example, and remind students that subject and verb are not inverted in an indirect question.

5 I wonder where she lives.
6 I'd like to know how many times she has been married.
7 Does anybody know how many children she has?
8 I wonder how many number one hits she has had.

5 Ask Students **A** to read the information on SB p155, and Students **B** to read the information on SB p156. Students take it in turns to ask and answer polite indirect questions to share their information. Monitor the activity closely to check that they are using indirect questions correctly.

ADDITIONAL MATERIAL

Workbook Unit 11
Exercises 1–5 Indirect questions
Exercises 6 Questions with a preposition at the end

WE LIKE ANIMALS, DON'T WE? (SB p88)

Question tags

The aim of this section is to introduce and practise question tags. However, don't expect your students to be using question tags accurately and appropriately from now on. It will take a long time before they use them without being prompted, or needing correction. The idea is to make students aware of them as a system so that they can begin to recognize them and see how important they are in spoken English.

1 Ask students to look at the photo of Gabriella and her mother. Ask *Where are they? What do you think they are talking about?*

T 11.2 Play the recording. Ask students to listen to the conversation and underline the question tags.

Now play the recording again. Pause after Gabriella's lines containing a question tag, and ask students if the intonation goes up or down. Note that here all the question tags go down. Model each question and get students to repeat, paying careful attention to pronunciation and falling intonation.

2 Ask the students to look at the photo of Karen and her assistant. Ask *Where are they? What do you think they are talking about?*

Ask students in pairs to complete the conversation with question tags from the box.

T 11.3 Play the recording so that students can check their answers. Then play it again, pausing after each question tag and asking students if the intonation goes up or down (this time all the tags go up).

Answers and tapescript
K = Karen   A = Karen's assistant
K Now, what's happening today? I've got a meeting this afternoon, **haven't I**?
A Yes, that's right. With Henry and Tom.

K And the meeting's here, **isn't it**?
A No, it isn't. It's in Tom's office, at 3 o'clock.
K Oh! I'm not having lunch with anyone, **am I**?
A No, you're free for lunch.
K Phew! And I signed all my letters, **didn't I**?
A Erm, no, you didn't, actually. They're on your desk, waiting for you.
K OK. I'll do them now. Thanks a lot.

GRAMMAR SPOT (SB p88)

1–2 Answer these questions as a class. These are difficult questions so don't be surprised if students don't know the answers.

Answers
1 Karen uses question tags to mean 'I'm not sure, so I'm checking.'
Gabriella uses question tags when she thinks the other person will agree – she's just chatting. We use question tags with falling intonation to encourage people to respond to what we're saying – it means 'Please talk to me.'
2 We repeat the auxiliary verb. If there is no auxiliary verb, we use *do/does/did*. A positive sentence usually has a negative tag, and a negative sentence usually has a positive tag.

Refer students to Grammar Reference 11.2 on SB p149.

3 Ask students to practise the two conversations with their partner.

SUGGESTION
This is an alternative way of practising the two conversations. First, ask the class to close their books. Ask two volunteers to try to say the conversations from memory. The first one is quite easy to remember, but you will need to give some prompts for the second. Then students do the same in pairs. Occasionally, asking students to memorize something is good practice.

PRACTICE (SB p89)

Question tags and intonation

This section practises form and intonation patterns of question tags.

1 Ask students in pairs to add tags to the sentences.

T 11.4 Play the recording so that the students can listen and check their answers. Play the recording again. Ask them to put arrows to show rising or falling intonation. Do the first as an example on the board.

Answers and tapescript

1 It isn't very warm today, **is it**?

2 You can cook, **can't you**?

3 You've got a CD player, **haven't you**?

4 Mary's very clever, **isn't she**?

5 There are a lot of people here, **aren't there**?

6 The film wasn't very good, **was it**?

7 I'm a silly person, **aren't I**?

8 You aren't going out dressed like that, **are you**?

T 11.4 Play the recording again, pausing for students to repeat. Language learners are sometimes reluctant to stretch their voice range so encourage varying intonation, and make sure their voices are falling or rising appropriately.

2 Ask students in pairs to match a response with a sentence in exercise 1.

T 11.5 Play the recording so that students can listen and check their answers.

Answers and tapescript

1 **A** It isn't very warm today, is it?
  B No, it's freezing.
2 **A** You can cook, can't you?
  B Me? No! I can't even boil an egg.
3 **A** You've got a CD player, haven't you?
  B Believe it or not, I haven't. I've got a cassette player, though.
4 **A** Mary's very clever, isn't she?
  B Yes. She's extremely bright.
5 **A** There are a lot of people here, aren't there?
  B I know! It's absolutely packed. I can't move!
6 **A** The film wasn't very good, was it?
  B It was terrible! The worst I've seen in ages.
7 **A** I'm a silly person, aren't I?
  B No, you're not. Everybody makes mistakes.
8 **A** You aren't going out dressed like that, are you?
  B Why? What's wrong with my clothes? I thought I looked really cool.

Ask students to practise the conversations in their pairs.

Conversations

This practice activity is deliberately controlled. Students are restricted as to which sentences they can make question tags for. It is easy to over-apply the rule of form without thinking about why you are using tags in the first place. Mistakes often result, for example:

I'm going to the shops, aren't I? Do you want anything, don't you?

Yes, I need a newspaper, don't I? I'll give you some money, won't I?

3 Ask students to look at the picture and read the conversation. Ask them in pairs to decide where the tags can go, and what the tags should be.

T 11.6 Play the recording so that students can listen and check their answers.

Answers and tapescript

A It's so romantic, **isn't it**?
B What is?
A Well, they're really in love, **aren't they**?
B Who?
A Paul and Mary.
B Paul and Mary aren't in love, **are they**?
A Oh yes, they are. They're mad about each other.

4 Ask students in pairs to look at the conversations on SB p156, choose one, and decide where the question tags could go. Go round monitoring and helping. Give students time to prepare and memorize their conversation, then ask them to act it out for the rest of the class. If there are mistakes, correct them carefully.

T 11.7 Play the recording so that students can listen and compare their answers. Ask if they are the same as the conversations the students prepared. There are occasions when more tags could be used than are in the sample answers, so be careful when accepting or rejecting students' suggestions.

Sample answers and tapescript

1 **A** You broke that vase, **didn't you**?
  B Yes, I did. I dropped it. I'm sorry.
  A You'll replace it, **won't you**?
  B Yes, of course I will. How much did it cost?
  A £300.
  B £300?! It wasn't *that* much, **was it**?
  A Yes, it was.
2 **A** Have you paid the electricity bill yet?
  B No, *you* paid it, **didn't you**?
  A No, I haven't paid it. I thought you paid it.
  B Me? But you *always* pay it, **don't you**?
  A No, I don't. I always pay the phone bill.
  B Oh, yes, sorry.
3 **A** We love each other, **don't we**?
  B Erm, I think so.
  A We don't ever want to be apart, **do we**?
  B Well ...
  A And we'll get married and have lots of children, **won't we**?
  B What? You haven't bought me a ring, **have you**?
  A Yes, I have. Diamonds are forever.
  B Oh, dear!

4 A Helen didn't win the lottery, **did she?**

B Yes, she did. She won £2 million!

A She isn't going to give it all away, **is she?**

B As a matter of fact she is.

A Wow. Not many people would do that, **would they?**

B Well, *I* certainly wouldn't.

5 A I think we're lost. Let's look at the map.

B Uh-oh.

A What do you mean, 'Uh-oh'? You didn't forget to bring the map, **did you?**

B Sorry.

A How are we going to get back to the campsite without a map?

B Well, we could ask a police officer, **couldn't we?**

A There aren't many police officers on this mountain!

ADDITIONAL MATERIAL

Workbook Unit 11
Exercise 7–9 Question tags

READING AND SPEAKING (SB p89)

How well do you know your world?

1 Put students in small groups to see how many of the questions they can answer. Then have a brief class discussion.

2 Ask students to put one of the lines before each question. This is more difficult than it looks, so you may want to elicit two or three examples to get the students started.

> **Sample answers**
> 1 **I think/I don't know if** animals have feelings.
> 2 **I think I know** what the Earth's oldest living things are.
> 3 **I wonder** what man-made things on Earth can be seen from space.
> 4 **I don't know/I'm not sure** what the most terrible natural disaster to have hit the Earth is.
> 5 **I think I know** why there isn't a row 13 on aeroplanes.
> 6 **I have no idea** why women live longer than men.
> 7 **I wonder if** Uncle Sam was a real person.

Discuss the ideas as a class.

3 Ask students to read the seven answers quickly to find out if they were right. The texts are quite long, so give them a strict time limit, for example, seven to ten minutes for all seven texts.

4 Do the first as an example with the whole class, then ask students in pairs to match the last lines with their texts.

> **Answers**
> 1 d   2 f   3 e   4 c   5 b   6 a   7 g

5 The aim of this exercise is to get the students to read the texts more intensively in order to identify what the underlined words refer to, and then to answer the questions. Ask students to do the exercise in their pairs.

> **Answers**
> 1 one = tree
> 2 this = Great Wall of China
> 3 they = animals
> 4 they = dinosaurs
> 5 he = a company worker
> 6 they = modern high-rise buildings
> 7 they = men

Now ask students to answer the questions.

> **Answers**
> 1 The White Mountains of California.
> 2 The Great Wall is mostly grey stone in a grey landscape.
> 3 Pet owners would say 'Yes', but many scientists are sceptical.
> 4 Probably because of a meteor that hit the Earth 65 million years ago.
> 5 His employer, Uncle Sam.
> 6 No, they don't.
> 7 They drink more than women and their behaviour is more aggressive.

6 This is a scanning task and should be done quickly. Ask students to work individually to find the answers, then check with a partner. Give them a strict time limit, for example, four minutes.

> **Answers**
> | | |
> |---|---|
> | 4,600 | the age of the oldest tree in the world |
> | 15 | the height in kilometres at which a plane flies |
> | 200 | the height in kilometres of a spacecraft orbiting the Earth |
> | 1906 | the year of a violent earthquake in Ecuador |
> | 1815 | the year of a volcanic eruption in Indonesia |
> | 65 million | the number of years ago that a meteor hit the Earth |
> | 14 | the number of the floor which follows 12 in a US skyscraper |
> | six | the number of years by which women generally outlive men |
> | 84 | the number of years' life expectancy for Japanese women |
> | 1766 | the year Uncle Sam was born |

Producing a class poster

The success of this sort of activity is dependent on the students' interest in achieving the task. Make sure you have access to the Internet or good reference books to help them. If you don't have the facilities for researching in class, you could set this part for homework and students can then work together to design the poster in the next lesson.

7 Put students in groups of four to think of questions. Go round monitoring and helping. In whole-class feedback, see if anyone can answer the questions.

8 Ask each group to choose two questions. Decide how much time to give students for their research. Inevitably, some groups will be quicker than others. Thirty to forty minutes to research and design the poster is probably reasonable. When students have researched the answers, get them to make a poster. Display the posters on the wall. Students circulate and read what their classmates have found out.

LISTENING AND SPEAKING (SB p92)

The forgetful generation

The aim of the listening is to improve students' ability to listen for gist and specific information.

1 **T 11.8** Play the recording. Ask students to listen and answer the questions.

> **Answers and tapescript**
> - They are talking about being forgetful.
> - In our modern lifestyle, we overload our memories.
>
> **T 11.8**
> **P = Presenter**
> **P** Hi, and welcome to *What's Your Problem?* How's your day been so far? Have you done all the things you planned? Kept all your appointments? Oh – and did you remember to send your mother a birthday card? If so, good for you! If not – well, you're not alone. Many of us in the busy twenty-first century are finding it more and more difficult to remember everything. Once upon a time we just blamed getting older for our absentmindedness, but now experts are blaming our modern lifestyle. They say that we have become 'the forgetful generation' and that day after day we overload our memories.

2 Put the students in small groups to discuss the questions. Then get one person from each group to summarize what was said for the class.

3 **T 11.9** Play the recording. Ask students to listen and take notes about Ellen, Josh, and Fiona.

Let students discuss their answers in pairs before checking with the whole class.

> **Answers and tapescript**
>
> | | What did they forget? | What did they do? |
> |---|---|---|
> | Ellen | She forgot that she was going to work not university. | She got the bus to university instead of work. |

	What did they forget?	What did they do?
Josh	He forgot where his parents lived.	He caught the train to the city where he lived as a child, not where his parents live now.
Fiona	She forgot to put her shoes on when she left home.	She left home wearing her slippers.

T 11.9
Ellen
Last year I finished university and I got a job in the same town, Canterbury. And one day, for some reason, rather than go to work for 9 o'clock, I got the bus and went to the university for an 11 o'clock lecture. I was sitting there, in the lecture room, and I thought to myself, 'Why don't I know anybody?' Then suddenly I remembered that I'd finished university and that I was two hours late for work!

Josh
I'm studying law in London now, and, erm, at the end of last term I packed my suitcase as usual and went to King's Cross station to catch the train home. I was sitting reading on the train, revising for my exams, and the inspector came to check my ticket. He looked at it and said, 'Thank you, sir. We'll be in Newcastle in about an hour.' Suddenly I thought, 'Newcastle!?! I don't want to go to Newcastle. My parents live in Plymouth!' You see, when I was a child I lived with my parents in Newcastle, but we moved to Plymouth when I was ten. I couldn't believe it. How could I have been so stupid?

Fiona
Some time ago I got dressed, ready to go to work. I put on my smart black suit. I'd been working at home the night before – preparing for a very important meeting the next day, and I remembered to put all the right papers into my briefcase. I left home and walked down to the bus stop. Just before I got on the bus, I looked down, and I was still wearing my fluffy, pink bedroom slippers!

4 **T 11.10** Ask students to listen to the rest of the programme, and answer the questions.

Let them check their answers in pairs before checking with the whole class.

> **Answers**
> 1 He's a Professor of Psychology.
> 2 Companies have far fewer employees, so one person does several jobs.
> 3 She began sentences but then couldn't remember what she was talking about.
> 4 She had a new job, she travelled a lot, she had a home and family to think about, and she had recently moved.
> 5 Professor Buchan helped her to recognize the problem. They

talked about her stressful lifestyle, and she realized that she wasn't going crazy and was able to help herself.

6 No, he doesn't.

7 Writing a list in a notebook, or on a piece of paper. He advises this because it is a very good feeling when you can cross something off.

8 He pretends that he has forgotten the professor's name.

T 11.10

P = Presenter   A = Alan Buchan

P Stories of forgetfulness like these are familiar to many of us, and experts say that such cases as Ellen's, Josh's, and Fiona's show that loss of memory is not just related to age, but can be caused by our way of life. Alan Buchan is a Professor of Psychology and he explains why.

A One of the problems, these days, is that many companies have far fewer employees. This means that one person often does several jobs. Jobs that before were done by many people are now done by a few. If you have five things to do at once, you become stressed and forgetful. I think many people in work situations, at a meeting or something, have the experience where they start a sentence and half way through it, they can't remember what they're talking about, and they can't finish the sentence.

P That's happened to me.

A It's a terrible feeling – you think you're going insane. I remember one patient who came to me so distressed because at three important meetings in one week, she found herself saying, mid-sentence, 'I'm sorry, I can't remember what I'm talking about.' This was a patient in a new job, which involved a lot of travelling. She also had a home and family to take care of and she'd recently moved. She had so many things to think about that her brain couldn't cope. It shut down.

P I can see the problem, but what's the solution? How did you help that patient?

A Well, part of the solution is recognizing the problem. Once we'd talked to this patient about her stressful lifestyle, she realized that she wasn't going crazy and she felt more relaxed and was able to help herself. But do you know one of the best ways to remember things, even in these days of personal or handheld computers?

P What's that?

A It's a notebook, or just a piece of paper! At the beginning of every day, write yourself a list of things you have to do – and it gives you a really good feeling when you cross things off the list as you do them!

P Well, there you have it! Thank you very much, Professor ... uh ... um ... ? Oh – Professor Alan Buchan!

What do you think?

Encourage a class discussion. With luck, one or two students will come up with some funny anecdotes about being forgetful.

What can your body do?

This section reviews vocabulary for parts of the body, then introduces and practises common collocations and idioms that refer to parts of the body.

1 Begin by drawing the outline of a body on the board and elicit as many words as you can by pointing to different parts and asking what they are. Say each word as you write it on the board. Be careful not to go on too long or deal with too many words. Alternatively, as suggested in the Student's Book, get students to come up to the board and write all the parts of the body they can think of in a list on the board or on the drawing. Go over the words with the whole class, and get students to repeat.

2 Ask students in pairs to decide which verb goes with which part of the body. Check the answers with the whole class.

Answers

kick:	foot, leg	climb:	feet, legs
lick:	tongue	hit:	hand, fist
bite:	mouth, teeth	stare:	eyes
hug:	arms, hands	point:	(index) finger
chew:	jaw, teeth	drop:	hand, fingers
think:	brain	kiss:	lips
hold:	fingers, hand, arms	whistle:	lips

3 Ask students in pairs to match a verb from exercise 2 with a noun or phrase from the box.

In the feedback, use mime to check meaning.

Answers

kick a football	climb a ladder
lick an ice-cream	hit a nail with a hammer
bite into an apple	stare into space
hug your grandmother	point a gun
chew gum	drop litter on the ground
think about the meaning of life	kiss me on the cheek
hold me in your arms	whistle a tune

4 Ask students to guess the meaning of the idioms. You can let them use dictionaries. Alternatively, let them complete the sentences first, and see if they can work out the meaning from context.

Ask students in pairs to complete the sentences. This can be a difficult exercise for students. Go round the room helping as necessary.

Answers

1 hold your breath	4 thought twice
2 hit the roof	5 kiss that money goodbye
3 kick the habit	6 Drop me a line

Words that join ideas

1 Ask students in pairs to join the sentences in different ways, using the words in brackets. Do one as an example.

Answers

1 George was rich, but he wasn't a happy man.
George was rich, although he wasn't a happy man.
Although George was rich, he wasn't a happy man.
George was rich. However, he wasn't a happy man.
2 Jo rang me from a phone box because she's lost her mobile.
Jo's lost her mobile, so she rang me from a phone box.

2 Ask students in pairs to complete the sentences.

Sample answers

1 Peter and I are in love. Actually, we**'re getting married soon.**
2 Naturally, when I was a child I didn't **understand anything about the political situation.**
3 She stood and waited for over an hour, but unfortunately, **the bus didn't come.**
4 My father didn't do very well at school. Nevertheless **he got a job in an office and now he runs his own business.**
5 Anyway, you've heard enough about me. What **have you been doing since I saw you last?**

3 Ask students in pairs to read the email and write the word or words that fit best.

Answers

1 so	5 of course	9 because
2 Unfortunately	6 Actually	10 In fact
3 but	7 but	11 Anyway
4 However	8 although	

Informal English

The aim here is to introduce informal language. It is important that students learn to recognize these items. However, don't encourage your students to use them. There are too many potential problems. Non-native speakers can often sound funny or inappropriate when trying to use such phrases.

1 Read the introduction and example. Point out that *quid* is an informal way of saying pounds.

Ask students in pairs to choose the words that fit best. This is more difficult than it might appear so allow them plenty of time.

T 11.11 Play the recording so that the students can listen and check their answers. Ask them to practise the conversations with their partner.

Answers and tapescript

1 A What do you say we break for lunch?
  B **Great idea.** We can grab a sandwich at the deli.
2 A **What are you up to?**
  B Nothing much. Just sitting around watching TV.
  A You're such a couch potato!
  B **Hey, give me a break!** I work hard all week. I like to relax at weekends.
3 A Quick! Give me your homework so I can copy it.
  B **No way!** Do your own homework!
4 A Did you mend the TV?
  B **Kind of.** Channel 4's OK, but we still can't get Sky.
  A Anything good on tonight?
  B **Dunno.** Look in the paper.
5 A What do you call that stuff you use to clean between your teeth?
  B What do you mean?
  A **You know!** It's like string. White.
  B **Oh!** You mean dental floss.
  A Yeah. That's it!

2 Ask students to look at the conversations again in more detail, and underline the examples of informal language.

Answers

1 What do you say = I suggest
  grab a sandwich = get/buy (quickly)
  deli = delicatessen
2 a couch potato = a lazy person who sits on the sofa (couch) watching TV all day
  give me a break = you're being unfair
3 No way! = certainly not!
4 Kind of = In one way yes, and in another way no. Not exactly.
  Anything good on tonight? = Is there anything good on TV?
  Dunno = I don't know
  paper = newspaper
5 stuff = uncountable word for *thing*
  You know! = you understand me
  It's like string = it's similar to string
  Oh! is used to express a variety of emotions, for example surprise, fear, happiness. Here it means 'I understand.'
  That's it! = That's right, that's what I mean.

Don't forget!

Workbook Unit 11
Exercise 10 Vocabulary and Pronunciation – A poem
Exercise 11 Pronunciation – Onomatopoeic words
Exercise 12 Phrasal verbs

Word list
Photocopy the Word list for Unit 11 (TB p160) for your students. Ask them to write in the translations, learn them at home, and/or write some of the words in their vocabulary notebooks.

12

Reported speech • Reporting verbs
Birth, marriage, and death
Saying sorry

Life's great events!

Introduction to the unit

This last unit of *New Headway Intermediate – the NEW edition* deals with reported speech not only as an aim in itself, but also as a useful way to pull together and revise many aspects of the tense system. The theme of weddings, births, and funerals has been chosen as an appropriate one with which to conclude the course because it brings together basic themes of life itself! The tone of the presentation sections is not meant to be serious – they include humorous material on the subject of weddings and marriage.

In the *Listening and speaking* section a Scottish woman tells the story of her niece's birth. The *Reading and speaking* section has a poem called *Funeral Blues,* by WH Auden, in which the writer describes his feelings about the death of a loved one.

The *Writing* section at the back of the book practises finding and correcting mistakes in a letter.

Language aims

Grammar – reported speech   The previous unit, Unit 11, dealt with indirect questions and focused on the problems of word order connected with them. The same word order problems apply to reported questions but with the added complication of the 'one tense back' rule, for example:

Direct speech:	'Where is she going?'	'What did they see?'
Indirect question:	I wonder where she is going.	I wonder what they saw.
Reported question:	He asked where she was going.	He asked what they had seen.

Tense usage in reported speech is quite straightforward and logical. The 'one tense back' rule is the same in many languages.

There are three main areas of reported speech: statements, questions, and commands. These are divided up in the following way in this unit.

The first presentation (*The wedding*) covers reported statements and questions in all tenses. It focuses on *say, tell,* and *ask* as reporting verbs.

The second presentation (*Go to jail!*) deals with reported commands and introduces other verbs which can be used as reporting verbs.

POSSIBLE PROBLEMS

When learning reported speech, students tend to have problems with form rather than meaning. There is often confusion about:

1 when to use *say* versus *tell*.

   *She said me that she lived in Paris. *She told that she lived in Paris.

2 the word order in reported questions.

   *He asked where was I going. *She asked me what did I want.
   *He asked do I smoke.

3 when to use *that*. Students often directly translate/transfer the use of that, used to report commands in L1, to reported commands in English.

   *He told that I come early. *She asked that I close the window.
   *He ordered that they went.

Vocabulary   The vocabulary fits the theme of the unit with a word sort on birth, marriage, and death. The activity also introduces some of the words needed for the listening and reading texts later in the unit.

Everyday English   This focuses on different ways of saying sorry. Students often confuse *Sorry* and *Excuse me,* so this section attempts to sort it out with discriminatory exercises. Different expressions are practised in various social situations.

Notes on the unit

TEST YOUR GRAMMAR (SB p94)

In this section, students are not required to consciously convert reported speech into direct speech. They are simply asked to fill in lines of a conversation.

The report of this proposal of marriage sounds very stilted and strange, but it is meant to be funny. The conversation highlights the notion of what reported speech is because it is *not* reported naturally, but literally, which is ultimately something students should try to avoid.

1   Ask students if they have ever received a proposal of marriage. Who from? When? Where? Have they ever proposed themselves? Then either ask them to read about John and Moira, or exaggerate the unnaturalness of the story by reading it aloud yourself to the class.

Ask students in pairs to complete the conversation. Give them about five minutes to do this. Go round monitoring and helping as necessary.

Ask students to practise the conversation with their partners, then ask volunteers to act out the marriage proposal for the class. Encourage them to exaggerate the humour of it, and hopefully, you will get some good stress and intonation practice!

> **Answers**
> **J = John   M = Moira**
> **J** Hi, Moira. How **are you**?
> **M** I'**m fine**, thanks.
> **J** It'**s great** to see you again. We **haven't** seen each other since Paris.
> **M** I **loved** Paris. **Can** we **go** back next spring?
> **J** There'**s** something I **have** to ask you. I **love** you. **Will** you **marry** me and come to Paris on honeymoon?
> **M** Yes, I **will**. I **love** you, too.

2   Discuss this question with the class.

> **Answer**
> The story is reported speech. The conversation is direct speech.

3   **T 12.1** Play the recording so that students can compare the conversations and decide what the differences are.

> **Tapescript**
> **J = John   M = Moira**
> **J** Moira! Hello there! How are you?
> **M** John! I'm just fine, thanks.
> **J** It's really great to see you again. We haven't seen each other since our trip to Paris.
> **M** Oh, John! I loved every minute in Paris. I'll never forget it as long as I live. Can we go back there next spring?
> **J** Moira, – er – first, there's something I want to ask you, something I have to ask you. Moira, I love you so much. Will

you marry me and come to Paris with me on honeymoon?
> **M** Oh, John! Yes, I will. I love you, too. •

THE WEDDING (SB p94)

Reported statements and questions

The aim of this section is to introduce and practise the form of reported statements and questions. It also teaches the difference between *say* and *tell*.

1   Set the scene by focusing students' attention on the photo and asking a few questions about students' own experiences of weddings. Ask *When did you last go to a wedding? What do people do at weddings? What do they talk about?* You can elicit words around the topic – words that collocate with wedding: *cake, ring, dress, bouquet, reception, day*, etc. Note, however, that the vocabulary section later in the unit covers this area.

Read the introduction, then ask students in pairs to match the lines.

T 12.2 Play the recording so that students can check their answers.

> **Answers and tapescript**
> **A = Adam   B = Beatrice**
> 1 **A** How do you know John and Moira?
>   **B** I went to the same school as Moira.
> 2 **A** Are you married?
>   **B** Yes, I am. That's my husband over there.
> 3 **A** Where did you meet your husband?
>   **B** Actually, I met him at a wedding.
> 4 **A** Have you travelled far to get here?
>   **B** Yes, we have. We flew in from Dublin yesterday.
> 5 **A** Do you live in Dublin?
>   **B** Yes, we do.
> 6 **A** So, where are you staying?
>   **B** We're staying at the Four Seasons Hotel.
> 7 **A** So am I. Can we meet there later for a drink?
>   **B** Sure. I'll introduce you to my husband.

2   Read Beatrice's report of what Adam said to her aloud, while the students follow in their books. The conversation in exercise 1 includes a variety of tenses. Thus, when it is reported it illustrates fully the 'one tense back' rule in reported speech.

GRAMMAR SPOT (SB p95)

1–4   Ask students in pairs to complete the sentences and discuss the questions. Tell them they can look back at Beatrice's report in the previous exercise for help.

> **Answers**
> 1 She said that they **were** married.
>   He asked me how I **knew** John and Moira.

She told him that she **had gone** to the same school as Moira.

2 The basic rule is 'one tense back.' This is illustrated by *we're* (Present Simple) which becomes *they were* (Past Simple), and *I went* (Past Simple) which becomes *she had gone* (Past Perfect). Also note that *we* becomes *they* and *I* becomes *she* here because we are reporting what someone else said.

Two other rules you may wish to remind students of are:

Both the Present Perfect and the Past Simple become the Past Perfect in reported speech.
And *yesterday* and *tonight* can become *the day before* or *that night* according to the immediacy of the reporting. For example, '*What's on TV tonight?*' *she asked* becomes *She asked what was on TV tonight* (if it is not tonight yet), or *She asked what was on TV that night* (if *that night* was a few days ago).

3 *Tell* must be used with a direct object: *she told him*. *Say* does not have a direct object: *she said* but it can be used with an indirect object: *she said to him*. *Tell* has the idea of passing on information, (*She told him a secret*), whereas *say* just conveys the idea of speaking, (*She said hello*).

Point out to your students that *that* is optional after *say* and *tell*. *She said they were married* and *She said that they were married* are both correct.

4 *If* is used to report *Yes/No* questions where there is no question word like *what* or *why*. So '*Are you married?*' *he asked* becomes *He asked **if** I was married*.

Refer students to Grammar Reference 12.1–12.3 on SB p150.

PRACTICE (SB p95)

What did Adam say?

This section practises form and intonation with reported speech. It pays particular attention to the short form *'d*, which can refer to both *had* and *would*.

1 Ask students in pairs to continue to report the conversation between Beatrice and her husband, Ron, in exercise 2. Get them to do this in writing as it may be difficult. Go round monitoring and helping as necessary. There will be a lot of little differences in the reporting, especially in the use of *say* and *tell*, so be flexible as long as students use them correctly. With the whole class, ask each pair to contribute a line of the reported conversation. Write answers on the board and correct any errors in the feedback.

T 12.3 Play the recording so that students can note any differences or additions to the conversation. They can read the tapescript on SB p132 while they listen, or immediately afterwards, to compare their answers.

Answers and tapescript

B = Beatrice   R = Ron

B I just met this really nice guy called Adam.

R Oh, yeah?

B He was very friendly. Do you know what he said? First, he asked me how I knew John and Moira. I told him that I had gone to the same school as Moira. Then he asked if I was married. Of course I said that I was!

R He asked you that?

B ... and next he asked where we'd met and I told him that we'd actually met at a wedding.

R You told him that?

B Sure. Then he wanted to know how long we had been here, and I said we had just got here yesterday and that we had flown in from Dublin. He asked if we lived in Dublin, so I told him that we did.

R What else did this guy want to know?

B Well, he asked where we were staying and it turns out that he's staying at the Four Seasons, too. Then he asked if I could meet him later for a drink, and I said we could and that I would introduce him to you.

R I'm not sure I want to meet this guy.

Model some of the sentences from the recording and ask students to repeat to provide controlled practice of the target language, particularly those sentences which contain the Past Perfect in contracted form. Remind your students that *'d* is the contracted form of *had*. The following sentences would be good for repetition work.

He asked where we'd met and I told him we'd met at a wedding.

He asked if we lived in Dublin, so I told him that we did.

He's a liar!

2 The aim of this activity is controlled oral practice with emphasis on good stress and intonation. Make sure students understand the meaning of *liar*.

There are a number of ways of approaching this exercise:

• Ask students to work in pairs to write the responses, then ask different pairs of students to say the lines. Correct them carefully.

• Ask students to do the exercise in pairs. Do the first as an example, then ask students to say the lines with their partners. Go round monitoring and checking that they have the form right. Don't worry too much at this stage about good stress and intonation.

• Go straight to the recording. Play it once for students to write in the responses. Then play it again, pausing for them to repeat.

114   Unit 12 · Life's great events!

T 12.4 Play the recording so that students can listen and check their answers.

Answers and tapescript
R = Ron   B = Beatrice
1 R Adam lives in Birmingham.
   B He told me he lived in Cambridge!
2 R He doesn't like his new job.
   B He told me he loved it!
3 R He's moving to Manchester.
   B Hang on! He told me he was moving to Australia!
4 R He went to Brighton on his last holiday.
   B Strange. He told me he'd been to Florida!
5 R He'll be 40 next week.
   B Really? He told me he'd be 30!
6 R He's been married three times.
   B But he told me he'd never been married!
   R You see! I told you he was a liar!

Ask students in pairs to practise the conversations again, but this time paying close attention to stress and intonation. Tell them that Beatrice is very upset at Adam's lies – that their stress and intonation must reflect this.

Discussing grammar

3 This exercise is to raise awareness of the changes in meaning when different tenses are used. Ask students in pairs to discuss the three pairs of sentences, then conduct whole-class feedback. Be flexible about how your students express the different meanings – they just need to have the general idea right. Ask them to decide what was actually said.

Answers
1 In the first sentence, *'d = had*. The question is asking about a past event.
   How did you travel to the wedding?
   In the second sentence, *'d = would*. The question is asking about a future event.
   How will you travel to the wedding?
2 The first sentence describes a current situation.
   I love John.
   In the second sentence, *'d = would*. The sentence is describing a future event.
   I will love John.
3 In the first sentence, they still live in Dublin.
   We live in Dublin.
   In the second sentence, *'d = had*. They don't live there now, but lived there at some time in the past.
   We lived/have lived in Dublin.

4 This is a purely mechanical exercise. It could be set as homework, but it is worthwhile doing in class to provide immediate consolidation of the grammar. You could go through it with the whole class, or you could ask students to do it in pairs.

Answers
1 He said (that) he was tired.
2 She asked me if I was leaving on Friday.
3 They said (that) they hadn't seen Jack for a long time.
4 They said (that) they'd flown to Tokyo.
5 I asked them which airport they'd flown from.
6 The announcement said (that) the flight had been cancelled.
7 He said (that) he'd call me/her later.
8 They told the teacher (that) they couldn't do the exercise.

ADDITIONAL MATERIAL

Workbook Unit 12
Exercises 1–3 Reported statements and questions
Exercises 4–7 Reported commands

GO TO PRISON! (SB p96)

Reported commands and requests

In this section a newspaper article '*A Marriage Made in Hell!*' provides the context for examples of reported commands and requests.

1 Ask students to look at the headline. Ask *What does the headline mean? Is it a good or a bad marriage?* Ask students to predict the story from the introduction, the photos, and the captions, then to read the article, name the people in the photos, and check their predictions.

Answers
From left to right:
Mr and Mrs West and their baby; Kenny and Kathleen Brady

SUGGESTION
It's a good idea to check students' general understanding of the article with some quick comprehension questions, such as:
How long have Kenny and Kathleen been married?
Why did the neighbours complain?
Why did Ann West complain?
Why did she call the police?
Why were Kenny and Kathleen arguing?
Did the judge think they were telling the truth?
Is this the first time the police have been called?
What is a marriage guidance counsellor? (Somebody who gives married couples advice when they have a problem with their marriage.) **Note:** *Marriage counsellor* introduced in Unit 2 SB p16 is American English.

2 Focus attention on the example, then ask students in pairs to complete the exercise. Some of the sentences are reported commands, others illustrate the use of other verbs to report speech.

Answers

2 The neighbours: *Neighbours complained that they could hear them shouting from across the street.*

3 Mrs Ann West: *I asked them nicely to stop because my baby couldn't get to sleep.*

4 Mr West: *My husband told them to stop (making a noise).*

5 Mr and Mrs West: *We called the police and asked them to come right away.*

6 Mr and Mrs Brady: *The Bradys admitted they had been arguing.*

7 Mrs Brady: *Mrs Brady said that she had accused Mr Brady of wasting their money on drinking and gambling.*

8 Mr and Mrs Brady: *They denied throwing the chair.*

9 The judge: *She reminded them that they had already had two previous warnings from the police.*

10 The judge: *She advised them to talk to a marriage guidance counsellor.*

GRAMMAR SPOT (SB p97)

1–3 Go through these with the whole class. Read them aloud and answer any questions. Ask students to give other examples of each type of sentence.

Answers

1 *He told them to stop making a noise* is a reported command.
She told them that she lived next door is a reported statement.

2 *I asked them to stop making a noise* is a reported request.
She asked me if I had met them before is a reported question.

Note that reported commands and reported requests are formed in the same way:

Verb + object + infinitive + *to*: ask/tell/order someone to do something.

3 *Complained, refused, admitted, accused, denied, reminded, advised* can all be used to report conversations.

Refer students to Grammar Reference 12.4 on SB p150.

SUGGESTION

Go through the form of each of the sentences in exercise 2 on p96 which use these verbs. Get students to write them in their notebooks for future reference.

complain that (+ clause)

admit (that) + clause

accuse (someone) *of* (verb) + *-ing*

deny (verb) + *-ing*

remind (someone) *that* (+ clause)

advise (someone) + *to* + infinitive

PRACTICE (SB p97)

Other reporting verbs

These exercises introduce students to other reporting verbs, which, with one exception, *refuse to do*, follow the same pattern as *ask someone to do something*.

They could be set for homework, but it is worthwhile doing them in class.

1 Check that students understand all the verbs. Read the example as a class; then put students in pairs to match the verbs with the direct speech.

Answers

2 a   3 e   4 g   5 d   6 h   7 f   8 c

2 Focus attention on the example, then ask students in pairs to report the sentences. Refer them to the list of Verb patterns on SB p158.

T 12.5 Play the recording so that students can check their answers.

Answers and tapescript

1 The postman told me to sign on the dotted line.
2 Maria asked Mark to translate a sentence for her.
3 Mary reminded her son to send Aunt Judy a birthday card.
4 John begged Moira to marry him.
5 John invited his boss to his wedding.
6 Tommy refused to go to bed.
7 Ben advised Tim to talk to his solicitor.
8 The teacher ordered Joanna to take the chewing gum out of her mouth.

ADDITIONAL MATERIAL

Workbook Unit 12
Exercise 6 Other reporting verbs
Exercise 7 *speak* and *talk*

Listening and note-taking

3 Remind students of the newspaper article about the fighting couple. Ask them to give you a very quick recap of the characters and story focusing their attention on the women in the two photos (SB p97) *Who are they? What happened?*

Divide the class into two groups. Tell them to imagine that they are all police officers on the case. Group **A** will listen to Kathleen Brady (the arguing wife) and Group **B** will listen to Ann West (the complaining neighbour). The idea is that students from the two groups report back to each other on what the women have said, thereby getting freer practice of reported speech.

T 12.6 **T 12.7** Play the recordings. Students take notes and then compare notes with others in their group.

If possible, put the groups next to separate tape recorders/CD players in different parts of the classroom or in different rooms to do the listening simultaneously. Alternatively, you could ask the groups to come to the front of the class and listen in turn to their recordings. The recordings are short, but students may still need to listen to them more than once.

T 12.6 **Kathleen Brady**
OK. We argue sometimes but not *that* often. Usually we just sit quietly and watch TV in the evenings. But sometimes … sometimes we argue about money. We don't have much, so I get very upset when Kenny spends the little we have on drinking or gambling. He promised to stop drinking, but he hasn't stopped. It's worse since he lost his job. OK, we were shouting, but we didn't throw a chair at Mr West. It … um … it just fell out of the window. And I'm really sorry that we woke the baby. We won't do it again. We love children. We'll babysit for Mr and Mrs West any time if they want to go out.

T 12.7 **Ann West**
Every night it's the same thing. They argue all the time. And we can hear every word they say. During the day it's not so bad because they're both out. But in the evenings it's terrible. Usually they start arguing about which TV show to watch. Then he slams the door and goes down the street to the pub. Last night he came back really drunk. He was shouting outside his front door, 'Open the door you … um … so and so.' I won't tell you the language he used! But she wouldn't open it; she opened a window instead and threw a plant at him. Tonight they threw a chair at my poor husband. They're so selfish. They don't care about our baby one bit.

4 Ask each student to find a partner from the other group and then report and compare the stories. They must find as many differences between the two stories as they can.

Go round monitoring and helping as necessary. Students may be reluctant to use a variety of reporting verbs and will need some gentle encouragement.

Sample answers (The differences are underlined.)
Group A
Kathleen admitted that they sometimes argued. She said that they sometimes argued about money, but they didn't argue often, and usually just watched TV quietly in the evenings. She told me that she got upset when Kenny gambled and drank, especially because he had promised to stop. She admitted shouting at Ann but denied throwing the chair – she said it had fallen out of the window. She apologized for waking the baby and said she loved children. She offered to babysit for Mr and Mrs West.

Group B
Ann complained that they argued every night. She said that she and Mr West could hear every word, but that it was not so bad during the day because Mr and Mrs Brady were both out. She told me that usually they argued about which TV show to watch and then Mr Brady went down the street to the pub. She said that last night he had come back really drunk and he had been shouting outside. He ordered his wife to open the door but she had refused to – she had opened the window and thrown a plant at him and tonight they had thrown a chair at Mr West. She said that they were selfish and didn't care about the baby.

5 Students can work in the same groups to produce written group reports for the classroom wall for the other group to read. Tell them to use the words in the box. Alternatively, you can set this for homework.

Refer students once again to the list of Verb patterns on SB p158.

VOCABULARY AND SPEAKING (SB p98)

Birth, marriage, and death

The aim here is to teach and practise key vocabulary around the topics of birth, marriage, and death.

1 Students can do this activity in pairs or small groups. Encourage them to use their dictionaries.

Check answers with the whole class. Ask questions to help students with some of the difficult words, for example, *Which word means a bed for a baby? a man who is getting married? a party after a wedding?*

If you prefer, you could draw three columns on the board and invite individual students to come up to the board and write in the words under the correct headings. Ask other students to correct any errors.

Answers

Birth	Marriage	Death
have a baby	wedding	funeral
pregnant	get engaged	wreath
midwife	bouquet	bury
cot	reception	widow*
nappy	groom	mourners
	honeymoon	coffin
	get divorced	

widow fits both the marriage and death sections.

2 Ask students in groups of two or three to complete the story. Give them 10 minutes to talk and brainstorm ideas and take notes. Then give them 10–15 minutes to write up the story. Or set the writing part for homework. Ask them to read their story to the class, or put the stories on the wall so students can circulate and read them.

3 Discuss the question in small groups or as a class.

Exercise 8 Vocabulary – Birth, death, and marriage

LISTENING AND SPEAKING (SB p98)

A birth

The listening has a prediction task and a specific information task. It is a springboard for the roleplay which follows.

1 The aim is to set the scene in a personalized fashion. You could start by telling your class what you know about the day you were born. Put the students into small groups, and encourage them to share stories. In the feedback, get students with interesting stories to share them with the whole class.

2 Focus attention on the photos. Ask some questions about the photo of the Isle of Mull *What problems might there be for someone expecting a baby here?* and the group photo *When do you think this photo was taken? Where are they?*

T 12.8 Play the recording. Ask students to answer the questions and identify the people in the photo. Ask students *Who must have taken the photo?* (the other midwife).

Note: We refer to the Isle of Mull as an *island* in the tapescript to assist students' comprehension.

> **Answers and tapescript**
> The people in the photo are Jane, the baby, Nick (Jane's husband), one of the midwives, and the lifeboat crew.
>
> **T 12.8**
> Well, my sister was expecting her first child and – er – she was living on a Scottish isle, the island of Mull … just off the west coast, and – er – the plan was that she would – er – travel to a friend's house on the mainland – er – there's a ferry of course – er – a week before the baby was due. That was the plan but – er – of course babies don't always … and – er – anyway, two weeks before the baby was due, she was at home and the baby started coming early so my sister had to be taken off the island by lifeboat, not by ferry. You see, it was really early in the morning and the ferry hadn't started running . Erm – but even the lifeboat didn't make it in time to actually get her to the mainland. You can imagine it's quite a small space to give birth in. She said it was kind of like lying in the aisle of an aeroplane or something, that's about all the space that you've got! Fortunately the lifeboat crew were marvellous – er – they're nearly all volunteers who … who man the lifeboats. You have like the captain of the boat and four crew members, and – er – in this case, a midwife from the hospital – and another midwife who was just passing, just on her way home, in fact. So, in this small space there were all these people standing around as she was giving birth – oh, and of course her husband Nick was there too – so it was quite crowded! Er – my sister was just pleased that there were no complications and that she

managed to get through it. And what was really nice, on the lifeboat, – erm – the crew had a bottle of champagne which I think they were saving for a special occasion and they did actually open it and – er – drink the health of the new baby. And then they also engraved her name and date of birth on the lifeboat's bell so that it's always remembered!

The lifeboatmen were encouraging my sister to name the baby after the lifeboat, 'cos lifeboats always have a name – and this one was called Mora Edith Macdonald. And so they wanted my sister to call the baby Mora – but she'd already got a name planned. But she did use Mora as a middle name. So my niece has the name Hazel Beth Mora Banner, – er – she has two middle names. One of the lifeboatmen joked – he said it was a good job she didn't give birth on the ferry because she'd have had to call the baby Caledonian McBrayne – that's the name of the ferry company. Actually the story – erm – it was featured in the local newspapers after the birth – erm – so there was a photo, somebody had a camera on the boat and took photos straight away. So the story appeared with that photo in all the local papers.

3 Ask students in pairs to choose the correct answer. You may need to play the recording again.

> **Answers and tapescript**
> 1 lifeboat
> 2 on the lifeboat
> 3 two midwives
> 4 lack of space
> 5 champagne
> 6 Hazel Beth Mora
> 7 put her name on the bell

Roleplay

Put the students in pairs. Read through the roles carefully, then give students four or five minutes to look at the tapescript on SB p133, or just the sentences in exercise 3, and prepare their roleplay. When they are ready, give a start signal, monitor and prompt. You could get one or two pairs to act out their conversations for the class.

READING AND SPEAKING (SB p99)

A death

The aim here is to read a poem for gist, then to interpret the poet's meaning. It asks the students to learn the poem by heart, which is fun, and good for pronunciation and intonation. The poem is called *Funeral Blues*, and it is written by WH Auden. The class may not know anything about the poet, but they may have heard the poem if they have seen the film *Four Weddings and a Funeral*.

Note that there is such a wealth of well-known writers past and present in English that it is a shame not to reflect this to some extent in language textbooks. If the literature extracts are carefully selected and handled, they can be of great interest to students, and may give them the confidence and motivation to try and read more.

> **NOTE ON THE POET**
> Wystan Hugh Auden (1907–1973) was born in York, England, and educated at Oxford University. He drove an ambulance for the Republicans in the Spanish Civil War in 1937. He won the Pulitzer Prize for Poetry in 1948 for *The Age of Anxiety* and went to live in the United States in 1939. He later became an American citizen. He died on 28 September 1973 in Vienna.

1 Read the question as a class. Ask students to predict from the title what the poem is about. (*Blues* means a feeling of sadness or depression, but is also a type of sad music, so the title could mean either feeling depressed at a funeral, or a song about a funeral in the blues style.)

2 Ask the students to close their books at this stage. Tell them that you want them to listen to the poem first, before they read it, to see how much they can understand.
   T 12.9 Ask everyone to relax and close their eyes, then play the recording. Ask the questions.

   Answers
   • The poet's loved one has died.
   • He can't understand how the world continues to go on. It all seems meaningless.
   • It can be fun to try to build this poem using any words or phrases your students can remember – many of the words seem to be quite memorable. Write them on the board.

3 **T 12.9** Play the recording again, and ask students to open their books and to read the poem silently as they listen. Tell them to answer the questions in pairs.

   Answers
   1 He wants the rest of the world to stop because he feels so grief-stricken.
   2 The lines of the first verse describe things that could possibly happen. The lines of the second and last verses describe impossible things.
   3 Verse three.
   4 This means that quite ordinary things look different. The whole world looks beautiful even if it is really not. The weather seems sunny even if it is raining; everyone you meet seems happy; buildings, the countryside are beautiful, etc. Nothing can make you feel unhappy. The poem describes the opposite of this when you lose someone you love dearly, nothing looks good and everything makes you feel unhappy. You cannot find a reason for living, and you wonder how anyone can.

Learning by heart
This can be immensely satisfying if it is done once in a while in an appropriate way.

4 Put the students in four groups and give each group a verse to learn. Give them a strict time limit – say six minutes – to learn it. Invite each group to say their verse with books closed. You can ask individuals from each group to come to the front of the class to recite it.

LISTENING AND SPEAKING (SB p100)

My Way
1 Tell students they will hear a song made famous by the singer Frank Sinatra. Write the two questions on the board to help students focus their attention as they listen.
   T 12.10 Play the recording. Discuss the questions as a class.

   Answers and tapescript
   • The message is that you should live life to the fullest and live the way you want. Don't let others tell you what to do or how to live.
   • The singer is reaching the end of his life.

   T 12.10
   My Way
   And now, the end is near
   And so I **face** the final curtain
   My friend, I'll say it clear
   I'll **state** my case, of which I'm certain
   I've lived a life that's full
   I've **travelled** each and every highway
   And more, much more than this,
   I did it my way.

   Regrets, I've had **a few**
   But then again, too few to mention
   I did what I **had** to do
   and saw it through without exemption,
   I planned each charted course,
   each careful **step** along the byway
   And more, much more than this,
   I did it my way.

   Yes, there were **times**,
   I'm sure you knew,
   When I bit off
   more than I could **chew**
   But through it all,
   when there was doubt
   I ate it up and spit* it out
   I faced it all and I stood **tall**
   and did it my way.

   I've loved, I've **laughed** and cried
   I've had my fill, my share of losing
   And now, as tears subside,

I find it all so **amusing**
To think I did all that
And may I say, not in a **shy** way,
'Oh, no, oh, no, not me, I did it my way.

For what is a man, what has he got?
If not himself, then he has **naught**.
To say the things he truly **feels**
and not the words of one who kneels,
The record shows I took the **blows**
and did it my way.
Yes, it was my way.

* In US English, *spit* has the Past Simple *spit*, rather than the British English *spat*.

2 In pairs, students complete the song.

Answers

1	face	9	tall
2	state	10	laughed
3	travelled	11	amusing
4	a few	12	shy
5	had	13	naught
6	step	14	feels
7	times	15	blows
8	chew		

T 12.9 Play the recording again so that students can check their answers.

WRITING (SB p119)

Correcting mistakes (2)

This activity revises language from the whole Student's Book.

1 Read the introduction to the class. Ask students in pairs to find the mistakes and mark them using the correction symbols from Unit 1 *Writing* (SB p103) wherever they can. Go round monitoring. Help students identify the appropriate correction symbol where necessary. Check answers as a class.

2 Ask students in pairs to produce a correct version. Go round monitoring and helping as necessary.

Answers (1 and 2)

Szerencs u. 43
3300 Eger
Hungary
Friday, 14 June

Dear Mr and Mrs Kendall

I **have been** home now **for** two weeks but I **had** to start work immediately, so this is the first time **that it is** possible for me to write. How are you all? Are you busy as usual? **Is** Tim **still working** hard for his exam next month? I ~~am~~ **miss** you a lot

and also all my friends from Dublin. Yesterday I**'ve received** a letter from my **Spanish** friend, Martina, and she told me about some of the other people I met. She **said** that Atsuko and Yuki **are going to** write **to** me from Japan. I am lucky because I made so many good **friends while** I was in Ireland. It was really interesting for me to meet people from so many different countries. I think that we not only improved our English (I hope **so**!) but we also **got to know** people from all over the world and this is important.
My family are fine. They had a good summer holiday by the lake. We are all very **excited** because my brother **is getting/is going to get** married just before Christmas and we like **his girlfriend very much**. They have **been looking** for a flat near the city centre but it is **not** easy to find one. If they **don't** find one soon they will have to stay here with us.
Please can you check something for me? I can't find my red scarf. I think **I might have left** it in the **cupboard** in my bedroom.
Please write soon. My family send best wishes to you all. I hope I can come back next year. **Staying** with you was a **really** wonderful experience for me. Thank you for **everything** and excuse my mistakes. **I have already forgotten** so **many** words.
Love
Kati
PS I hope you like the photo. It's nice, isn't it?

3 In small groups students discuss a time when they have stayed at somebody else's home. What was the experience like for them? Then ask students to work individually to make notes in preparation for writing a thank-you letter to someone they have stayed with. They could write the letter for homework, and bring it back to class for other students to help correct.

EVERYDAY ENGLISH (SB p101)

Saying sorry

The aim here is to introduce and practise different ways of saying sorry. Students often confuse the expressions in the box. Write them on the board and elicit or pre-teach their meanings.

(I'm) sorry and *I'm so sorry* – is an apology and a regret.

Excuse me – is to attract someone's attention.

Pardon? – (polite) when you can't hear someone clearly.

What? – (not polite) when you can't hear someone clearly.

1 Ask students in pairs to complete the conversations.

T 12.11 Play the recording so that students can listen and check their answers. Then ask them to act out the conversations in pairs with proper stress and intonation.

Answers and tapescript

1 **A** Excuse me, can you tell me where the post office is?
   B **I'm sorry**, I'm a stranger here myself.
2 **A** Ouch! That's my foot!
   B **I'm sorry**. I wasn't looking where I was going.
3 **A** **Excuse me**, what's that creature called?
   B It's a Diplodocus.
   A **Pardon?**
   B A Diplodocus. D-I-P-L-O-D-O-C-U-S.
   A Thank you very much.
4 **A** I failed my driving test for the sixth time!
   B **I'm so sorry.**
5 **A** **Excuse me**! We need to get past. My little boy isn't feeling well.
6 **A** Do you want your hearing aid, Grandma?
   B **Pardon?**
   A I said: Do you want your hearing aid?
   B **What?**
   A DO YOU WANT YOUR HEARING AID?!
   B **I'm sorry**, I can't hear you. I need my hearing aid.

2 Ask students in pairs to complete the activity. If you don't have much time, you could divide the situations among small groups, and then get individual students to act them out in front of the class.

Sample answers

1 Hello, I'm sorry about that. I think we must have been cut off.
2 Excuse me, please. Thank you. Oh excuse me. I'm getting off at the next stop. Sorry, I have a big suitcase.
3 Excuse me! ... um ... Excuse me! Excuse me, please! Waiter! Could we have another large bottle of mineral water, please? Thanks.
4 Oh, I'm so sorry to hear that. Of course I understand. We'll get together another time.
5 Excuse me. I wonder if you could help me. I thought this jumper was a medium, but when I got home, I realized it was the wrong size. Can I exchange it?
6 Oh, no! Of course, you're a vegetarian! I'm so sorry. How stupid of me. Don't worry. I'll make you an omelette if you like.

Don't forget!

Workbook Unit 12
Exercise 9 Pronunciation – Word stress
Exercise 10 Pronunciation – *had* or *would*?
Exercise 11 Phrasal verbs

Word list
Photocopy the Word list for Unit 12 (TB p160) for your students. Ask them to write in the translations, learn them at home, and/or write some of the words in their vocabulary notebooks.

EXTRA IDEAS UNIT 12

On p133 of the Teacher's Book, there is an English folk tale with suggested discussion questions and an activity on reported speech to exploit it.

If you have time, and feel your students would benefit, photocopy it to use in class as follow-up material to Unit 12.

The answers to the activities are on p149 of the Teacher's Book.

Stop and check 4
(TB pp140–141). A suggestion for approaching the *Stop and check* tests is in the introduction on TB p5.

Progress test 2
There is a Progress test for Units 7–12 on TB pp145–148.

Photocopiable material

Extra ideas Units 1–3

Reading and speaking

Living in the modern world

1 We live in a world of amazing, new technology. But how up-to-date are you with this new, technological world? Complete the questionnaire and check your score in the key.

2 Discuss these questions with a partner.

- How modern and technological are you? Are there any new inventions that you don't have, which you would like to try?

- Which technological inventions in the questionnaire were luxury items, or not even invented, twenty years ago?

- What new technological inventions will change our lives in the near future?

How **up-to-date** are you?

COMMUNICATIONS

1 **How do you keep in touch with friends who live far away or abroad?**
   A I write them letters.
   B I send them emails.
   C I give them a call.
   D We chat on the videophone.

2 **How often do you check your emails?**
   A Once a day.
   B I never get any.
   C More than once a day.
   D At least once a week.

3 **An acquaintance asks for a way of contacting you. Do you give him/her ...?**
   A your home phone number
   B your mobile phone number
   C your email address
   D your home address

4 **How often do you text friends?**
   A At least once a day.
   B I've never done it.
   C More than five times a day.
   D Not very often.

5 **How many different covers do you have for your mobile?**
   A 2
   B 3
   C more than 3
   D I didn't know you could get different covers.

ENTERTAINMENT

6 **You decide to buy tickets for the theatre. Do you ... ?**
   A buy them at the box office
   B buy them on the phone
   C buy them online
   D use a text message to buy them

7 **You fancy watching a film tonight. Do you ... ?**
   A rent a DVD
   B rent a video cassette
   C download the movie from the Internet
   D check out what's on cable or satellite movie channels
   E have a look to see if there is anything on the main channels

8 **In your music collection, which of the following are most numerous?**
   A CDs
   B cassettes
   C LPs/vinyl
   D minidiscs

9 **Which of the following do you have in your home entertainment system?**
   A a flat screen TV
   B a DVD player
   C a play station
   D surround sound
   E a digital radio
   F a personal CD player
   G interactive TV

10 **Where do you find out about the news?**
   A from the newspaper
   B from the radio
   C from the Internet
   D from the TV

11 **Which of the following can't you do yet?**
   A access text messages on a mobile
   B send an email attachment
   C set the timer on the video
   D set up a website
   E record from one CD to another

QUESTIONNAIRE KEY

1 A 0, B 2, C 1, D 3
2 A 2, B 0, C 3, D 1
3 A 1, B 2, C 3, D 0
4 A 2, B 0, C 3, D 1
5 A 1, B 2, C 3, D 0
6 A 0, B 1, C 2, D 3
7 A 2, B 1, C 3, D 3, E 0
8 A 2, B 0, C 0, D 3
9 One point for each thing you have.
10 A 0, B 0, C 3, D 1
11 Minus 1 for each thing you can't do.

31–40 You are very up-to-date and modern. But remember that you can have a conversation with friends without using a mobile.

21–30 You are fairly modern. You like mobiles, DVDs and emails, but you don't let it control your life.

11–20 You aren't very up-to-date. If you have a mobile, you never switch it on. You still watch videos, not DVDs.

0–10 You live in The Stone Age. You remember black and white TV and typewriters.

Extra ideas Units 1–3

Song

1 It's winter. It's cold and grey. It's raining, and you're feeling miserable. Close your eyes. Imagine you're somewhere warmer, somewhere you'd rather be. *Where are you? Who are you with? What are you doing?* Open your eyes and tell the class about your dream.

2 What's the connection between these words?
   a church, preacher, knees, pray
   b sun, California, L.A. (Los Angeles)

3 You are going to listen to a song called 'California Dreamin''. Answer the questions.
   a Do you think the singer is in his home town?
   b How is he feeling?

4 Look at the song and choose the best word in *italics* to fill each gap. Remember that songs usually rhyme!

   Listen and check.

5 Discuss these questions with your partner.
   a Why does the preacher like the cold?
   b The singer says 'If I didn't tell her, I could leave today.' What do you think he means? What do you think is the story behind the song?

Poem

1 Read the poem. Use your dictionary to look up new words and phrases.

2 Find examples of present active and passive forms.

3 Learn the poem by heart.

California Dreamin'

All the leaves are (1) *brown*/*green*
And the sky is (2) *blue*/*grey*
I've been for a (3) *walk*/*run*
On a winter's (4) *night*/*day*
I'd be safe and (5) *warm*/*hot*
If I was in L.A.

California dreamin'
On such a winter's (6) *night*/*day*

(7) *Stopped*/*Walked* into a church
I (8) *passed*/*noticed* along the way
Well I got (9) *up*/*down* on my knees
And I began to (10) *sing*/*pray*
You know the preacher likes the (11) *heat*/*cold*
He knows I'm gonna (12) *stay*/*leave*

California dreamin'
On such a winter's (13) *night*/*day*

All the leaves are (14) *brown*/*green*
And the sky is (15) *blue*/*grey*
I've been for a (16) *walk*/*run*
On a winter's (17) *night*/*day*
If I didn't tell her
I could leave today

California dreamin'
On such a winter's (18) *night*/*day*

A MAN IS MADE

A man is made
Of flesh and blood
Of eyes and bones and water.
The very same things make his son
As those that make
His daughter.

A tree is made
Of leaf and sap,
Of bark and fruit and berries.
It keeps a bird's nest
In its boughs
And blackbirds eat the cherries.

A table's made
Of naked wood
Planed as smooth as milk. I wonder
If tables ever dream of sun,
Of wind, and rain, and thunder?

And when man takes
His axe and strikes
And sets the sawdust flying –
Is it a table being born?
Or just a tree that's dying?

Extra ideas Units 4–6

Song

1   Are you optimistic or pessimistic? Complete the questionnaire for you. Then ask and answer the questions with a partner.

Check your answers in the key. Are you optimistic or pessimistic?

Can you think of a day when everything went wrong? Tell your partner about it.

	YOU	YOUR PARTNER
1 I'm usually lucky.		
2 Everything I do always goes wrong.		
3 I always say, things can only get better.		
4 If I go to the beach, it's usually cloudy.		
5 You don't know if you can do something until you try.		
6 I often feel sorry for myself.		
7 I get depressed when things go wrong.		
8 I always look on the bright side.		
9 I give up easily.		
10 There's always a light at the end of the tunnel.		

2   You are going to listen to a song called 'Why does it always rain on me?' Listen and answer the questions.
   a   Is the singer feeling optimistic or pessimistic?
   b   Why do you think he feels this way? Have a guess.

3   Look at the song and choose the best word in *italics* to fill in each gap. Listen and check.

4   Can you explain these lines? Discuss them with your partner.
   a   Why does it always rain on me?
   b   I'm seeing a tunnel at the end of all these lights.
   c   Is it because I lied when I was 17?

5   Read what some people have said about the singer and the song. Which do you agree with?

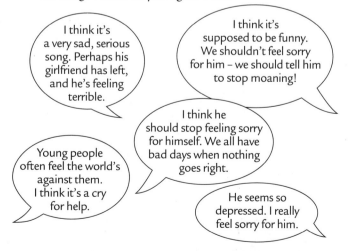

I think it's a very sad, serious song. Perhaps his girlfriend has left, and he's feeling terrible.

I think it's supposed to be funny. We shouldn't feel sorry for him – we should tell him to stop moaning!

I think he should stop feeling sorry for himself. We all have bad days when nothing goes right.

Young people often feel the world's against them. I think it's a cry for help.

He seems so depressed. I really feel sorry for him.

How would *you* describe the singer's feelings and what do you think the song is about?

Why does it always rain on me?

I can't (1) *be awake /* (sleep) tonight
Everybody's saying everything's alright
Still I can't (2) *close / open* my eyes
I'm seeing a tunnel at the end of all
   (3) *this darkness / these lights*

(4) *Sunny / Rainy* days
Where have you gone?
I get the (5) *typical / strangest* feeling you belong

Why does it always rain on me?
Is it because I (6) *lied / told the truth* when I was 17?
Why does it always rain on me?
Even when the sun is (7) *behind the clouds / shining*
I can't avoid the (8) *lightning / crying*

Oh, where did the (9) *grey / blue* skies go?
And why is it raining so?
It's so (10) *warm / cold*

Repeat

Student A1

You want to speak to Mr James in the Service Department at Ford Garages.

You want your car serviced. If Mr James isn't there, be prepared to leave a message and give your phone number. Say how long you'll be on that number.

Student B1

You work for Ford Garages. Someone phones for Mr James from the Service Department, but he's not there at the moment.

Explain the situation, and offer to take a message. Get all the information you need.

Remember! You answer the phone. Begin by saying, 'Hello. Ford Garages. Can I help you?'

Student A2

You want to book two nights at the Palace Hotel. Decide which dates you want, and what sort of room you want. You need to know the price of the room and what is included. Does the hotel need a deposit? Can you pay by credit card?

Be prepared to give your name, address, and details of your credit card.

Student B2

First you are the telephonist at the Palace Hotel. Answer the phone and say, 'Hello. Palace Hotel. How can I help you?' Put the caller through to Reservations.

Now you work in Reservations! Answer the phone and say, 'Hello. Reservations. Can I help you?' Someone wants to book a room. Ask the dates, and what sort of room is required.

Remember to get the person's name, address, and details of their credit card.

Student A3

You need a plumber desperately! Your washing machine is pouring water all over the floor.

You phone Chris, a local plumber. He's probably out at work, so you might have to leave a message on his answer phone.

Be prepared to leave a message, giving your name and number, and explaining the situation. Ask him to get in touch as soon as possible.

Student B3

Your name is Chris, and you're a plumber. Decide what message to record onto your answer phone. Remember that customers might be phoning, so you must tell them when you'll phone back.

When the phone rings, deliver your recorded message.

Student A4

You phone your friend Jo to invite her to go to the cinema. You, Mary, and Steve have arranged to meet outside the cinema at 7.00. Would Jo like to join you?

Jo will probably be out, so be prepared to leave a message on her answer phone.

Student B4

Your name is Jo. Decide what message to record onto your answer phone at home.

When the phone rings, deliver your recorded message!

Student A5

You phone the International School of English for a brochure. When the phone rings, ask for the Admissions Department. You want to know course dates and fees. You also want to know when the next course starts.

Be ready to give your name and address.

Student B5

First you are the telephonist at the International School of English. Answer the phone and say, 'Good morning! International School of English'. Put the caller through to the Admissions Department.

Now you work in the Admissions Department! Answer the phone and say 'Hello. Admissions. How can I help you?'

The caller wants information from you about course dates and fees. Be ready to give the information about your school.

The caller also wants a brochure, so you'll have to get their name and address.

1 Congratulations!
You have won £5 MILLION!

Now you have to make some decisions.
Are you going to keep your win a secret, or will you go to a big London hotel to receive your cheque from a famous film star? Of course, the press will be there, and your photo will be in all the newspapers.

If you want to remain anonymous,
GO TO 10

If you want to go to the hotel and the press conference,
GO TO 15

Extra ideas Units 7–9 **A maze**

Instructions *You have won a lot of money on the lottery. You have to decide as a group how to collect your win and what to do with it once you have it.*

1 In your groups read aloud card number 1.
2 Talk together until you *all* agree what to do next.
3 If you decide to remain anonymous, ask your teacher for card number 10. If you decide to go to the hotel and the press conference, ask your teacher for card number 15.
4 Continue to follow the instructions on each maze card until the maze comes to an end. For each card make sure you *all* agree what to do next.

10

You want to try to keep your win a secret from the world. But what about your family? Are you going to tell your relatives?

No.
GO TO 12

Yes.
GO TO 18

2

You have a reputation for being kind and generous, so you feel you're handling your new wealth quite well.
Meanwhile, you have to make another big decision. Are you going to carry on in your old job, or are you going to give up work? After all, you don't need the money any more.

If you're going to carry on working,
GO TO 7

If you're going to stop working,
GO TO 13

15

You've received your cheque at a big press conference, after which your name and photograph appeared in all the newspapers. As a result you get thousands of letters begging for money. What are you going to do?

Give all of them £10.
GO TO 2

Give some money to the people who sound genuine, but nothing to the crazy ones.
GO TO 8

Give nothing to anyone.
GO TO 11

18

You tell your relatives, and they're all very pleased, especially when you give them all £1,000 each. They're a little bit jealous, but you were generous, so that's all right.
Anyway, you have to make another big decision. Are you going to carry on in your old job, or are you going to give up work? After all, you don't need the money any more.

If you're going to carry on working,
GO TO 7

If you're going to stop working,
GO TO 13

12

Your relatives find out that you've won a lot of money, and they feel very upset that you didn't tell them. Can things ever be the same again?
Anyway, you have to make another big decision. Are you going to carry on in your old job, or are you going to give up work? After all, you don't need the money any more.

If you're going to carry on working,
GO TO 7

If you're going to stop working,
GO TO 13

8

The press keeps asking people about you. They don't write about the people you have given to, but they write article after article about the people you didn't give to. You don't feel that you're handling your new wealth very well.
Anyway, you have to make another big decision. Are you going to carry on in your old job, or are you going to give up work? After all, you don't need the money any more.

If you're going to carry on working,
GO TO 7

If you're going to stop working,
GO TO 13

11

The press keep asking people about you and what you're doing with all your money. When they find out that you haven't given a penny to anyone, they write horrible things about you. As a result you feel awful. You aren't handling this new wealth at all well.

Meanwhile, you have to make another big decision. Are you going to carry on in your old job, or are you going to give up work? After all, you don't need the money any more.

If you're going to carry on working,
GO TO 7

If you're going to stop working,
GO TO 13

21

You just carry on working as usual. People think you're a little strange, and you're getting a reputation for being a bit of an eccentric. Why, if you've got so much money, do you carry on doing your old job?

You could spend a few hundred pounds on one or two things for your flat.
GO TO 14

You could go on a shopping spree to New York, and buy presents for everyone you know. For goodness sake, you can afford it, so why not enjoy it?
GO TO 3

7

You've decided to carry on in your old job, at least for the time being. Of course, by now everyone at work knows you're a multi-millionaire. What are you going to do?

Throw a huge party for all your work colleagues.
GO TO 9

Just carry on working and ignore everyone's comments.
GO TO 21

14

You spend a tiny percentage of your money, and invest the rest in the bank.

This new wealth isn't doing very much for you. It certainly isn't making you very happy.

Why don't you give it all away to charity, or to someone who might do something more creative with it?
GO TO 17

Why not just carry on working? If that's what you want to do, then do it.
GO TO 19

9

You have a huge party, and everyone has a wonderful time. All your work colleagues think you're a great person, and love you very much. That's what they all said at the end of the party, anyway, after the champagne had been flowing all night.

You carry on working for another six months, and you've still got all this money in the bank. You can't just ignore it. You've got to do something with it.

You could spend a few hundred pounds on one or two things for your flat.
GO TO 14

You could go on a shopping spree to New York, and buy presents for everyone you know. For goodness sake, you can afford it, so why not enjoy it?
GO TO 3

3

You go to New York and have a great time. Everyone loves their presents.

You've still got loads of money. What are you going to do with it?

Give a lot to various charities, both at home and in other countries.
GO TO 16

Give up work now. You'd like a new challenge.
GO TO 6

Carry on working, doing the same old thing.
GO TO 4

33

You try to fight your drug addiction alone, but you can't do it. You keep falling back into bad habits.

There is one last thing you can try. You can go to the Betty Ford Clinic in California, where they have a very good success rate with people like you.

Unfortunately, it will cost the rest of your money.

What are you going to do?

Go to the clinic. What's the point of your money if you haven't got your health?
GO TO 40

Keep trying to give up your addiction. If you haven't got any money, how can you buy the drugs you need?
GO TO 32

24

You go to the detoxification centre, and six weeks later you are cured of your addictions.
While you're in the centre, you meet some born-again religious fanatics. They say that if you give them all your money, you will be saved.

If you want to give them all your money,
GO TO 36

If you don't want to give them a penny,
GO TO 34

40

You find the meaning of life.

You're cured – completely cured, and the world seems a beautiful place again.

You could even try to get your old job back!

You have come to the end of this activity.

Well done!

? Was it worth having so much money? Maybe people just shouldn't have so much more than others?

17

You feel an awful lot better now that you don't have to worry about all that money. You're relieved, and you've found true happiness. Having so much money was quite an experience, but you think that you are probably better off without it.

You have come to the end of this activity.

Well done!

36

You give all your money to the religious group and go to live with them in a community in California.

You find true happiness, and live with the group for the rest of your life.

You have come to the end of this activity.

Well done!

16

You're feeling good. You seem to be getting a balance of what to do with your money. Spend some and save some.

One day you get a phone call. It's your Uncle Ernie who you haven't heard from for years. He asks for £100,000 or he will tell the press stories about you from your childhood. What are you going to do?

Give him the money.
GO TO 5

Not give him the money.
GO TO 20

32

You live a life which is dominated by your drug habit, which you never manage to control. You're an addict for the rest of your life.

You have come to the end of this activity.

Bad luck!

? Was the money worth it?

? Weren't you happy when you were just doing your old job, and had friends to go out with on a Friday night? What you would give to be able to go back to those days!

19

Your life grinds on until you die of boredom. Money didn't do much for you, did it? You didn't seem to find much to do with it, either.

You have come to the end of this activity.

Bad luck!

34

You come out of the centre cured. You feel a little disillusioned with life. What is money for? It doesn't seem to bring much happiness.

You could invest it in a friend's business. You trust her, and you would be doing something useful with your money.
GO TO 35

You could use your money to help homeless people and drug addicts. This would be a constructive thing to do with your money.
GO TO 38

5

You give Uncle Ernie the money, and this keeps him quiet.

You're getting fed up with the responsibility of having so much money, and so many people keep sending you begging letters. You feel it's time for a major decision in your life.

Why not give it all away? It would be the end of all your troubles. You could go back to life as it used to be.
GO TO 17

Or you could just decide never, ever give anyone any money ever again. After all, it's yours to do with what you want.
GO TO 28

4

Your life grinds on until you die of boredom. Money didn't do much for you, did it? You didn't seem to find much to do with it, either.

You have come to the end of this activity.

Bad luck

28

You live a rich, miserable existence for the rest of your life.

You have come to the end of this activity.

Bad luck

? Maybe you would have been happier without the money. Who knows?

20

You decide not to give Uncle Ernie the money he asked for. As a result, he tells stories about you to the press, which are then published.

You're getting fed up with all this attention from the press, and you've had enough of the responsibility of handling so much money.

You decide to give it all away.
GO TO 17

13

You've stopped work because you have so much money, and you don't see why you should carry on getting up so early in the morning if you don't have to. So what are you going to do?

Go on a world cruise. Here's your big chance to see the world!
GO TO 29

You could buy your local football team. You've always been interested in football, and the club needs some money urgently. You could be manager!
GO TO 22

Buy some fantastic clothes and a Mercedes sports car, and start going to the most fashionable restaurants and night clubs.
GO TO 25

6

You've finally given up work. You've got all this time and all this money. What on earth are you going to do?

You could do some charity work at your local hospital. You feel it would do you good to think of other people for a change.
GO TO 27

You could invest all your money in a new business that you've read about in the papers. It promises to double your money within six months.
GO TO 30

27

You've found true happiness. You've managed to be both rich and happy, which is no easy thing to do. You've balanced wealth with care and concern for other people.

You have come to the end of this activity.

Well done!

30

You've invested all your money in a new business venture. It goes wrong and you lose it all. Everything. You don't have a penny left.

This is the best thing that could happen to you. Suddenly you don't have a care in the world. All the worries about what to do with so much money have disappeared. You go back to your old job, where you're very happy until you retire.

You have come to the end of this activity.

Well done!

29

You're on a world cruise. You meet another millionaire on board the ship, but this is a multi-multi-millionaire. He/she is also single. If you two got married, you would be rich forever. However, you don't actually love him/her.

If you decide to get married,
GO TO 23

If you decide it would be crazy to get married,
GO TO 26

25

You start to have a great time, going out every night and not getting home till dawn. Suddenly a lot of people seem to like you. Is it because you're the one who pays for everything?

At a night club one evening, a friend of yours shows you some white powder and says, 'Here! Try this!'

What are you going to do?

Try it. Why not? A little won't do you any harm.
GO TO 37

Don't touch it. You'd be mad.
GO TO 31

23

You got married with the intention of becoming super rich, but it becomes clear within six months that you don't get on with your new husband/wife. Inevitably you get divorced.

Meanwhile, you have more decisions to make. You have spoken to your accountant about what to do with your money. Your accountant has two suggestions.

Invest your money in high-risk schemes. You could make another fortune.
GO TO 39

Invest your money in low-risk schemes. You won't make a lot, but you won't lose it either.
GO TO 42

39

You've invested all your money in risky schemes, and you've lost the lot. You don't have a penny left. Naughty, naughty! You were too greedy, weren't you?

You have come to the end of this activity.

Bad luck!

? Maybe you can get your old job back? Was it worth having so much money?

38

You've found true happiness and the meaning of life. You've managed to be both rich and happy, which is not easy. You've balanced spending money on yourself and using it to help others.

You have come to the end of this activity.

Well done!

22

You're the manager of a football team. You're doing well. It is the last game of the season. If you win this match, you will win the championship.

Just make sure you win, you could offer your opponents a bribe to lose the match. You're pretty sure you could get away with it.

What are you going to do?

Offer a bribe.
GO TO 43

Play fair.
GO TO 46

42

You chose low-risk investments, which provide you with an income for life. Not a fortune, but enough to keep you, your family and friends happy for the rest of your life.

You have come to the end of this activity.

Well done!

35

Your friend runs away with all your money. What a friend! With friends like that, who needs enemies?

You're broke. You've lost the lot.

You have come to the end of this activity.

Bad luck!

? Maybe you could get your old job back? Maybe that's when you were happiest in your whole life?

31

Well done. You resisted the temptation to try the illegal drug. You could have become addicted. Maybe these friends aren't so friendly after all.

You decide to get some financial advice. Your accountant has two suggestions.

Invest your money in high-risk schemes. You could make another fortune.
GO TO 52

Invest your money in low-risk schemes. You won't make a lot, but you won't lose it, either.
GO TO 53

26

Thank goodness you chose not to get married. He/she wasn't a millionaire at all, but a con artist. You nearly lost the lot!

Meanwhile, you have more decisions to make. You have spoken to your accountant about what to do with your money. Your accountant has two suggestions.

Invest your money in high-risk schemes. You could make another fortune.

GO TO 39

Invest your money in low-risk schemes. You won't make a lot, but you won't lose it, either.

GO TO 53

45

You invest what you have left in the scheme and you lose the lot. Every penny.

You have come to the end of this activity.

Bad luck!

? Maybe you weren't meant to be a football manager? Maybe you would have been happier just staying in your old job?

43

You bribed the opposition and you won the championship. Everything seems to be going OK.

Unfortunately, there are some rumours about you and your dishonesty going round.

What are you going to do?

You can deny everything.

GO TO 41

You can come clean and admit that you did wrong.

GO TO 44

47

You invest all your money in a new business venture. It goes wrong and you lose it all. Everything. You don't have a penny left.

This is the best thing that could happen to you. Suddenly, you don't have a care in the world. All the worries about what to do with so much money have disappeared. You go back to your old job, where you are very happy until you retire.

You have come to the end of this activity.

Well done!

37

Unfortunately, one thing leads to another, and you've started drinking and taking drugs. You're losing control of your life.

What are you going to do?

Get yourself to a detoxification centre. You need help.

GO TO 24

Fight it alone. You've never needed anyone's help before, and anyway you can stop taking drugs whenever you want.

GO TO 33

48

When you come out of prison, you give up on football. There are so many dishonest people in the game.

You decide to ask for your old job back, and you're in luck! You go back to work, and stay there until it's time for your retirement. You live out your days poor, but you are a wise and happy person.

You have come to the end of this activity.

Well done!

41

You deny all knowledge of any wrong doing. The case goes to court, and you're found guilty. You're sentenced to four years in prison.

While you're in prison, you meet someone who says he knows how to make a fortune, probably not legally. When you get out of prison, what are you going to do?

Invest in this man's scheme. You need the money badly.

GO TO 45

Go on the straight and narrow. You've learned your lesson.

GO TO 48

49

You carry on with the football team. Things go from bad to worse. You suffer from stress, you start drinking too much alcohol, and your team is relegated to the lower division.

You finally have a heart attack, and you're forced to resign from the club.

You live out your life older, poorer and wiser.

You have come to the end of this activity.

Bad luck!

44

You admit that you offered the other team a bribe. You're fined several thousand pounds, and the Board of Directors forgives you.

However, you're going off the idea of being involved in football. The game is full of dishonest people.

What are you going to do?

Sell the team and do something else with the money.
GO TO 47

Carry on with the team. Things have to get better soon.
GO TO 49

51

You decide not to give yourself all the stress and hard work, and you're happy being the manager of your local team.

You carry on in the job for years. There are ups and downs, but by and large you are happy.

You have come to the end of this activity.

Well done!

46

You play fair and resist the temptation to bribe the opposition. You win the championship and become a famous manager.

You're offered the chance of being the manager of your country's football team. What an honour! However, it would mean more work and more stress. Is it the kind of thing you want?

If you decide to accept the job,
GO TO 50

If you decide not to take it,
GO TO 51

53

You invest your money in low-risk schemes, but you still make loads of money. You can't stop making money.

What are you going to do?

Give half of it away to charity. You don't need it, and you've got enough to live on.
GO TO 54

Invest all of it in environmental education to make everyone aware of how we need to take care of the world and its animals.
GO TO 55

50

You become the manager of your country's football team. Unfortunately, after two years your luck runs out. You haven't won a game for nine months, and you are sacked. You're poor and on the street.

You have come to the end of this activity.

Bad luck!

? **Was it a good idea to go into football?**

? **Was it worth winning all that money? You could have just stayed in your old job. Maybe they would take you back?**

55

Your ideas work wonderfully and the world is saved! You're made a Sir or Lady, and you go to Buckingham Palace to receive your award.

Everyone says what a wonderful person you are.

You have come to the end of this activity.

Well done!

52

You invest every penny you have in a high-risk scheme. Unfortunately, there's a stock market collapse and you lose the lot. It has all gone.

This is the best thing that could happen to you. Suddenly, you don't have a care in the world. All the worries about what to do with so much money have disappeared. You go back to your old job, where you are very happy until you retire.

You have come to the end of this activity.

Well done!

54

You find true happiness. You've managed to be both rich and happy, and you've balanced spending your money on yourself, and using it to benefit other people.

You have come to the end of this activity.

Well done!

Extra ideas Units 10–12

Unit 10 Suggestion
Prepositions of time

For each time expression, put *in*, *at*, *on*, or nothing.

a	____ March	i	____ two days ago
b	____ 1986	j	____ the weekend
c	____ 14 May	k	____ Christmas
d	____ Monday	l	____ last year
e	____ last Monday	m	____ the end of April
f	____ summer	n	____ the morning
g	____ 8 o' clock	o	____ Monday morning
h	____ the 1960s		

Reading and speaking

1   You are going to read *Lazy Jack*, an English folk tale. Work in small groups and discuss the following:

   a   What is a folk tale? How are they different from other stories?

   b   What are some folk tales from your culture?

2   Read the story.

Language Work

3   Read these sentences from the text. Change the direct speech into reported speech and the reported speech into direct speech.

   a   Jack's mother told him that she wouldn't support him anymore.

   _____

   b   'You have to find a job!' she ordered.

   _____

   c   'I'll do that next time,' replied Jack.

   _____

   d   The doctors said she had no chance of recovering until someone could make her laugh.

   _____

   e   'The first man who makes my daughter laugh has my permission to marry her,' the father promised.

   _____

Lazy Jack

ONCE UPON A TIME, there was a young man called Jack. He lived with his mother, and they were very poor. Jack's mother worked hard, but Jack was so lazy that he did nothing but lie in the sun. One day Jack's mother told him that she would no longer support him. 'Find a job!' she ordered.

On Monday Jack was hired by a farmer. At the end of the day, the farmer paid Jack a penny. Since Jack had never had any money, he accidentally dropped the penny in the river.

When he got home and told his mother what had happened, she said, 'You should have put it in your pocket!'

'I'll do that next time,' replied Jack.

On Tuesday Jack worked for a dairy farmer, who gave him a bottle of milk. Jack put the bottle in his pocket. By the time he got home, all of the milk had spilled.

Jack's mother said, 'You should have carried it on your head!'

'I'll do that next time,' replied Jack.

The next day, Jack worked for a baker, who offered only a mean old cat as payment. Jack tried carrying the cat on his head, but it scratched him so much that he had to let it go.

When he got home and told his mother, she said, 'You should have tied it with a string and dragged it behind you.'

'I'll do that next time,' replied Jack.

Jack's next job was with a butcher, who paid Jack with a large piece of fresh meat. Jack tied the meat with a string and dragged it home. By the time he got home, the meat was completely spoiled.

'You should have carried it on your shoulder,' said Jack's mother.

'I'll do that next time,' replied Jack.

On Friday, Jack's employer was a cattle farmer, who rewarded Jack with a donkey. Jack lifted the donkey onto his shoulders and started walking home. Now, along the way, there lived a rich man with his daughter. The daughter was a beautiful girl who was deaf and couldn't speak. She had never laughed, and the doctors said she had no chance of recovering until someone could make her laugh. 'The first man who makes my daughter laugh,' her father promised, 'has my permission to marry her.'

The young woman happened to be looking out the window when Jack was walking by with the donkey on his shoulders. The sight was so funny that she burst into laughter and immediately recovered her speech and hearing. Her father kept his promise: Jack married the girl and became a rich gentleman. Jack's mother lived with them, and her final years were happy ones.

Stop and check 1

General revision

Look at the letter from Claudia, a student in England, to her friend Julie. There are 32 gaps. After some gaps there is a verb in brackets. Put the verb in the correct tense.

Example: Last week I **visited** (visit) Liverpool.

When there is no verb in brackets, write *one* suitable word – a preposition, an adverb, an auxiliary verb, an article, etc.

Example: I came **to** York to learn English.

Dear Julie,

I (1)_____ (arrive) in England three days (2)_____.
I (3)_____ (stay) with a family in a suburb of York. They're really nice. Mr Jones (4)_____ (work) in York. Mrs Jones has just had a baby, so she (5)_____ (not work) at the moment. I (6)_____ (not ask) her what she does yet, but I (7)_____ (think) she's (8)_____ accountant.

    I (9)_____ (have) a good time here, (10)_____ everything is very expensive. Yesterday I (11)_____ (take) the train (12)_____ York to do some sightseeing. Something really embarrassing happened (13)_____ I was there. After I (14)_____ (visit) the Viking Museum, I (15)_____ (decide) to do some shopping. Earlier in the day, I (16)_____ (see) a beautiful sweater in a department store, so I (17)_____ (go) back (18)_____ (buy) it. The shop assistant (19)_____ (put) it into a bag when I realized that I (20)_____ (forget) my purse with my credit cards! So, unfortunately, I couldn't buy (21)_____ after all.

    Anyway, after that I went to York Minster. I have never seen such a beautiful cathedral! It (22)_____ built between 1200 and 1470. In 1984 it (23)_____ (be) struck by lightning during a storm, and there was a terrible fire. But they've rebuilt it since then. While I (24)_____ (walk) back to the station, I (25)_____ (meet) Frank. Do you remember him? I haven't heard from him (26)_____ over a year. When we last (27)_____ (see) him, he (28)_____ (work) in a bank. Now he (29)_____ (study) English here at the same school as me! What a coincidence! Last night we went to (30)_____ cinema together and saw a horror film. Frank was terrified, but I (31)_____ enjoyed it!

    That's about all the news for now. Write soon and tell me about your holiday in Portugal. What was Lisbon (32)_____?
Write back soon.
Love, Claudia

| 32 |

Questions

Read the interview with Andre Agassi (**A**), the famous tennis player. Complete the interviewer's (**I**) questions.

Example
I How long **have you been playing tennis?**
A I've been playing tennis since I was 3 or 4.

I Where _____ ?
A I was born in Las Vegas, Nevada.
I When _____ ?
A I won Wimbledon in 1992.
I How long _____ ?
A I've been a professional tennis player since 1986.
I How often _____ ?
A I play tennis every day.
I What _____ ?
A I'm preparing for a match against Pete Sampras.

| 5 |

Auxiliary verbs

Complete the sentences using the correct auxiliary verb. Some are positive, some are negative.

Example
What time **did** you get up this morning?

1 What _____ you doing when the phone rang?
2 _____ you ever read any Ernest Hemingway?
3 I'm sorry. I can't drive you to the station because my car _____ being serviced.
4 How long _____ she been studying English?
5 In France they say *bon appétit*. But in Britain people _____ usually say anything before they start their meal.

6 _____ you go to work yesterday?

7 'Where _____ BMW cars made?'
'In Germany.'

8 I _____ watch the film last night. Was it good?

9 _____ Janet never been abroad before? No, it was her first time.

10 What _____ she studying last year?

[10]

Vocabulary

1 Do these words and phrases come after *play, do, make, go,* or *have*? Put them in the correct columns.

~~volleyball~~	a meeting	a nice time		on holiday
aerobics	golf	faces	sightseeing	sports	skiing
jogging	a headache	a party	home	the shopping
a mistake	a shower	basketball	a phone call
a decision	your homework	the washing

play	do	make	go	have
volleyball				

[22]

2 Choose the word that is different from the others and say why it is different. Think about the meaning and the grammar!

Example
a farmer   a ski instructor   a traffic warden   a secretary
A farmer, a ski instructor, and a traffic warden all work outside. A secretary works inside.

1 want   know   enjoy   understand

2 oil painting   portrait   palette   drawing

3 literature   writer   correspondent   journalist

4 beautiful   eventually   loudly   immediately

5 newspaper   play   novel   poem

6 as soon as   while   before   however

7 teepee   mansion   hotel   bed and breakfast

8 do   have   make   be

9 ski   snowboard   read   jog

10 was   been   seen   done

[10]

Active or passive?

Put the verbs in parentheses into the correct tense. Some are active, some are passive.

Reuters News Agency

Martin Webb **has worked** (work) for the Reuters News Agency for ten years. He describes the company.

'Reuters is one of the world's biggest news agencies. It (1)_____ (supply) news and stock market prices to media and financial institutions all over the world. It (2)_____ (start) by Paul Reuter in 1849 – with pigeons! Reuter (3)_____ (be born) in 1816 in Germany. During the 1840s he (4)_____ (employ) as a bank clerk in Berlin. German bankers (5)_____ (need) to know the prices on the Paris stock exchange, but the French telegraph system only went as far as Belgium. From there the information (6)_____ (send) to Germany by train. The journey (7)_____ (take) nine hours. The same information (8)_____ (carry) by Paul Reuter's pigeons in only two hours!

'Reuters (9)_____ (change) a lot since those days. Over the past 50 years, we've opened offices in many different countries – and we (10)_____ still _____ (expand). Now, news and stock market prices (11)_____ (send) all over the world within seconds.'

[11]

Translate

Translate the sentences into your language. Translate the ideas, not word for word.

1 When I arrived, the children were going to bed.

2 When I arrived, the children went to bed.

3 When I arrived, the children had gone to bed.

4 *Hamlet* was written by William Shakespeare.

5 She's working at home today.

6 Do you know the answer?

7 She works in a bank.

8 What did you think of the film?

9 What's she like?

10 What does she look like?

[10]

TOTAL [100]

Stop and check 2

General revision

Look at the letter from Julie to her friend Claudia, who's a student in England. There are 28 blanks. Sometimes you have to choose the correct verb.

Example: I must /(had to)/ could take the train because there weren't any buses.

When there is a blank, write *one* suitable word – an article, a relative pronoun, an adjective, a noun, etc.

Example: I got back __from__ Japan last week.

Dear Claudia,

Thanks for your letter. I'm pleased **(1) to hear / hearing / hear** that you're having a good time in York. How is the English course going? **(2) Are you allowed to / Do you have to** do lots of homework? What's your teacher **(3)_____** ? Is he friendly? You **(4) have to / should / must** write and tell me more!

I had **(5)_____** wonderful time in Japan. My friend, Akiko, invited me **(6) stay / to stay / staying** with her family in Kyoto. Do you remember her? She's the girl **(7)_____** visited me last summer. They have a house on a hill just outside Kyoto. There was a beautiful **(8)_____** of the city from my bedroom window. Akiko's family were incredibly kind and hospitable, and wouldn't let **(9) that I pay / me pay / me to pay** for anything. We ate out a lot. Japanese **(10)_____** is delicious – lots of vegetables, fish, and rice. The weather was really nice. It was warm and **(11)_____** , except on the last day, when it turned cloudy and chilly. I loved **(12) visit / visiting / to visit** the temples and gardens – the autumn colours were quite spectacular. **(13) I'll send / I send / I'm sending** you some photos when I've had them developed. We went everywhere by train. I think Japan has **(14)_____** best trains in the world. They're never late!

I **(15) had to / must / could** learn Japanese customs very quickly! In Japan you **(16) don't have to / aren't allowed to** wear your shoes in the house – you wear slippers **(17)_____** the host provides. And you **(18) have to / are allowed to** make a loud noise when you drink tea! (In fact, it's polite if you do!) I caught a cold while I was there, but I **(19) couldn't / shouldn't / didn't have to** blow my nose in public as it's considered to be rude.

Tomorrow my mother and father **(20) came / were going to come / are coming** to stay for a few days. I **(21) must / can** clean up the house before they arrive! Tomorrow evening **(22) we're going / we'll go / we're going** to go to the theatre, and on Wednesday Ann has invited us all **(23) go out / going out / to go out** for dinner. Apart from that, I haven't made any plans – perhaps **(24) I'm taking / I'll take / I'm going to take** them for a drive in the country. Or we could go to Stratford and visit the house **(25)_____** Shakespeare was born.

Anyway, I **(26) must / can** stop writing now – it's nearly midnight and I have to get up early tomorrow. Write again soon and let me **(27) know / knowing / to know** how you're getting along. Give my love to Frank when you see him. Hope **(28) see / seeing / to see** you soon!
Love,
Julia

| 28 |

Future forms

Complete Harry and Kate's conversation using the verb in brackets in the correct form (*will*, *going to*, or the Present Continuous).

Harry __Are__ you __going__ (go) on holiday at Easter? (1)_____ you _____ (go) away?

Kate Oh, I don't know .... In the summer we (2)_____ (visit) friends in Italy, so I think perhaps we (3)_____ (stay) in this country at Easter. What about you?

Harry We (4)_____ (rent) a cottage near Edinburgh. It (5)_____ (be) our first visit to Scotland. Jane (6)_____ (have) a baby in the summer, so we can't do anything too adventurous or tiring.

Kate Scotland – what a good idea! Maybe we (7)_____ (do) the same.

Harry Maybe we (8)_____ (see) you there!

| 16 |

can, must, and should

Read the following extract from a guidebook to Thailand. Fill in the blanks with *can*, *can't*, *must*, *mustn't*, *should*, or *shouldn't*. (Sometimes more than one answer is correct.)

Visas

Visitors to Thailand **must** apply for a visa. You (1)_____ enter the country without one.

Customs regulations

- You (2)_____ bring in up to 200 cigarettes.
- You (3)_____ bring in guns or drugs.
- You (4)_____ bring in one litre of wine or spirits.
- Cars (5)_____ be brought into Thailand for personal use, but you (6)_____ have a valid Driving Licence.
- You (7)_____ have at least US $250 with you. If you don't, you (8)_____ enter the country.

Advice to travellers

- It's usually very hot in Thailand, so you (9)_____ bring summer clothes.
- You (10)_____ drink tap water. (It's not always dangerous, but it's safer to buy bottled drinking water.)
- Traveller's cheques get a better exchange rate than cash, so you (11)_____ bring traveller's cheques with you.
- You (12)_____ tip taxi drivers. They don't expect tips, and they might be embarrassed.
- You (13)_____ make international phone calls from hotels as they are very expensive. You (14)_____ use the government telephone offices.
- You (15)_____ have medical insurance.

[ ] 15

like

Read the answers. Write questions with *like*.

Example: **What does she look like?**
She's tall and slim, and she wears glasses.

1 _____ ?
She's a little reserved but very friendly when you get to know her.

2 _____ ?
He's short with dark brown hair.

3 _____ ?
A disaster! It rained on Saturday, and we sat in a traffic jam most of Sunday!

4 _____ ?
They love playing tennis, and they like going skiing in the winter.

5 _____ ?
I don't know. We could go to the theatre.

6 _____ ?
He's really nice. Very outgoing and easy to talk to.

[ ] 12

Vocabulary

Match a word in **A** with its opposite in **B**.

A	B		A	B
young	clear		outgoing	poor
boring	delicious		industrial	talkative
polluted	historic		sunny	hot
disgusting	rude		formal	agricultural
modern	interesting		rural	shy
foggy	clean		freezing	cloudy
polite	tasteless		wealthy	cosmopolitan
tasty	elderly		quiet (people)	casual

[ ] 16

Translate

Translate the sentences into your language. Translate the ideas, not word for word.

1 Passengers must have a valid ticket.
2 You shouldn't steal from other people.
3 Nurses have to wear uniforms.
4 Do you have to go to school tomorrow?
5 You should eat more fruit.
6 Teenagers don't have to go to work.
7 Would you mind opening the window?
8 Your shoes will be ready next Thursday.
9 I'll phone you tonight.
10 She's going to study maths at university next year.
11 I'm having lunch with my mother tomorrow.
12 How are your parents?
13 What's Peter like?

[ ] 13

TOTAL [100]

Stop and check 3

General revision

1 Look at the letter from Alberto, who's staying in Bristol, in England, to his friend Paul. There are 33 gaps. After some gaps there is a verb in brackets. Put the verb in the correct tense.

Example: I **haven't visited** (not visit) Alcatraz yet.

When there is no verb in brackets, write *one* suitable word – a modal verb, an auxiliary verb, a conjunction, an adverb, etc.

Example: I'll write again **when** I have time.

Dear Paul,

My stay in England is coming to an end. In ten days' time I (1)_____ (be) back in Brazil. I can hardly believe that I (2)_____ (be) in Bristol for three months. The time (3)_____ (go) so quickly! Yesterday I (4)_____ (take) my final exams. As soon as I (5)_____ (get) the results, I (6)_____ (let) you know.

I'd really like to have a holiday (7)_____ the course finishes, but I have to go straight back to Brazil. If I (8)_____ (have) more time, I (9)_____ visit Scotland. Unfortunately I (10)_____ (not see) much of Britain – I (11)_____ even _____ (not be) to London yet!

I really like England. The people are friendly, the countryside's lovely, and the food's actually quite good. My friend Pablo loves it here. He even says he wouldn't (12)_____ living here. But for me the problem is the weather. I think I'd (13)_____ live somewhere warmer and drier. Recently it's been (14)_____ terrible – raining every day.

My host family (15)_____ (be) really nice to me. They've looked (16)_____ me very well. I'll miss them. But I'm looking (17)_____ to seeing my family again. My parents were planning to move to São Paulo. They might (18)_____ moved already. I (19)_____ (not hear) from them for a while. My brother (20)_____ (be) made redundant, so now he (21)_____ (look for) a new job. It (22)_____ be very hard for him and his wife. He says he (23)_____ have to move to another town where there are more jobs, but he's not sure.

Yesterday I (24)_____ (go) to the cinema with Pablo to see *Gladiator*. It's the fifth time Pablo (25)_____ (see) it! He (26)_____ really like it. Well, (27)_____ do I, but I wouldn't want to see it that many times!

I (28)_____ (apply) for a lot of jobs recently. Yesterday I (29)_____ (apply) for one with the United Nations. It (30)_____ be great if I (31)_____ (get) it, but I haven't got a very good chance. They want someone with fluent English and French, and my French isn't very good any more.

Anyway, I haven't picked up my plane ticket (32)_____ , so I have to go into town now and do that. See you next week. I'll give you a call (33)_____ I get home. Take care.
Best wishes,
Alberto

33

Present Perfect: active and passive

Complete the text with verbs from the box. Put them into the Present Perfect active or passive.

die	find	block	be	bury	advise
speak	hear	crash	kill	discover	

Here is the news. Donald Brash, who was Foreign Secretary for four years in the 1960s, (1)_____ . Mr. Brash was 79. Politicians from both the Labour and Conservative Parties (2)_____ warmly of his achievements.

Gale-force winds are causing chaos in southern England. Many roads (3)_____ by fallen trees and there (4)_____ a number of serious accidents involving lorries and coaches. The police (5)_____ motorists to stay at home unless their journey is absolutely necessary.

Three men who disappeared yesterday while climbing in the Appalachians (6)_____ safe and well.

Archaeologists (7)_____ the tomb of a Pharaoh near Cairo. The tomb (8)_____ in the sand for over 4,000 years.

And some late news. We (9)_____ just _____ that a plane (10)_____ at Prague Airport. First reports say that over 50 people (11)_____ . We'll bring you more news of this disaster as soon as we have it.

11

Conditionals and time clauses

Join a phrase in **A** with a time expression in **B** and a phrase in **C** to make 12 sentences. Use each conjunction twice.

A	B	C
I'd buy a new house	when	you go to work in the morning?
I'll clean up the house	if	you see her.
I'll call you	before	he gets the job?
If you want a ticket, you should phone the theatre	as soon as	my guests arrive.
What will he do		I won the lottery.
I'm watching TV at the moment, but I promise I'll help you		dinner is ready.
You'll recognize her		the ticket office opens.
Do you have breakfast		this programme finishes.

☐ 8

Vocabulary

1 Complete the story with phrasal verbs from the box. If the verb has an object, make sure it is in the correct position.

Example: He gave me a form and I __filled it in__ (it).

look for	go back	bring back	take back	sort out
make up	be in	give back	try on	be away

Last week I went to a clothes shop. I said to the assistant, 'I **(1)**_____ (a sweater) for my boyfriend. I like the blue one and the red one in the window, but I can't **(2)**_____ (my mind) which one to buy.' 'No problem,' said the assistant. 'Take them both and ask your boyfriend to **(3)**_____ (them). Then you can **(4)**_____ (the one he doesn't want) and I'll **(5)**_____ (you) (your money).' Well, my boyfriend chose the blue one, so I **(6)**_____ (the red one) to the shop. There was a different assistant. She said, 'I'm sorry. The assistant you spoke to made a mistake. We can't give you your money back.' I asked to see the manager. 'I'm afraid she **(7)**_____ on holiday,' said the assistant. 'Well, can I see the assistant manager?' 'No, he **(8)**_____ not _____ today, either. But he'll be here tomorrow, and he can **(9)**_____ (your problem) then.' I **(10)**_____ the next day and the assistant manager apologized and allowed me to return the red sweater.

☐ 10

2 Copy the chart. Put the adjectives in the correct columns.

tired	surprised	difficult	tasty	cold
astonished	beautiful	funny	impossible	filthy
pretty	frightened	delicious	terrified	dirty
exhausted	hilarious	freezing		

Base adjective	Strong adjective

☐ 18

3 Complete the sentences with adjectives from Exercise 2.

Example: Jack told a very __funny__ joke last night. We couldn't stop laughing!

1 Put the fire on. It's absolutely _____ in here!

2 I was very _____ to see him. I thought he was in Australia!

3 'How was your exam?' 'It was quite _____, but I managed to answer all the questions.'

4 We walked 20 kilometres. I was absolutely _____ when I got home!

5 'How was the meal?' 'It was very _____. I really enjoyed it.'

6 'What's the weather like?' 'It's quite _____, so put a coat on.'

☐ 6

Translate

Translate these sentences into your own language. Translate the ideas, not word for word.

1 He has lived in Berlin for ten years.

2 If I won the lottery, I'd travel around the world.

3 When I get home, I'll have a bath.

4 She might have gone out.

5 I saw the film yesterday.

6 If it's a nice day on Sunday, we'll have a picnic.

7 He must be furious!

☐ 14

TOTAL ☐ 100

Stop and check 4

General revision

Look at the letter from Mary, who is on holiday, to her friend Ana, who lives in France. There are 25 gaps. After some gaps there is a verb in brackets. Put the verb in the correct tense.

Example: I __have been learning__ (learn) English for two years.

When there is no verb in brackets, write *one* suitable word – a preposition, an auxiliary verb, a conjunction, an adverb, etc.

Example: I last saw her __in____ 1993.

> Dear Ana,
>
> Thanks for your letter. It was great to **(1)**_____ (hear) from you. So, what **(2)**_____ I _____ (do) recently? Well, my friend, Jennifer, **(3)**_____ (stay) with me for the past two weeks. I don't think you've met Jennifer, **(4)**_____ you? I **(5)**_____ (know) her since we were at university together. She's the one that **(6)**_____ (try) to get a job in Africa since she **(7)**_____ (graduate) last year. She hasn't had much luck, unfortunately.
>
> Anyway, we are having a great time. The weather **(8)**_____ (be) wonderful for weeks now, so we **(9)**_____ (drive) round the countryside. I wonder **(10)**_____ you are having such good weather in France. We have visited quite a few of the little villages around Oxford. I didn't know there **(11)**_____ (be) so many nice places to see here. Then, Jennifer said she **(12)**_____ never _____ (be) to Stonehenge, so we went there, too. **(13)**_____ Saturday, Harry **(14)**_____ (invite) Jennifer and me to dinner. He cooked a delicious meal. But I'm a bit worried about him – he **(15)**_____ (drink) too much recently. He **(16)**_____ (drink) two bottles of wine **(17)**_____ we were there on Saturday. He said he **(18)**_____ (be) under a lot of pressure at work since his promotion. But alcohol won't help, **(19)**_____ it?
>
> Jennifer **(20)**_____ (go back) to London the day **(21)**_____ tomorrow. She's asked me **(22)**_____ go with her. I'd love to, but unfortunately I haven't got **(23)**_____ time. I have more visitors arriving **(24)**_____ the end of the week!

> I have no **(25)**_____ when I'm next coming to France, but I hope it won't be too long. Take care.
> Love, Mary

[ ] 25

Indirect questions

Complete the answers.

Example: Has Pam gone to bed?
I don't know __if she's gone to bed__ .

1 Where does James live?
   I have no idea _____
2 Do you want to go out tonight?
   I'm not sure _____
3 Have I passed the exam?
   I'm sorry. I can't tell you _____
4 How many languages are there in the world?
   I haven't got a clue _____
5 Who's that woman over there?
   I can't remember _____
6 Did Ben buy some more sugar?
   I don't know _____

[ ] 12

Reported statements and questions

Turn the direct speech into reported speech.

Examples
Jim How are you? (direct speech)
Jim asked Sue __how she was__ . (reported speech)
Sue I'm fine, thanks. (direct speech)
Sue replied __that she was fine__ . (reported speech)

1 **Jim** I haven't seen you for ages. What have you been doing?
   Jim said _____
   and asked her _____
   Sue I've been abroad. I spent a year in Taiwan.
   Sue replied _____
   She said _____

       Photocopiable

2 **Jim** What do you think of Taiwan?

Jim asked her _____

Sue The people are very friendly and the food is great.

Sue said _____

and that _____

3 **Jim** Are you going to stay in this country now?

Jim asked her _____

Sue I'll probably stay for a while. Are you driving back to Manchester today?

Sue said _____

Then she asked Jim _____

4 **Jim** Yes, I am.

Jim said _____

Sue Can you give me a lift?

Sue asked him _____

| 24 |

Reported commands

Fill in the blank with the verb from the box that can be used to report the direct speech.

invited	told	ordered	asked	begged
warned	advised	refused	offered	reminded

1 'Would you like to spend the weekend with us?'

They _____ her to spend the weekend with them.

2 'Could you open the window, please?'

She _____ him to open the window.

3 'Go to bed immediately!'

Kate's mother _____ her to go to bed immediately.

4 'Don't forget to post the letter!'

He _____ me to post the letter.

5 'Park the car behind the van.'

The instructor _____ him to park behind the van.

6 'Please, please, turn down the music!'

Dan's sister _____ him to turn down the music.

7 'Don't play with matches. They're very dangerous.'

He _____ the children not to play with matches.

8 'I'll give you a lift to the airport.'

She _____ to give him a lift to the airport.

9 'I won't lend you any more money.'

Jeff _____ to lend me any more money.

10 Teacher to student: 'You need to study harder.'

She _____ him to study harder.

| 20 |

Vocabulary

Match a word in **A** with a word in **B** to make compound nouns.

A	B
tooth	paper
shopping	tan
fire	card
air	paste
credit	works
tea	room
hair	conditioning
toilet	dresser
sun	pot
waiting	centre

| 10 |

Translate

Translate these sentences into your own language. Translate the ideas, not word for word.

1 I've been learning English for three years.

2 How long have you known your teacher?

3 She speaks good English, doesn't she?

4 They told me that I had to go home.

5 She told him to do his homework carefully.

6 He said he'd been married before.

7 How long are you here for?

8 I don't know where she lives.

9 I'm sorry, I can't help you.

| 9 |

TOTAL | 100 |

Progress test 1

Exercise 1 Tenses

Put the verb in brackets in the correct tense. The tenses used are Present Simple, Present Continuous, Past Simple, Past Continuous, Past Perfect, and future with *will*. There are also examples of the infinitive.

Example: Yesterday I __went__ (go) to the city centre. I wanted __to do__ (do) some shopping.

Mrs Hay **(1)**_____ (drive) along a country road when she **(2)**_____ (see) a man at the side of the road. He **(3)**_____ (wave) and pointing at his car. Mrs Hay **(4)**_____ (stop) and **(5)**_____ (ask) the man if he was all right.

'My car's broken down,' said the man.

'Where do you want **(6)**_____ (go)?' asked Mrs Hay.

'London,' replied the man.

'Well, I **(7)**_____ (not go) to London, but I **(8)**_____ (give) you a lift to the station, if you like.'

On the way to the station they chatted.

'**(9)**_____ you _____ (work) in London?' asked Mrs Hay.

'No, I don't. I **(10)**_____ (run) my own business in Oxford. But today I **(11)**_____ (have) dinner with a friend in London – we always **(12)**_____ (have) dinner together on the last Friday of every month. I promised **(13)**_____ (meet) her at six o'clock.'

'There's a train at 1.30. I don't think you **(14)**_____ (be) late.'

When they arrived at the station, a train **(15)**_____ (stand) at the platform.

'That's your train,' said Mrs Hay. 'You **(16)**_____ (catch) it if you're quick.'

After the man **(17)**_____ (get out) of the car, Mrs Hay **(18)**_____ (drive away). A few minutes later she realized that she **(19)**_____ (make) a mistake – it was the wrong train. She went back to the station, but the train wasn't there. It **(20)**_____ already _____ (leave)! She went into the station and asked at the information

desk where the train was going. 'Edinburgh.' the information clerk told her.

'Where does it stop next?' asked Mrs Hay.

'It's the express service,' the clerk told her. 'It doesn't stop until it gets to Edinburgh.'

$\boxed{20}$

Exercise 2 Auxiliary verbs

Complete the sentences with the correct form of *be*, *do*, or *have* in the positive or negative.

1 That's Peter over there. He _____ wearing a red jacket.

2 '_____ you ever been to Spain?'
   'Yes, I went there in 2000.'

3 'Where _____ you live?'
   'I live in San Francisco.'

4 She's not allowed to drive. She _____ passed her driving test yet.

5 Tea _____ grown in India and China.

6 Who _____ you play tennis with yesterday?

7 When I arrived, they _____ having dinner.

8 She _____ usually go shopping on Saturdays. She prefers to go during the week.

$\boxed{8}$

Exercise 3 Irregular past tense

What is the Past Simple of the following irregular verbs?

1 become _____

2 catch _____

3 fall _____

4 fly _____

5 grow _____

6 lose _____

7 think _____

8 wear _____

9 write _____

$\boxed{9}$

© Oxford University Press **Photocopiable**

Exercise 4 Question formation

Look at the chart.

	Pierre	Donna and Mike
Nationality	French	Canadian
Occupation	Teacher	Students
City	Paris	Toronto
Holiday last year	2 weeks in Morocco	A month in the US
Next holiday	3 weeks in Italy	2 weeks in Greece, visiting ancient ruins

Using the information in the chart, write an appropriate question.

Example
Where do Donna and Mike come from?
They come from Canada.

1 _____
   He comes from France.
2 _____
   He lives in Paris.
3 _____
   Morocco.
4 _____
   Three weeks.
5 _____
   They're students.
6 _____
   A month.
7 _____
   Because they're very interested in ancient ruins.

[7]

Exercise 5 Verb patterns

Choose the correct verb form.

1 He invited me *stay* / *to stay* / *staying* at his house.
2 I can't stand *clean* / *to clean* / *cleaning*.
3 Write soon and let me *know* / *to know* / *knowing* what your plans are.
4 Joe forgot *post* / *to post* / *posting* the letter.
5 I don't mind *cook* / *to cook* / *cooking*, as long as I don't have to do the shopping.

6 The climb was very long and tiring, so we often stopped *have* / *to have* / *having* a rest.
7 He's a very funny person. He always makes me *laugh* / *to laugh* / *laughing*.
8 His mother told Ben *wash* / *to wash* / *washing* his hands before dinner.

[8]

Exercise 6 Correct the sentences

There is one mistake in each of the following sentences. Find it and write the corrected sentence below.

1 Where are you born?
   _____
2 On weekdays they're usually getting up at 6.30.
   _____
3 'Where's James?' 'He does the washing up in the kitchen.'
   _____
4 During I was on holiday I read six novels.
   _____
5 I no could swim until I was twelve.
   _____
6 You shouldn't to take photographs in the theatre.
   _____
7 We didn't allowed to wear jewellery at school.
   _____
8 You mustn't pay in cash. You can also pay by credit card.
   _____
9 Bob's a police officer. He have to wear a uniform.
   _____
10 Student to teacher: 'Must I to finish this exercise tonight?'
   _____
11 I don't think you must hitch-hike. It could be dangerous.
   _____
12 'We haven't got any milk left.' 'Haven't we? I'm going to the shop to buy some.'
   _____

[12]

Exercise 7 Numbers

Match the numbers and words.

1	1934	a	nineteen euros and thirty-four cents
2	19.34%	b	nineteen and three-quarters
3	193.4	c	nineteen point three four percent
4	€ 19.34	d	nineteen thirty-four
5	19 ¾	e	a hundred and ninety-three point four

5

Exercise 8 Word order

Put the words in the correct order.

1 watching / while / TV / I / rang / was / phone / the

_____

2 do / what / you / get / have / time / up / to ?

_____

3 at / we / school / aren't / smoke / to / allowed

_____

4 she / been / Russia / has / to / ever ?

_____

5 to / our / with / friends / us / invited / stay / them

_____

6 think / win / I / Mexico / the / don't / will / match

_____

7 Seoul / is / husband / in / next / my / to / year / going / work

_____

8 phone / had / couldn't / she / lost / him / number / she / his / because

_____

8

Exercise 9 Word formation

Write the nationality or the profession.

1 Brazil _____   4 novel _____
2 Greece _____   5 poem _____
3 Japan _____

Write the adjectives.

6 cloud _____   9 wind _____
7 fog _____   10 rain _____
8 sunshine_____

10

Exercise 10 Everyday English

What would you say in these situations?

1 You are in a cafe. Offer to buy your friend a cup of coffee.

_____

2 You arrive late for a meeting. Apologize and say why you are late.

_____

3 Your brother has just come home from the cinema. Ask him for his opinion of the film.

_____

4 You are on a bus. Politely ask the passenger next to the window to open the window.

_____

5 Somebody asks you, 'What does your teacher look like?' What do you say?

_____

6 You are in a clothes shop. You are looking at some sweaters but you don't want to buy anything. The shop assistant comes up to you and says, 'Can I help you?' What do you say?

_____

7 You are in a hotel at reception. Ask the receptionist to order you a taxi to go to the station.

_____

7

Exercise 11 Vocabulary

Complete the sentences.

1 'Are you a v_____?'
   'Yes, I am. I never eat meat.'
2 The English painter Thomas Gainsborough painted many p_____ of people.
3 The air in the city centre is very p_____.
   You can hardly breathe when the traffic's heavy!
4 Many countries have their own f_____
   t_____ – special stories for children.
5 'These vegetables are delicious. Did you get them at the supermarket?'
   'No, they're h_____.'
6 I've just finished reading a b_____ about Ernest Hemingway. He had an interesting life.

6

TOTAL 100

Progress test 2

Exercise 1 Tenses and verb forms

Put the verb in parentheses in the correct tense. Some verbs are passive, and there are also examples of the second conditional, indirect questions, infinitives, gerunds, and reported statements and requests.

Example

I **started**_____ (start) teaching five years ago. I really like **teaching**_____ (teach) children.

An Interview with Sarah Jenkins

Sarah Jenkins is an English teacher. She **(1)**_____ (work) in a language school in Brighton. She **(2)**_____ (teach) English since she **(3)**_____ (leave) university five years ago. I asked her first if she **(4)**_____ (enjoy) teaching English.

'Yes, I do,' she replied. 'It's hard work, but it's very rewarding.'

'**(5)**_____ you ever _____ (work) abroad?'

'Yes,' replied Sarah, 'I **(6)**_____ (spend) two years in Madrid. But the school closed and I **(7)**_____ (be) made redundant. Luckily, some of my students asked me if I **(8)**_____ (continue) to teach them privately, so I stayed in Madrid.'

'And how long **(9)**_____ you _____ (teach) in Brighton?' I asked.

'Since I came back from Madrid, three years ago.'

I then asked Sarah what the most memorable moment of her career was.

'Well, a funny thing **(10)**_____ (happen) while I **(11)**_____ (work) at the school in Madrid. I had a student called Gloria. On some days, she was the best student in the class. But on other days she performed really badly. I tried very hard **(12)**_____ (help) her, but things only got worse. Then, one day, I met Gloria on the street and asked her about her boyfriend. (The day before she **(13)**_____ (tell) me a sad story about him.) She looked surprised and told me that her name **(14)**_____ (be) Victoria, not Gloria. She continued, 'My twin sister and I **(15)**_____ (take turns) in your classes since September – two for the price of one!' After that, it was much easier to teach them. At the beginning of each class I simply asked, 'Are you Gloria or Victoria today?'

Finally, I asked Sarah about her plans for the future.

'Well, I'm very interested in teaching young children, so next September I **(16)**_____ (do) a special training course.'

'And are you going to stay in Britain, or would you like to work abroad again?'

'I **(17)**_____ (promote) recently. I'm now Director of Studies. So I think I **(18)**_____ (stay) here for a few more years. Of course, if someone **(19)**_____ (offer) me a well-paid job in Italy or Greece, I **(20)**_____ (take) it, but that's not very likely!'

	20

Exercise 2 Conditionals

Using the prompts, write a sentence in either the first or the second conditional.

1 'Are you coming to town with me this afternoon?'
'Perhaps. If I / finish / decorating the living room, I / come / with you.'

_____

2 'I don't have any money. If I / have / some money, I / buy / you lunch.'

_____

3 'I always go on holiday to Italy. If the weather in Scotland / be / better, I / go / on holiday / there.'

_____

4 'I've got so much work to do!' 'I'm sorry. I have a lot of work, too. If I / have / more time, I / help / you.'

_____

5 'I'm a teacher. If I / be / the Minister for Education, I / spend / more money on schools.'

_____

6 'I've lost my address book.'
'If I / find it, I / bring it to you.'

_____

7 'I have a temperature. If I / feel better tomorrow / I go back to school.'

_____

	7

Exercise 3 Passives

Make these active sentences passive.

1 Do they still build ships in Scotland?
   Are _____

2 Do you think aliens will ever visit the Earth?
   Do you think the Earth _____

3 The Chinese invented printing.
   Printing _____

4 You mustn't take photographs in the museum.
   Photographs _____

5 They have recently discovered oil near Argentina.
   Oil _____

6 They're planning a big celebration to mark the start of the Olympics.
   A big celebration _____

7 The police think someone might have murdered him.
   The police think he _____

8 They didn't know the bones were human until they had carried out a number of tests.
   They didn't know the bones were human until a number of tests _____

9 In the next decade, car manufacturers are going to make more electric cars.
   In the next decade, _____

10 If the car is fitted with an alarm, they can't steal it.
   If the car is fitted with an alarm, it _____
   _____

[10]

Exercise 4 Modals

Finish each sentence (b) so that it means the same as sentence (a).

Example
(a) He has black hair and brown eyes. I'm sure he's not Swedish.
(b) He has black hair and brown eyes. He can't **be Swedish**.

1 (a) The dog's barking. I'm sure he's hungry.
   (b) The dog's barking. He must _____

2 (a) There's no food in his bowl. I'm certain he hasn't eaten anything since this morning.
   (b) There's no food in his bowl. He can't
   _____

3 (a) Sally hasn't been in touch with me. Perhaps she phoned while I was out.
   (b) Sally hasn't been in touch with me. She could
   _____

4 (a) Ah, the phone's ringing. Maybe it's Sally.
   (b) Ah, the phone's ringing. It could _____

5 (a) Why did the car crash? Perhaps the driver didn't see the red light.
   (b) Why did the car crash? The driver might
   _____

6 (a) I'm sure it was Tom I saw at the theatre last night.
   (b) It must _____

7 (a) Why is that man standing at the side of the road? Perhaps he's trying to hitch a lift
   (b) Why is that man standing at the side of the road?
   He might _____

[7]

Exercise 5 Time expressions

Complete the sentences with *in*, *on*, *at*, *ago*, *for*, *since*, or nothing.

1 I left college _____ 2002.
2 What are you doing _____ next Thursday?
3 I like to go to bed _____ midnight on Saturdays.
4 He came to live here four years _____.
5 He'd been painting _____ many years before he sold his first picture.
6 Shakespeare was born _____ 23 April, 1564.
7 Spring begins _____ March.
8 We always eat turkey _____ Christmas.
9 _____ you left, there have been many changes.
10 I started my new job _____ last Monday.
11 His dog died five months _____ and he still misses him.
12 I've been studying Spanish _____ I was 11 years old.

[12]

Exercise 6 Reported statements and questions

Put the direct speech into reported speech.

1 'I always play football on Saturdays,' he said.
   _____

2 'We've been waiting since six o'clock,' she said.
   _____

3 'Where did you go last night?' she asked me.
   _____

4 'Will you stay in a hotel?' I asked him.
   _____

5 'I'm really looking forward to my holiday,' he said.
   _____

6 'Do you like living alone?' she asked me.
   _____

   [6]

Exercise 7 Reported commands

Use the verbs in the box to change the direct speech into reported speech. Not all the verbs are used.

| ask beg refuse offer remind advise order invite |

1 'Don't forget to take all your belongings with you,' said the driver to the passengers as they left the coach.
   As the passengers left the coach, the driver _____
   _____

2 'If I were you, I wouldn't visit that area late at night,' said the travel agent to the young couple.
   The travel agent _____

3 'Would you like to stay at my house?' said Peter to James.
   Peter _____

4 'I won't eat my vegetables!' said Timmy.
   Timmy _____

5 'I'll give you a lift into town,' said Ray to Mary.
   Ray _____

6 'Put that diamond necklace down!' the police officer said to the burglar.
   The police officer _____

   [6]

Exercise 8 Correct the sentences

There is one mistake in each of the following sentences. Find it and write the corrected sentence below.

1 How long do you live in Miami?
   _____

2 Yesterday evening I have seen a really funny film.
   _____

3 I'll phone you as soon as I'll arrive.
   _____

4 If I win a million pounds, I'd buy a Ferrari.
   _____

5 I work in this office since 1999.
   _____

6 'I went to Canada last year.' 'So have I.'
   _____

7 If you have a headache, you should to take an aspirin.
   _____

8 'What's the matter?' 'I've just been seeing a car accident.'
   _____

9 Could you tell me how much does this cost?
   _____

10 She said me that she was hungry.
   _____

   [10]

Exercise 9 Everyday English

What would you say in these situations?

1 Somebody phones your house and wants to speak to your son, but he isn't at home. Tell the caller where your son is and offer to take a message.
   _____
   _____
   _____

2 You phone the travel agent to inquire about flights to the US. The office is closed so you leave a message on the answer phone. Introduce yourself, say why you are phoning, ask the travel agent to call you back, leave your number, and end the call.
   _____
   _____
   _____

3 Your friend says she has a headache. Make helpful suggestions.

_____

_____

_____

4 Your brother phones you and says he's just won £100,000 in the lottery. Suggest things he could do with the money.

_____

_____

_____

5 You have arranged to go to the cinema with your friend. But on that day your sister has an accident and is taken to hospital. You want to visit her in the evening and have to cancel the appointment with your friend. What will you say to him?

_____

_____

_____

6 Your friend tells you he has just failed to get the job he really wanted.

_____

_____

_____

| 6 |

Exercise 10 Adjectives

Use *un-*, *in-*, or *im-* to make these adjectives negative.

1 tidy   _____
2 possible   _____
3 sensitive   _____
4 patient   _____
5 sociable   _____
6 comfortable   _____

| 6 |

Exercise 11 Phrasal verbs

Match a verb from **A** with an adverb/preposition from **B** to complete the sentences. Put the verbs in the correct form.

A	B
pick	out
look	up
cut	off
go	
take	

1 This is a very bad storm. I hope the lights don't _____ .

2 We _____ from JFK airport at half past two and landed in London only a few hours later.

3 Hello? Hello? Is anyone there? Oh no, we've been _____ .

4 He found it very difficult to _____ Japanese while he was working there.

5 Could you _____ *torch* in your dictionary? I don't know what it means.

| 5 |

Exercise 12 Compound nouns

Complete the sentences with a compound noun formed with *room*, *card*, or *traffic*.

1 I'm sorry I'm late. I got stuck in a _____ in the town centre.

2 I don't have any cash. Can I pay by _____ ?

3 'Have you got her work number?' 'Yes, she gave me a _____ at our last meeting.'

4 'What's the matter?' 'I parked outside the bank. A _____ saw me and gave me a parking ticket!'

5 Good morning. Please take a seat in the _____ and Dr Cooper will see you when he's ready.

| 5 |

TOTAL | 100 |

Answer keys

Extra ideas Units 1–3

Song – California Dreamin'

2 1 *Church*, *preacher*, *knees*, and *pray* are all connected with going to church. A preacher is another name for a minister in some Christian churches.
  2 Los Angeles, often abbreviated to L.A. (/el 'eɪ/), is a city in California. California is usually sunny.

3 a No. His hometown is probably Los Angeles. He is somewhere far away and much colder.
  b He wishes he was in California, so possible answers are that he feels homesick, depressed, sad – he has some kind of problem.

4   2 grey   8 passed
    3 walk   9 down
    4 day   10 pray
    5 warm   11 cold
    6 day   12 stay
    7 stopped   13 day
    Note: Point out that   14 brown
    walked into is better   15 grey
    English. We usually   16 walk
    say *stopped at*, not   17 day
    stopped into. This   18 day
    is an example of
    poetic licence.

5 a Because he knows the singer will stay in the church to keep out of the cold. Cold weather means more church-goers.
  b There are many interpretations possible. Perhaps the singer has a secret, and he knows he has to tell 'her', but if he does, it means he won't be able to go home. One possible story is that his girlfriend is in California, but for some reason he has to end the relationship. He's been for a walk to think about what he should do. He doesn't know whether to tell her and end the relationship, or not tell her and be able to go back and see her in L.A.

Poem – A Man Is Made

2 **Passive:**
  is made (×3)   Is ... being born

  Active:
  make (×2)   wonder   strikes   keeps
  dream   sets   eat   takes   's dying

Extra ideas Units 4–6

Song – Why Does it Always Rain on Me?

2 a He is pessimistic.
  b There are many possible answers. Perhaps his girlfriend has left him. Perhaps he has heard some bad news. Perhaps he always feels like this.

3   2 close
    3 these lights
    4 Sunny
    5 strangest
    6 lied
    7 shining
    8 blue
    9 lightning
   10 cold

4 a *Why does it always rain on me?* means *Why do bad things always happen to me?*
  b *I'm seeing a tunnel at the end of all these lights* is a play on the expression, *I can see the light at the end of the tunnel*, which means, even though times are bad now, they will be OK in the future. The singer seems to be saying that even though there are good things happening now, it will end badly. It's quite a funny play on words.
  c *Is it because I lied when I was 17?* can be interpreted literally: Are these things happening because he lied? It is more likely, however, that the singer is speaking more generally. He's saying, *What terrible thing have I done to deserve this?*

5 Students' own ideas. However, the song is so miserable, and the singer is such a moaner, that it is probably best to guide the students to recognize that this song is quite funny and tongue-in-cheek. Basically, it is a young person, sitting slumped in his room, feeling ridiculously sorry for himself. It will probably depend on the ages of your students as to how they wish to interpret this.

Extra ideas Units 10–12

Prepositions of time

  a in   f in   k at
  b in   g at   l *nothing*
  c on   h in   m at
  d on   i *nothing* n in
  e *nothing* j at   o on

2 a Jack's mother told him, 'I won't support you any more.'
  b Jack's mother/She ordered him to find a job.
  c Jack said he would do it next time.
  d 'She has no chance of recovering until someone can make her laugh,' said the doctors.
  e The father promised that the first man who made his daughter laugh would have his permission to marry her.

Stop and check 1

General revision

1	arrived	17	went
2	ago	18	to buy
3	'm staying	19	was putting
4	works	20	'd forgotten
5	isn't working	21	it
6	haven't asked	22	was
7	think	23	was
8	an	24	was walking
9	'm having	25	met
10	although/but	26	for
11	took	27	saw
12	to	28	was working
13	while	29	's studying
14	'd visited	30	the
15	decided	31	really
16	'd seen	32	like

Questions

Where were you born?
When did you win Wimbledon?
How long have you been a professional tennis player?
How often do you play tennis?
What are you doing now/at the moment?

Auxiliary verbs

1	were	6	Did
2	Have	7	are
3	is	8	didn't
4	has	9	Had/Has
5	don't	10	was

Vocabulary

1

play	do
golf	aerobics
basketball	sports
	the shopping
	your homework
	the washing

make	go	have
faces	on holiday	a meeting
a mistake	sightseeing	a nice time
a phone	jogging	a headache
call	skiing	a party
a decision	home	a shower

2 1 enjoy (others not used with -ing)
   2 palette (others are works of art)
   3 literature (others are people who write)
   4 beautiful (an adjective; others are adverbs)
   5 newspaper (not fiction)
   6 however (all the others join sentences together)

7 teepee (only one made of material: skins, cloth, or canvas / not holiday accommodation)
8 make (a main verb; others can be auxiliaries)
9 read (it's an activity you do sitting down)
10 was (it's in the past tense)

Active or passive?

1	supplies	7	took
2	was started	8	was carried
3	was born	9	has changed
4	was employed	10	are … expanding
5	needed	11	are sent
6	was sent		

Translate
(self check)

Stop and check 2

General revision

1	to hear	15	had to
2	Do you have to	16	aren't allowed to
3	like	17	which
4	must	18	are allowed to
5	a	19	couldn't
6	to stay	20	are coming
7	who	21	must
8	view	22	we're going
9	me pay	23	to go out
10	food	24	I'll take
11	sunny/dry/clear	25	where
12	visiting	26	must
13	I'll send	27	know
14	the	28	to see

Future forms

1 Are … going
2 're going to visit / 're visiting
3 'll stay
4 're going to rent / 're renting
5 'll be/is
6 is going to have / 's having
7 'll do
8 'll see

can, must, and should

1	can't	9	should
2	can	10	shouldn't
3	can't/mustn't	11	should
4	can	12	shouldn't
5	can	13	shouldn't
6	must	14	should
7	must	15	should
8	can't		

like

1 What's she like?
2 What does he look like?
3 What was the weekend like?
4 What do they like doing?
5 What would you like to do?
6 What's he like?

Vocabulary

A	B
young	elderly
boring	interesting
polluted	clean
disgusting	delicious
modern	historic
foggy	clear
polite	rude
tasty	tasteless
outgoing	shy
industrial	agricultural
sunny	cloudy
formal	casual
rural	cosmopolitan
freezing	hot
wealthy	poor
quiet (people)	talkative

Translate
(self check)

Stop and check 3

General revision

1	'll be / 'm going to be	18	have
2	've been	19	haven't heard
3	's gone	20	was / 's been
4	took	21	's looking for
5	get / 've got	22	must
6	'll let	23	may/might
7	when	24	went
8	had	25	's seen
9	'd	26	must
10	haven't seen	27	so
11	haven't … been	28	've applied
12	mind	29	applied
13	rather	30	would
14	really/absolutely	31	got
15	's been/are	32	yet
16	after	33	when
17	forward		

Present Perfect: active and passive

1 has died
2 have spoken
3 have been blocked
4 have been
5 have advised
6 have been found
7 have discovered
8 has been buried
9 have … heard
10 has crashed
11 have been killed

Conditionals and time clauses

I'd buy a new house if I won the lottery.
I'll clean up the house before my guests arrive.
I'll call you when dinner is ready.
If you want a ticket, you should call the theatre as soon as the ticket office opens.
What will he do if he gets the job?
I'm watching TV at the moment, but I promise I'll help you as soon as this programme finishes.
You'll recognize her when you see her.
Do you have breakfast before you go to work in the morning?

Vocabulary

1
1 'm looking for a sweater
2 make up my mind/make my mind up
3 try them on
4 bring back the one he doesn't want/bring the one he doesn't want back
5 give you your money back/give you back your money
6 took the red one back/took back the red one
7 's away
8 's ... in
9 sort out your problem/sort your problem out
10 went back

2
Base	Strong
tired	exhausted
surprised	astonished
difficult	impossible
tasty	delicious
cold	freezing
funny	hilarious
pretty	beautiful
frightened	terrified
dirty	filthy

3
1 freezing
2 surprised
3 difficult
4 exhausted
5 tasty
6 cold

Translate

(self check)

Stop and check 4

General revision

1 hear
2 have ... been doing
3 has been staying
4 have
5 've known
6 's been trying
7 graduated
8 's been
9 've been driving
10 whether/if
11 were
12 'd ... been
13 On/Last
14 invited
15 's been drinking
16 drank
17 while
18 's been
19 will
20 's going back
21 after
22 to
23 the/enough
24 at
25 idea

Indirect questions

1 I have no idea where James lives.
2 I'm not sure if/whether I want to go out tonight.
3 I'm sorry. I can't tell you if/whether you've passed the exam.
4 I haven't got a clue how many languages there are in the world.
5 I can't remember who that woman over there is.
6 I don't know if/whether Ben bought some more sugar.

Reported statements and questions

1 Jim said (that) he hadn't seen Sue for ages and asked her what she'd been doing.
Sue replied (that) she'd been abroad. She said (that) she'd spent a year in Taiwan.
2 Jim asked her what she thought of Taiwan.
Sue said (that) the people were very friendly and (that) the food was great.
3 Jim asked her if/whether she was going to stay in this country now.
Sue said (that) she'd probably stay for a while. Then she asked Jim if/whether he was driving back to Manchester that day.
4 Jim said (that) he was.
Sue asked him if/whether he could give her a lift.

Reported commands

1 invited
2 asked
3 ordered
4 reminded
5 told
6 begged
7 warned
8 offered
9 refused
10 advised

Vocabulary

toothpaste
shopping centre
fireworks
air conditioning
credit card
tea pot
hairdresser
toilet paper
suntan
waiting room

Translate

(self check)

Progress test 1

Exercise 1
1	was driving	11	'm having
2	saw	12	have
3	was waving	13	to meet
4	stopped	14	'll be
5	asked	15	was standing
6	to go	16	'll catch
7	'm not going	17	'd got out
8	'll give	18	drove away
9	Do … work	19	'd made
10	run	20	'd … left

Exercise 2
1	's	5	is
2	Have	6	did
3	do	7	were
4	hasn't	8	doesn't

Exercise 3
1	became	6	lost
2	caught	7	thought
3	fell	8	wore
4	flew	9	wrote
5	grew		

Exercise 4
1 Where does Pierre come from?
2 Where does he live?
3 Where did he go on holiday last year?
4 How long is he going to spend in Italy?
5 What do Donna and Mike do?
6 How long did they spend in the US?
7 Why are they going to Greece?

Exercise 5
1	to stay	5	cooking
2	cleaning	6	to take
3	know	7	laugh
4	to post	8	to wash

Exercise 6
1 Where were you born?
2 On weekdays they usually get up at six thirty.
3 'Where's James?'
'He's doing the washing up in the kitchen.'
4 While I was on holiday I read six novels.
5 I couldn't swim until I was 12.
6 You shouldn't take photographs in the theatre.
7 We weren't allowed to wear jewellery at school.
8 You don't have to pay in cash. You can also pay by credit card.
9 Bob's a police officer. He has to wear a uniform.
10 Student to teacher: 'Must I / Do I have to finish this exercise tonight?

11 I don't think you should hitch-hike. It could be dangerous.
12 'Haven't we? I'll go to the shop to buy some.'

Exercise 7
1 d   2 c   3 e   4 a   5 b

Exercise 8
1 While I was watching TV, the phone rang.
2 What time do you have to get up?
3 We aren't allowed to smoke at school.
4 Has she ever been to Russia?
5 Our friends invited us to stay with them.
6 I don't think Mexico will win the match.
7 My husband is going to work in Seoul next year.
8 She couldn't call him because she had lost his number.

Exercise 9
1	Brazilian	6	cloudy
2	Greek	7	foggy
3	Japanese	8	sunny
4	novelist	9	windy
5	poet	10	rainy

Exercise 10
(These are sample answers. Variations are possible.)
1 Can I/Let me buy you a cup of coffee.
2 Sorry I'm late. I got held up in traffic.
3 What did you think of the film?
4 Would you mind opening the window, please?
5 She's short with long, dark hair.
6 No, thanks. I'm just looking.
7 Could you call me a taxi to go to the station, please?

Exercise 11
1	vegetarian	4	fairy tales
2	portraits	5	home-grown
3	polluted	6	biography

Progress test 2

Exercise 1
1	works
2	's been teaching
3	left
4	enjoyed
5	Have … worked
6	spent
7	was
8	would continue
9	have … been teaching
10	happened
11	was working
12	to help
13	'd told
14	was
15	have been taking turns
16	'm doing/'m going to do
17	was promoted/'ve been promoted
18	'll stay
19	offered (or offers)
20	'd take (or 'll take)

Exercise 2
1 'If I finish decorating the living room, I'll come with you.'
2 'If I had some money, I'd buy you lunch.'
3 'If the weather in Scotland was/were better, I'd go on holiday there.'
4 'If I had more time, I'd help you.'
5 'If I were the Minister for Education, I'd spend more money on schools.'
6 'If I find it, I'll bring it to you.'
7 'If I feel better tomorrow, I'll go back to school.'

Exercise 3
1 Are ships still built in Scotland?
2 Do you think the Earth will ever be visited by aliens?
3 Printing was invented by the Chinese.
4 Photographs mustn't be taken in the museum.
5 Oil has recently been discovered near Argentina.
6 A big celebration is being planned to mark the start of the Olympics.
7 The police think he might have been murdered.
8 They didn't know the bones were human until a number of tests had been carried out.
9 In the next decade, more electric cars are going to be made.
10 If the car is fitted with an alarm, it can't be stolen.

Exercise 4

1 He must be hungry.
2 He can't have eaten anything since this morning.
3 She could have phoned while I was out.
4 It could be Sally now.
5 The driver might not have seen the red light.
6 It must have been Tom I saw at the theatre last night.
7 He might be trying to hitch a lift.

Exercise 5

1	in	7	in
2	(nothing)	8	at
3	at	9	Since
4	ago	10	(nothing)
5	for	11	ago
6	on	12	since

Exercise 6

1 He said that he always played football on Saturdays.
2 She said that they'd been waiting since six o'clock.
3 She asked me where I had been the night before.
4 I asked him if/whether he would stay in a hotel.
5 He said he was really looking forward to his holiday.
6 She asked me if/whether I liked living alone.

Exercise 7

1 As the passengers left the bus, the driver reminded them to take all their belongings with them.
2 The travel agent advised the young couple not to visit that area late at night.
3 Peter invited James to stay at his house.
4 Timmy refused to eat his vegetables.
5 Ray offered (to give) Mary a lift to the airport.
6 The police officer ordered the burglar to put down the diamond necklace.

Exercise 8

1 How long have you lived/have you been living in Miami?
2 Yesterday evening I saw a really funny film.
3 I'll phone you as soon as I arrive.
4 If I won a million pounds, I'd buy a Ferrari.
5 I've worked/'ve been working in this office since 1999.
6 'I went to Canada last year.'
   'So did I.'
7 If you have a headache, you should take an aspirin.

8 'What's the matter?'
   'I've just seen a car accident.'
   Or 'I just saw a car accident.'
9 Could you tell me how much this costs?
10 She told me/said to me that she was hungry.

Exercise 9

(These are sample answers. Variations are possible.)
1 I'm sorry, he isn't in. He just went out to the shops. Can I take a message?
2 Hello. My name is Bill Smith. I'm calling to inquire about flights to the US. Could you call me back, please? My number is 555-7157. Thank you.
3 You'd better take an aspirin. And maybe you should go and lie down for a while.
4 Why don't you buy a new car?/If I were you, I wouldn't spend it, I'd invest it.
5 I'm sorry, but I'm afraid I can't go to the cinema with you tonight. My sister's had an accident and is in the hospital. I really want to visit her this evening.
6 I am sorry. But I'm sure you'll get a job soon.

Exercise 10

1 untidy
2 impossible
3 insensitive
4 impatient
5 unsociable
6 uncomfortable

Exercise 11

1 go out
2 took off
3 cut off
4 pick up
5 look up

Exercise 12

1 traffic jam
2 credit card
3 business card
4 traffic warden
5 waiting room

Word list

Here is a list of most of the new words in the units of *New Headway Intermediate – the NEW edition* Student's Book.

adj = adjective
adv = adverb
US = American English
coll = colloquial
conj = conjunction
pl = plural
prep = preposition
pron = pronoun
pp = past participle
n = noun
v = verb

Unit 1

achievement *n* /ə'tʃiːvmənt/
advertisement *n* /əd'vɜːtɪsmənt/
afford (can't) *v* /ə'fɔːd/
ages *n* /'eɪdʒɪz/
amazing *adj* /ə'meɪzɪŋ/
ambassador *n* /aem'baesədə(r)/
amount *n* /ə'maʊnt/
ancient *adj* /'eɪnʃənt/
apologize *v* /ə'pɒlədʒaɪz/
architectural *adj* /ɑːkɪ'tektʃərəl/
assassinate *v* /ə'saesɪneɪt/

benefit *v* /'benəfɪt/
break (from work) *n* /breɪk/
bright *adj* /braɪt/
brochure *n* /'brəʊʃə(r)/
builder *n* /'bɪldə(r)/
butterfly *n* /'bʌtəflaɪ/

celebrity *n* /sə'lebrəti/
century *n* /'sentʃəri/
come round *v* /ˌkʌm 'raʊnd/
commercialized *adj*
    /kə'mɜːʃəlaɪzd/
communicate *v* /kə'mjuːnɪkeɪt/
computer *n* /kəm'pjuːtə(r)/
corn *n* /kɔːn/

destroy *v* /dɪ'strɔɪ/
dishwasher *n* /'dɪʃwɒʃə(r)/
drug abuse *n* /'drʌg əˌbjuːs/

email *n, v* /'iːmeɪl/
estimate *v* /'estɪmeɪt/

famine *n* /'faemɪn/
freezing *adj* /'friːzɪŋ/
full-time *adj* /ˌfʊl 'taɪm/

galaxy *n* /'gaeləksi/
get stuck *v* /ˌget 'stʌk/
giant adj, *n* /'dʒaɪənt/
go mad *v* /ˌgəʊ 'maed/
go out with (sb) *v* /ˌgəʊ 'aʊt wɪð/
goodwill *adj* /ˌgʊd'wɪl/
gorgeous *adj* /'gɔːdʒəs/
greed *n* /griːd/

hang on (= wait) informal *v*
    /ˌhaeŋ 'ɒn/
health care *n* /'helθ ˌkeə(r)/
hectic *adj* /'hektɪk/
huge *adj* /hjuːdʒ/
humble *adj* /'hʌmbl/

inconvenience *n* /ˌɪnkən'viːniəns/
increase *v* /ɪn'kriːs/
interactivity *n* /ˌɪntəraek'tɪvəti/
Internet *n* /'ɪntənet/

knowledge *n* /'nɒlɪdʒ/

leap *n, v* /liːp/
lift (= ride in a car) *n* /lɪft/
loo (= toilet) informal *n* /luː/

mankind *n* /ˌmaen'kaɪnd/
mess *n* /mes/
mobile phone *n* /ˌməʊbaɪl 'fəʊn/

musical instrument *n* /ˌmjuːzɪkl 'ɪnstrəmənt/
noticeable *adj* /'nəʊtɪsəbl/
nuclear weapon *n*
    /ˌnjuːkliə 'wepn/

observatory *n* /əb'zɜːvətri/
Olympic Games *n* /əˌlɪmpɪk 'geɪmz/
online *adj* /ɒn'laɪn/
order *n, v* /'ɔːdə(r)/

packing and postage *n* /ˌpaekɪŋ ən 'pəʊstɪdʒ/
payment *n* /'peɪmənt/
perform *v* /pə'fɔːm/
pet *n* /pet/
pick up *v* /ˌpɪk 'ʌp/
popcorn *n* /'pɒpkɔːn/
process *v* /'prəʊses/

race (of people) *n* /reɪs/
ray (the sun's rays) *n* /reɪ/
record *v* /rɪ'kɔːd/
revolutionize *v* /ˌrevə'luːʃənaɪz/
rise *v* /raɪz/

save (a life) *v* /ˌseɪv/
skid *v* /skɪd/
solar system *n* /'səʊlə ˌsɪstəm/
space probe *n* /'speɪs ˌprəʊb/
sparkling *adj* /'spɑːklɪŋ/
stage *n* /steɪdʒ/
stand/(can't stand) *v* /'staend/
stand for (sth) *v* /'staend fə/
statement *n* /'steɪtmənt/
step *n, v* /step/
stuff (= things in general) informal *n* /stʌf/
surely *adv* /'ʃʊəli/
swimming costume *n* /'swɪmɪŋ ˌkɒstjuːm/

take part *v* /ˌteɪk 'pɑːt/
take place *v* /ˌteɪk 'pleɪs/
text message *n* /'tekst ˌmesɪdʒ/
text *v* /tekst/
try on *v* /ˌtraɪ 'ɒn/
the UN *n* /ðə ˌjuː 'en/
user *n* /'juːzə(r)/

vegetarian *n* /ˌvedʒɪ'teəriən/

web page *n* /'web ˌpeɪdʒ/
website *n* /'websaɪt/
wing *n* /wɪŋ/
wonder *n* /'wʌndə(r)/

Unit 2

absolutely *adv* /ˌaebsəˈluːtli/
aerobics *n* /eəˈrəʊbɪks/
allow *v* /əˈlaʊ/
arrangement *n* /əˈreɪndʒmənt/
bargain *n* /ˈbɑːgɪn/
busy *adj* /ˈbɪzi/
charity *n* /ˈtʃaerəti/
cheer (sb) up *v* /ˌtʃɪə(r) ˈʌp/
cheque *n* /tʃek/
clown *n* /klaʊn/
coach *v* /kəʊtʃ/
convenience *n* /kənˈviːniəns/
(be) crazy about (sth) *v* /ˈkreɪzi əbaʊt/
decimal *n, adj* /ˈdesɪml/
decorate *v* /ˈdekəreɪt/
deep *adj* /diːp/
definitely *adv* /ˈdefɪnətli/
distract *v* /dɪˈstraekt/
dry ski slope *n* /ˌdraɪ ˈskiː sləʊp/
energetic *adj* /enəˈdʒetɪk/
event *n* /ɪˈvent/
exhausted *adj* /ɪgˈzɔːstɪd/
fancy *adj* /ˈfaensi/
feed *v* /fiːd/
football pitch *n* /ˈfʊtbɔːl ˌpɪtʃ/
goggles *pl n* /ˈgɒglz/
graduate *n* /ˈgraedjʊət/
guess *v* /ges/
health *n* /helθ/
injection *n* /ɪnˈdʒekʃn/
interior designer *n* /ɪnˌtɪəriə dɪˈzaɪnə(r)/
jogger *n* /ˈdʒɒgə(r)/
journalist *n* /ˈdʒɜːnəlɪst/
kid *n* /kɪd/
laugh *v* /lɑːf/
laughter *n* /ˈlɑːftə(r)/
lawyer *n* /ˈlɔːjə(r)/
leisure *n, adj* /ˈleʒə(r)/
lobby *n* /ˈlɒbi/
loose-fitting *adj* /ˈluːs ˌfɪtɪŋ/
magic trick *n* /ˌmaedʒɪk ˈtrɪk/
marriage counsellor *n US* /ˈmaerɪdʒ ˌkaʊnsələ(r)/
master's degree *n* /ˈmɑːstəz dɪˌgriː/
medicine *n* /ˈmedsn/
mind *n* /maɪnd/
nonsense *n* /ˈnɒnsəns/
operation *n* /ɒpəˈreɪʃn/
otherwise *adv* /ˈʌðəwaɪz/
pack *v* /paek/
participate *v* /pɑːˈtɪsɪpeɪt/
percentage *n* /pəˈsentɪdʒ/
plait *n* /plaet/
privileged *n* /ˈprɪvəlɪdʒd/
race about *v* /ˌreɪs əˈbaʊt/
raise *v* /reɪz/
rarely *adv* /ˈreəli/
reduced *adj* /rɪˈdjuːst/
relax *v* /rɪˈlaeks/

research scientist *n* /ˈriːsɜːtʃ ˌsaɪəntɪst/
resort (ski resort) *n* /rɪˈzɔːt/
response *n* /rɪˈspɒns/
rubber *adj* /ˈrʌbə(r)/
sale *n* /seɪl/
sensitive *adj* /ˈsensətɪv/
shorts *n* /ʃɔːts/
sick *adj* /sɪk/
silly *adj* /ˈsɪli/
sleep *n, v* /sliːp/
slightly *adv* /ˈslaɪtli/
suburb *n* /ˈsʌbɜːb/
supportive *adj* /səˈpɔːtɪv/
tell a lie *v* /tel ə ˈlaɪ/
tights *n* /taɪts/
tip (= advice) *n* /tɪp/
tiring *adj* /ˈtaɪrɪŋ/
totally *adv* /ˈtəʊtəli/
treat *v* /triːt/
unemployment *n* /ˌʌnɪmˈplɔɪmənt/
unwind *v* /ʌnˈwaɪnd/
useless *adj* /ˈjuːsləs/
volleyball *n* /ˈvɒlibɔːl/
ward *n* /wɔːd/
waterproof *adj* /ˈwɔːtəpruːf/
web page designer *n* /ˈweb peɪdʒ dɪˌzaɪnə(r)/
wedding anniversary *n* /ˈwedɪŋ aenɪˌvɜːsəri/
worry *n, v* /ˈwʌri/
yell *v* /jel/
zookeeper *n* /ˈzuːkiːpə(r)/

Unit 3

accidentally *adv* /ˌaeksɪˈdentli/
act (of a play) *n* /aekt/
amazement *n* /əˈmeɪzmənt/
award *n, v* /əˈwɔːd/
awful *adj* /ˈɔːfl/
battle *n* /ˈbaetl/
beat *v* /biːt/
bet *v* /bet/
birth *n* /bɜːθ/
boast *v* /bəʊst/
breathe *v* /briːð/
brush *n* /brʌʃ/
chapter *n* /ˈtʃaeptə(r)/
chat *v* /tʃaet/
childhood *n* /ˈtʃaɪldhʊd/
commit suicide *v* /kəˌmɪt ˈsuːɪsaɪd/
depression *n* /dɪˈpreʃn/
diamond *n* /ˈdaɪəmənd/
dig *v* /dɪg/
disgusting *adj* /ˌdɪsˈgʌstɪŋ/
draw (a picture) *v* /drɔː/
DVD *n* /ˌdiː viː ˈdiː/
emperor *n* /ˈempərə(r)/
encourage *v* /ɪnˈkʌrɪdʒ/
exhibition *n* /eksɪˈbɪʃn/
eyesight *n* /ˈaɪsaɪt/
fail *v* /feɪl/
fascinated *adj* /ˈfaesɪneɪtɪd/
fearless *adj* /ˈfɪələs/
feature *n* /ˈfiːtʃə(r)/
fight *v* /faɪt/
genius *n* /ˈdʒiːniəs/
hang out (= relax) informal *v* /ˌhaeŋ ˈaʊt/
heart failure *n* /ˈhɑːt ˌfeɪljə(r)/
homesick *adj* /ˈhəʊmsɪk/
honour *n, v* /ˈɒnə(r)/
hunting *n* /ˈhʌntɪŋ/
impressed *adj* /ɪmˈprest/
influenza *n* /ˌɪnfluˈenzə/
lifelike *adj* /ˈlaɪflaɪk/
masterpiece *n* /ˈmɑːstəpiːs/
match (in sport) *n* /maetʃ/
mile *n* /maɪl/
moral *n* /ˈmɒrəl/
nationality *n* /ˌnaeʃˈnaeləti/
nature *n* /ˈneɪtʃə(r)/
necklace *n* /ˈnekləs/
neighbourhood *n* /ˈneɪbəhʊd/
old-fashioned *adj* /ˌəʊld ˈfaeʃnd/
only (child) *adj* /ˈəʊnli/
outdoor *adj* /ˈaʊtdɔː(r)/
palace *n* /ˈpaeləs/
palette *n* /ˈpaelət/
pigeon *n* /ˈpɪdʒən/
pleased *adj* /pliːzd/
point *v* /pɔɪnt/
portrait *n* /ˈpɔːtreɪt/
recognize *v* /ˈrekəgnaɪz/
refuse *v* /rɪˈfjuːz/
religious *adj* /rɪˈlɪdʒəs/
report (in writing) *n* /rɪˈpɔːt/

sand *n* /saend/
scary *adj* /ˈskeəri/
score *v* /skɔː(r)/
scream *v* /skriːm/
shotgun *n* /ˈʃɒtgʌn/
sign *v* /saɪn/
sink *v* /sɪŋk/
sketch *n, v* /sketʃ/
skip *v* /skɪp/
soldier *n* /ˈsəʊldʒə(r)/
spill *v* /spɪl/
spoiled (child) *adj* /spɔɪlt/
star *v* /stɑː(r)/
strict *adj* /strɪkt/
suffer *v* /ˈsʌfə(r)/
sweetcorn *n* /ˈswiːtkɔːn/
teepee *n* /ˈtiːpiː/
terrified *adj* /ˈterɪfaɪd/
thoroughly *adv* /ˈθʌrəli/
treasure *n* /ˈtreʒə(r)/
triangle *n* /ˈtraɪaeŋgl/
unless *adv* /ʌnˈles/
upset *adj* /ʌpˈset/
vine *n* /vaɪn/
vineyard *n* /ˈvɪnjɑːd/
war correspondent *n* /ˈwɔː kɒrɪˌspɒndənt/
war *n* /wɔː(r)/
warrior *n* /ˈwɒriə(r)/
wave *v* /weɪv/
wound *v* /wuːnd/

Unit 4

banquet *n* /'bæŋkwɪt/
behave *v* /bɪ'heɪv/
bill *n* /bɪl/
bow (greeting) *n*, *v* /baʊ/
break *v* /breɪk/
briefcase *n* /'briːfkeɪs/
budget *n* /'bʌdʒɪt/
business card *n* /'bɪznɪs ˌkɑːd/
casually *adv* /'kæʒʊəli/
chew (gum) *v* /tʃuː/
choice *n* /tʃɔɪs/
chopstick *n* /'tʃɒpstɪk/
cleanliness *n* /'klenlɪnəs/
code *n* /kəʊd/
colleague *n* /'kɒliːg/
complain *v* /kəm'pleɪn/
cool (= OK) informal *adj* /kuːl/
dish *n* /dɪʃ/
driving licence *n*
    /'draɪvɪŋ ˌlaɪsəns/
drop off *v* /ˌdrɒp 'ɒf/
engaged *adj* /ɪn'geɪdʒd/
extension (phone) *n* /ɪk'stenʃn/
fasten *v* /'fɑːsn/
(be) fed up with *v* /ˌfed 'ʌp wɪð/
gathering *n* /'gæðərɪŋ/
gift *n* /gɪft/
global *adj* /'gləʊbl/
guest *n* /gest/
guidebook *n* /'gaɪdbʊk/
heel *n* /hiːl/
host *n* /həʊst/
hostess *n* /həʊ'stes/
interrupt *v* /ɪntə'rʌpt/
kilt *n* /kɪlt/
loads of things (= lots of things)
    pl n /'ləʊdz əv θɪŋz/
make-up *n* /'meɪk ʌp/
manners (= behaviour) *pl n*
    /'mænəz/
military service *n* /ˌmɪlətri 'sɜːvɪs/
minus *n*, *adj* /'maɪnəs/
modest *adj* /'mɒdɪst/
name tag *n* /'neɪm tæg/
noodle *n* /'nuːdl/
plus *n* /plʌs/
pocket money *n* /'pɒkɪt ˌmʌni/
polite *adj* /pə'laɪt/
potluck lunch *n* /ˌpɒtlʌk 'lʌntʃ/
pray *v* /preɪ/
pursue *v* /pə'sjuː/
rainy season *n* /'reɪni ˌsiːzn/
raw *adj* /rɔː/
responsibility *n* /rɪˌspɒnsə'bɪləti/
reverse n, *adj* /rɪ'vɜːs/
rule *n* /ruːl/
rush *v* /rʌʃ/
seatbelt *n* /'siːtbelt/
short-sleeved *adj* /'ʃɔːt sliːvd/
sign of respect *n*
    /saɪn əv rɪ'spekt/
skateboarding *n* /'skeɪtbɔːdɪŋ/
skewer *n* /'skjuːə(r)/
socialize *v* /'səʊʃəlaɪz/
spray *n*, *v* /spreɪ/
status *n* /'steɪtəs/
stranger *n* /'streɪndʒə(r)/
stuffy (a room) *adj* /'stʌfi/
suncream *n* /'sʌnkriːm/
supply *v* /sə'plaɪ/
tip (= suggestion) *n* /tɪp/
travellers' cheque *n*
    /'trævələz ˌtʃek/
trouble *n* /'trʌbl/
vaccination *n* /ˌvæksɪ'neɪʃn/
valuable *adj* /'væljʊəbl/
welcome *n*, *v* /'welkəm/
yawn *v* /jɔːn/

Unit 5

acting *n* /'æktɪŋ/
blow *v* /bləʊ/
chilly *adj* /'tʃɪli/
clear *adj* /klɪə(r)/
climate *n* /'klaɪmət/
cloud *n* /klaʊd/
cloudy *adj* /'klaʊdi/
confess *v* /kən'fes/
crossing *n* /'krɒsɪŋ/
deer *n* /dɪə(r)/
degree (of temperature) *n*
    /dɪ'griː/
depart *v* /dɪ'pɑːt/
descent *n* /dɪ'sent/
dramatically *adv* /drə'mætɪkli/
eastbound *adj* /'iːstbaʊnd/
enquiry *n* /ɪn'kwaɪəri/
en-suite *n* /ˌɒn 'swiːt/
exciting *adj* /ɪk'saɪtɪŋ/
experience *n* /ɪk'spɪəriəns/
face *v* /feɪs/
ferry *n* /'feri/
fog *n* /fɒg/
foggy *adj* /'fɒgi/
forecast *n* /'fɔːkɑːst/
haircut *n* /'heəkʌt/
heaven *n* /'hevn/
heavy (rain) *adj* /'hevi/
helipad *n* /'helɪpæd/
honeymoon *n*, *v* /'hʌnimuːn/
horizontal *adj* /ˌhɒrɪ'zɒntl/
hurry *n*, *v* /'hʌri/
ice *n* /aɪs/
icy *adj* /'aɪsi/
igloo *n* /'ɪgluː/
item *n* /'aɪtəm/
land (a plane) *v* /lænd/
laze *v* /leɪz/
library *n* /'laɪbrəri/
lightning *n* /'laɪtnɪŋ/
loaf *n* /ləʊf/
lowland *adj* /'ləʊlənd/
luggage *n* /'lʌgɪdʒ/
melt *v* /melt/
millionaire *n* /ˌmɪljə'neə(r)/
must-dos *pl n* /'mʌst ˌduːz/
non-smoking *adj*
    /ˌnɒn 'sməʊkɪŋ/
nose around *v* /ˌnəʊz ə'raʊnd/
paint *n* /peɪnt/
pile *n* /paɪl/
pleasant *adj* /'plezənt/
potter *v* /'pɒtə(r)/
practise *v* /'præktɪs/
qualification *n* /ˌkwɒlɪfɪ'keɪʃn/
rain *n* /reɪn/
rainy *adj* /'reɪni/
rare *adj* /reə(r)/
reach *v* /riːtʃ/
reception (wedding) *n* /rɪ'sepʃn/
recommend *v* /rekə'mend/
remote *adj* /rɪ'məʊt/
removal man *n* /rɪ'muːvl ˌmæn/
rhino *n* /'raɪnəʊ/
rough *adj* /rʌf/
shampoo *n* /ʃæm'puː/
shaped *adj* /ʃeɪpt/
shine *v* /ʃaɪn/
sleeping bag *n* /'sliːpɪŋ bæg/
smooth *adj* /smuːð/
snow *n*, *v* /snəʊ/
snowy *adj* /'snəʊi/
spice *n* /spaɪs/
spoil *v* /spɔɪl/
spring *n* /sprɪŋ/
stamp *n* /stæmp/
steak *n* /steɪk/
storm *n* /stɔːm/
stormy *adj* /'stɔːmi/
struggle *v* /'strʌgl/
temperature *n* /'temprɪtʃə(r)/
thunderstorm *n* /'θʌndəˌstɔːm/
tip (money) *n* /tɪp/
ton *n* /tʌn/
top *n* /tɒp/
towel *n* /taʊl/
travel agency *n* /'trævl eɪdʒənsi/
tube *n* /tjuːb/
vast *n* /vɑːst/
view *n* /vjuː/
weather *n* /'weðə(r)/
wind *n* /wɪnd/
windy *adj* /'wɪndi/
winter *n* /'wɪntə(r)/
yoghurt *n* /'jɒgət/

Unit 6

anchovy *n* /ˈæntʃəvi/
appearance *n* /əˈpɪərəns/
bacon *n* /ˈbeɪkən/
basil *n* /ˈbæzəl/
cause *v* /kɔːz/
(go) clubbing *n* /ˌɡəʊ ˈklʌbɪŋ/
consumer *n* /kənˈsjuːmə(r)/
cosmopolitan *adj*
    /ˌkɒzməˈpɒlɪtən/
cross *adj* /krɒs/
cynical *adj* /ˈsɪnɪkl/
delicious *adj* /dɪˈlɪʃəs/
deliver *v* /dɪˈlɪvə(r)/
disease *n* /dɪˈziːz/
disgusting *adj* /dɪsˈɡʌstɪŋ/
dry clean *v* /ˌdraɪ ˈkliːn/
eel *n* /iːl/
evolve *v* /ɪˈvɒlv/
external *adj* /ekˈstɜːnl/
fantastic *adj* /fænˈtæstɪk/
fast food *n* /ˌfɑːst ˈfuːd/
fatal *adj* /ˈfeɪtl/
fight *n* /faɪt/
finally *adv* /ˈfaɪnəli/
focal point *n* /ˈfəʊkl ˌpɔɪnt/
forever *adv* /fəˈrevə(r)/
fresh *adj* /freʃ/
frozen *adj* /ˈfrəʊzn/
garlic *n* /ˈɡɑːlɪk/
generally *adv* /ˈdʒenərəli/
gradually *adv* /ˈɡrædjuəli/
grateful *adj* /ˈɡreɪtfl/
gravitate *v* /ˈɡrævɪteɪt/
grumble (= complain) *v*
    /ˈɡrʌmbl/
handsome *adj* /ˈhænsəm/
herring *n* /ˈherɪŋ/
home-grown *adj* /ˌhəʊm ˈɡrəʊn/
(have) in common /ɪn ˈkɒmən/
junk food *n* /ˈdʒʌŋk fuːd/
karaoke *n* /kæriˈəʊki/
kettle *n* /ˈketl/
lane (road) *n* /leɪn/
locked *adj* /lɒkt/
look forward to *v*
    /ˌlʊk ˈfɔːwəd tə/
mend *v* /mend/
migrate *v* /maɪˈɡreɪt/
miss *v* /mɪs/
mix *n, v* /mɪks/
notice board *n* /ˈnəʊtɪs ˌbɔːd/
oil *n* /ɔɪl/
orchestra *n* /ˈɔːkɪstrə/
outside *prep* /ˈaʊtsaɪd/
pea *n* /piː/
pineapple *n* /ˈpaɪnæpl/
popularity *n* /ˌpɒpjəˈlærəti/
prayer *n* /ˈpreə(r)/
producer *n* /prəˈdjuːsə(r)/
promise *v* /ˈprɒmɪs/
promotion *n* /prəˈməʊʃn/
put the world to rights
    /ˌpʊt ðə ˌwɜːld tə ˈraɪts/
rave *v* /reɪv/
rectangular *adj* /rekˈtæŋɡələ(r)/
reputation *n* /ˌrepjəˈteɪʃn/
rude *adj* /ruːd/
safe *adj* /seɪf/
salmon *n* /ˈsæmən/
seldom *adv* /ˈseldəm/
shrimp *n* /ʃrɪmp/
simple *adj* /ˈsɪmpl/
skyscraper *n* /ˈskaɪskreɪpə(r)/
slice *n* /slaɪs/
squid *n* /skwɪd/
starving *adj* /ˈstɑːvɪŋ/
stereotype *n* /ˈsteriəʊtaɪp/
stove *n* /stəʊv/
succeed *v* /səkˈsiːd/
tasteless *adj* /ˈteɪstləs/
tasty *adj* /ˈteɪsti/
Thai *adj* /taɪ/
topping *n* /ˈtɒpɪŋ/
truly *adv* /ˈtruːli/
tuna *n* /ˈtjuːnə/
turn down (volume) *v*
    /ˌtɜːn ˈdaʊn/
ultimate *adj* /ˈʌltɪmət/
universal *adj* /juːnɪˈvɜːsl/
upright *adj* /ˈʌpraɪt/
varied *adj* /ˈveərɪd/
vegetable *n* /ˈvedʒtəbl/
wealthy *adj* /ˈwelθi/

Unit 7

advice *n* /ədˈvaɪs/
advise *v* /ədˈvaɪz/
amazingly *adv* /əˈmeɪzɪŋli/
ankle *n* /ˈæŋkl/
announce *v* /əˈnaʊns/
application *n* /ˌæplɪˈkeɪʃn/
back off (= retreat) *v* /ˌbæk ˈɒf/
box office *n* /ˈbɒks ˌɒfɪs/
broke (= have no money)
    informal *adj* /brəʊk/
career *n* /kəˈrɪə(r)/
carry on *v* /ˌkæri ˈɒn/
championship *n* /ˈtʃæmpiənʃɪp/
chase *v* /tʃeɪs/
circus *n* /ˈsɜːkəs/
come across (= find) *v* /ˌkʌm
    əˈkrɒs/
come up with *v* /ˌkʌm ˈʌp wɪð/
cover *v* /ˈkʌvə(r)/
crane *n* /kreɪn/
cut off (isolate) *v* /ˌkʌt ˈɒf/
cut off (telephone) *v* /ˌkʌt ˈɒf/
CV (= curriculum vitae) *n*
    /ˌsiː ˈviː/
damage *n* /ˈdæmɪdʒ/
delighted *adj* /dɪˈlaɪtɪd/
descendant *n* /dɪˈsendənt/
disappointed *adj* /ˌdɪsəˈpɔɪntɪd/
documentary *n* /ˌdɒkjəˈmentri/
elect *v* /ɪˈlekt/
end up *v* /ˌend ˈʌp/
excitement *n* /ɪkˈsaɪtmənt/
fascinating *adj* /ˈfæsɪneɪtɪŋ/
few /fjuː/
flood *n* /flʌd/
fluent *adj* /ˈfluːənt/
fluently *adv* /ˈfluːəntli/
flyer (= publicity leaflet) *n*
    /ˈflaɪə(r)/
force (sb to do sth) *v* /fɔːs/
forecaster *n* /ˈfɔːkɑːstə(r)/
genuine *adj* /ˈdʒenjuːɪn/
get on with (sb) *v* /ˌget ˈɒn wɪð/
girder *n* /ˈɡɜːdə(r)/
give up (= stop) *v* /ˌɡɪv ˈʌp/
guy (= man) informal *n* /ɡaɪ/
hand down (give to a younger
    relative) *v* /ˌhænd ˈdaʊn/
hand out (= distribute) *v*
    /ˌhænd ˈaʊt/
headline *n* /ˈhedlaɪn/
heavyweight *adj* /ˈheviweɪt/
height *n* /haɪt/
hit *v* /hɪt/
hold (= wait) *v* /həʊld/
homeless *adj* /ˈhəʊmləs/
hunter *n* /ˈhʌntə(r)/
hurricane *n* /ˈhʌrɪkən/
in charge /ˌɪn ˈtʃɑːdʒ/
indoors *adv* /ɪnˈdɔːz/
interpersonal *adj* /ˌɪntəˈpɜːsənl/
interview *n, v* /ˈɪntəvjuː/
ironworker *n* /ˈaɪən,wɜːkə(r)/
journalism *n* /ˈdʒɜːnəlɪzm/
just in case /ˌdʒʌst ɪn ˈkeɪs/
knock out (make unconscious) *v*
    /ˌnɒk ˈaʊt/
lay off (= make redundant) *v*
    /ˌleɪ ˈɒf/
leader *n* /ˈliːdə(r)/
leave a message *v* /ˌliːv ə ˈmesɪdʒ/
look (sth) up *v* /ˌlʊk ˈʌp/
mayor *n* /ˈmeə(r)/
meteorologist *n* /ˌmiːtiəˈrɒlədʒɪst/
nasty *adj* /ˈnɑːsti/
Nobel Prize *n* /ˌnəʊbel ˌpraɪz/
novelist *n* /ˈnɒvəlɪst/
of course *adv* /əv ˈkɔːs/
organize *v* /ˈɔːɡənaɪz/
outdoors *adv* /aʊtˈdɔːz/
particularly *adv* /pəˈtɪkjələli/
photocopier *n* /ˈfəʊtəʊˌkɒpiə(r)/
pride *n* /praɪd/
put (sb) through (on the phone) *v*
    /ˌpʊt ˈθruː/
put up with (sth) (= tolerate) *v*
    /ˌpʊt ˈʌp wɪð/
recapture *v* /ˌriːˈkæptʃə(r)/
resign *v* /rɪˈzaɪn/
resignation *n* /ˌrezɪɡˈneɪʃn/
retire *v* /rɪˈtaɪə(r)/
retirement *n* /rɪˈtaɪəmənt/
round (of a boxing fight) *n*
    /raʊnd/
sacrifice *n* /ˈsækrɪfaɪs/
scandal *n* /ˈskændəl/
seek *v* /siːk/
shoulder *n* /ˈʃəʊldə(r)/
skeleton *n* /ˈskelɪtən/
skill *n* /skɪl/
slowdown *n* /ˈsləʊdaʊn/
take a message *v* /ˌteɪk ə ˈmesɪdʒ/
take (sth) away (= remove) *v*
    /ˌteɪk əˈweɪ/
take up *v* /ˌteɪk ˈʌp/
training *n* /ˈtreɪnɪŋ/
turn on *v* /ˌtɜːn ˈɒn/
twist *v* /twɪst/
vacancy *n* /ˈveɪkənsi/
washing-up *n* /ˌwɒʃɪŋ ˈʌp/
widespread *adj* /ˈwaɪdspred/

Unit 8

actually *adv* /ˈaektʃəli/
address *n* /əˈdres/
afford (can't afford) *v* /əˈfɔːd/
AIDS (= acquired immune deficiency syndrome) *n* /eɪdz/
alone *adj* /əˈləʊn/
amnesty *n* /ˈaemnəsti/
angry *adj* /ˈaeŋgri/
appeal *n* /əˈpiːl/
appreciate *v* /əˈpriːʃieɪt/
astonished *adj* /əˈstɒnɪʃt/
attractive *adj* /əˈtraektɪv/
awake *adj* /əˈweɪk/

beg *v* /beg/
belief *n* /bɪˈliːf/
blanket *n* /ˈblaeŋkɪt/
book (a holiday) *v* /bʊk/
boss *n* /bɒs/
both /bəʊθ/
burglar *n* /ˈbɜːglə(r)/

calm *adj* /kɑːm/
camp *n* /kaemp/
cancer *n* /ˈkaensə(r)/
carpet *n* /ˈkɑːpɪt/
chimney *n* /ˈtʃɪmni/
circumstance *n* /ˈsɜːkəmstɑːns/
conservation *n* /ˌkɒnsəˈveɪʃn/
crisis *n* /ˈkraɪsɪs/
crowd *n* /kraʊd/
curtain *n* /ˈkɜːtn/

dedicate *v* /ˈdedɪkeɪt/
demand *n* /dɪˈmɑːnd/
desperately *adv* /ˈdespərətli/
die *v* /daɪ/
dirty *adj* /ˈdɜːti/
disastrous *adj* /dɪˈzɑːstrəs/
dream *v* /driːm/
drive *n* /draɪv/
drop dead *v* /ˌdrɒp ˈded/
dump (sb) (= end a romantic relationship) informal *v* /dʌmp/

earn *v* /ɜːn/
economic *adj* /iːkəˈnɒmɪk/
embassy *n* /ˈembəsi/
emergency supplies *pl n* /ɪˌmɜːdʒənsi səˈplaɪz/
endangered species *n* /ɪnˌdeɪndʒəd ˈspiːʃiːz/
enormous *adj* /ɪˈnɔːməs/
establish *v* /ɪˈstaeblɪʃ/
ethnic *adj* /ˈeθnɪk/

fantasize *v* /ˈfaentəsaɪz/
fee n /fiː/
fit together (a jigsaw) *v* /ˌfɪt təˈgeðə(r)/
fithy *adj* /ˈfɪlθi/
floor *n* /flɔː(r)/
fluid *n* /ˈfluːɪd/
fortunately *adv* /ˈfɔːtʃənətli/
frightened *adj* /ˈfraɪtnd/
funny *adj* /ˈfʌni/
furious *adj* /ˈfjʊəriəs/

get rid of (= discard) *v* /ˌget ˈrɪd əv/
ghost *n* /gəʊst/
grow *v* /grəʊ/
growl *v* /graʊl/
guard *n* /gɑːd/

heart attack *n* /ˈhɑːt əˌtaek/
heat *n* /hiːt/
heavily *adv* /ˈhevəli/
hilarious *adj* /hɪˈleəriəs/
horrible *adj* /ˈhɒrəbl/
hospice *n* /ˈhɒspɪs/
hound (= pursue) *v* /haʊnd/
housing *n* /ˈhaʊzɪŋ/
human rights *pl n* /ˌhjuːmən ˈraɪts/
hungry *adj* /ˈhʌŋgri/

incredibly *adv* /ɪnˈkredəbli/
incurable *adj* /ɪnˈkjʊərəbl/
invest *v* /ɪnˈvest/
island *n* /ˈaɪlənd/

jigsaw *n* /ˈdʒɪgsɔː/
just *adv* /dʒʌst/

knock *n*, *v* /nɒk/

land *n* /laend/
last *v* /lɑːst/
leave (sth) behind (= forget) *v* /ˌliːv bɪˈhaɪnd/
loan *n* /ləʊn/
lottery *n* /ˈlɒtəri/
loudly a*dv* /ˈlaʊdli/

mansion *n* /ˈmaenʃn/
medical supplies *pl n* /ˈmedɪkl səˌplaɪz/
menacingly *adv* /ˈmenəsɪŋli/
miserable *adj* /ˈmɪzrəbl/
misery *n* /ˈmɪzəri/

nearly *adv* /ˈnɪəli/

organization *n* /ˌɔːgənaɪˈzeɪʃn/

pay-rise *n* /ˈpeɪ ˌraɪz/
penniless *adj* /ˈpenɪləs/
photography *n* /fəˈtɒgrəfi/
pick up (= collect) *v* /ˌpɪk ˈʌp/
post office *n* /ˈpəʊst ˌɒfɪs/
post *v* /pəʊst/
pour *v* /pɔː(r)/
pretty *adj* /ˈprɪti/
prisoner of conscience *n* /ˌprɪznər əv ˈkɒnʃəns/
prize *n* /praɪz/
psychiatrist *n* /saɪˈkaɪətrɪst/
purpose *n* /ˈpɜːpəs/
put pressure on (sb) *v* /ˌpʊt ˈpreʃər ɒn/

ragged *adj* /ˈraegɪd/
receptionist *n* /rɪˈsepʃənɪst/
relative *n* /ˈrelətɪv/
release *v* /rɪˈliːs/
rescue *n* /ˈreskjuː/
research *n* /rɪˈsɜːtʃ/
routine *n* /ruːˈtiːn/
run (my nose is running) *v* /rʌn/
run out of *v* /ˌrʌn ˈaʊt əv/

sanity *n* /ˈsaenəti/
shelter *n* /ˈʃeltə(r)/

smash *v* /smaeʃ/
solicitor *n* /səˈlɪsɪtə(r)/
space shuttle *n* /ˈspeɪs ˌʃʌtl/
spending spree *n* /ˈspendɪŋ ˌspriː/
stand *v* /staend/
suddenly *adv* /ˈsʌdənli/
superb *adj* /suːˈpɜːb/
surprised *adj* /səˈpraɪzd/
survive *v* /səˈvaɪv/

tempt *v* /temt/
the press *n* /ðə ˈpres/
thrilled *adj* /θrɪld/
tired *adj* /ˈtaɪəd/
turn out *v* /ˌtɜːn ˈaʊt/

violently *adv* /ˈvaɪələntli/
visa *n* /ˈviːzə/

waste *v* /weɪst/
wide *adj* /waɪd/
windfall *n* /ˈwɪndfɔːl/
wildlife reserve *n* /ˈwaɪldlaɪf rɪˌzɜːv/
wild-looking *adj* /ˈwaɪld ˌlʊkɪŋ/
winner *n* /ˈwɪnə(r)/

Unit 9

advantage *n* /əd'vɑːntɪdʒ/
agony aunt *n* /'ægəni aːnt/
ambitious *adj* /æm'bɪʃəs/
annoyed *adj* /ə'nɔɪd/
background *n* /'bækɡraʊnd/
care *v* /keə(r)/
cheat *v* /tʃiːt/
cheerful *adj* /'tʃɪəfl/
clearly *adv* /'klɪəli/
complexion *n* /kəm'plekʃn/
concentrate *v* /'kɒnsəntreɪt/
conscious *adj* /'kɒnʃəs/
contented *adj* /kən'tentɪd/
cruel *adj* /kruːəl/
crutches *pl n* /'krʌtʃɪz/
curly *adj* /'kɜːli/
date *n* /deɪt/
daydream *n, v* /'deɪdriːm/
deal with (sth) *v* /'diːl wɪð/
definite *adj* /'defɪnət/
depend on (sb) *v* /dɪ'pend ɒn/
depressed *adj* /dɪ'prest/
disadvantage *n* /ˌdɪsəd'vɑːntɪdʒ/
drawer *n* /drɔː(r)/
drop *v* /drɒp/
easygoing *adj* /ˌiːzi'ɡəʊɪŋ/
envy *v* /'envi/
expert *n, adj* /'ekspɜːt/
finance *n* /'faɪnæns/
forget *v* /fə'ɡet/
gambling *n* /'ɡæmblɪŋ/
generation *n* /ˌdʒenə'reɪʃn/
hand-me-down *adj* /'hænd mi ˌdaʊn/
hardworking *adj* /ˌhɑːd'wɜːkɪŋ/
hate *v* /heɪt/
housework *n* /'haʊswɜːk/
husband *n* /'hʌzbənd/
I suppose. /ˌaɪ sə'pəʊz/
impatient *adj* /ɪm'peɪʃnt/
in front of *prep* /ɪn 'frʌnt əv/
in the meantime /ˌɪn ðə 'miːntaɪm/
kind *adj* /kaɪnd/
lorry driver *n* /'lɒri ˌdraɪvə(r)/
memory *n* /'meməri/
mood *n* /muːd/
moody *adj* /'muːdi/
notice *v* /'nəʊtɪs/
nun *n* /nʌn/
nurse *n* /nɜːs/
obsessed *adj* /əb'sest/
oversleep *v* /ˌəʊvə'sliːp/
passion *n* /'pæʃn/
plaster *n* /'plɑːstə(r)/
point of view *n* /ˌpɔɪnt əv 'vjuː/
put off (doing sth) (= postpone) *v* /ˌpʊt 'ɒf/
rather *adv* /'rɑːðə(r)/
relationship *n* /rɪ'leɪʃnʃɪp/
reliable *adj* /rɪ'laɪəbl/
relieved *adj* /rɪ'liːvd/
resentment *n* /rɪ'zentmənt/
reserved *adj* /rɪ'zɜːvd/
reunion *n* /ˌriː'juːniən/
sense of humour *n* /ˌsens əv 'hjuːmə(r)/
share *n* /ʃeə(r)/
sociable *adj* /'səʊʃəbl/
take care of (sb) *v* /ˌteɪk 'keər əv/
talkative *adj* /'tɔːkətɪv/
tolerant *adj* /'tɒlərənt/
twin *n* /twɪn/
unsure *adj* /ˌʌn'ʃʊə(r)/
untidy *adj* /ˌʌn'taɪdi/
ups and downs *pl n* /ˌʌps ən 'daʊnz/
vet *n* /vet/
veterinary assistant *n* /ˌvetnri ə'sɪstənt/

Unit 10

air conditioning *n* /'eə kənˌdɪʃnɪŋ/
airport *n* /'eəpɔːt/
audition *n, v* /ɔː'dɪʃn/
autobiographical *adj* /ˌɔːtəbaɪəʊ'ɡræfɪkl/
award *n* /ə'wɔːd/
ban *v* /bæn/
birthday card *n* /'bɜːθdeɪ ˌkɑːd/
blond *adj* /blɒnd/
button *n* /'bʌtn/
can't bear (sth) *v* /ˌkɑːnt 'beə(r)/
cast *v* /kɑːst/
casting director *n* /'kɑːstɪŋ dəˌrektə(r), dɪ-, daɪ-/
ceiling *n* /'siːlɪŋ/
cello *n* /'tʃeləʊ/
changing room *n* /'tʃeɪndʒɪŋ ˌruːm/
chemistry *n* /'keməstri/
classical music *n* /ˌklæsɪkl 'mjuːzɪk/
clear *v* /klɪə(r)/
collector *n* /kə'lektə(r)/
compose *v* /kəm'pəʊz/
concert *n* /'kɒnsət/
concerto *n* /kən'tʃeətəʊ/
conductor *n* /kən'dʌktə(r)/
constantly *adv* /'kɒnstəntli/
credit card *n* /'kredɪt ˌkɑːd/
debt *n* /det/
dust *v* /dʌst/
dynamite *n* /'daɪnəmaɪt/
engineer *n* /ˌendʒɪ'nɪə(r)/
estate agent *n* /ɪ'steɪt ˌeɪdʒənt/
explosion *n* /ɪk'spləʊʒn/
explosives *pl n* /ɪk'spləʊsɪvz/
fake *adj* /feɪk/
figure *n* /'fɪɡə(r)/
fire engine *n* /'faɪər ˌendʒɪn/
fireplace *n* /'faɪəpleɪs/
fireworks *pl n* /'faɪəwɜːks/
found *v* /faʊnd/
hairbrush *n* /'heəbrʌʃ/
hairdresser *n* /'heədresə(r)/
headache *n* /'hedeɪk/
hippie *n* /'hɪpi/
history *n* /'hɪstri/
hurt *v* /hɜːt/
immaculate *adj* /ɪ'mækjələt/
lecture *n, v* /'lektʃə(r)/
legendary *adj* /'ledʒəndri/
make up (= invent) *v* /ˌmeɪk 'ʌp/
memorabilia *n* /ˌmemərə'bɪliə/
metallic *adj* /mə'tælɪk/
movies *n US* /'muːviz/
optimism *n* /'ɒptɪmɪzəm/
originally *adv* /ə'rɪdʒənəli/
out-of-work *adj* /ˌaʊt əv 'wɜːk/
ponytail *n* /'pəʊniteɪl/
press *v* /pres/
profile *n* /'prəʊfaɪl/
promote *v* /prə'məʊt/
react *v* /ri'ækt/
reckon (= think) informal *v* /'rekən/
redecorate *v* /ˌriː'dekəreɪt/
revise (for an exam) *v* /rɪ'vaɪz/
role *n* /rəʊl/
rugged *adj* /'rʌɡɪd/
scholarship *n* /'skɒləʃɪp/
shopping centre *n* /'ʃɒpɪŋ ˌsentə(r)/
shopping list *n* /'ʃɒpɪŋ ˌlɪst/
shopping spree *n* /'ʃɒpɪŋ ˌspriː/
soundtrack *n* /'saʊndtræk/
state of the art *adj* /ˌsteɪt əv ði 'ɑːt/
sunglasses *pl n* /'sʌnɡlɑːsɪz/
sunset *n* /'sʌnset/
tale *n* /teɪl/
teacup *n* /'tiːkʌp/
teapot *n* /'tiːpɒt/
tear (in your eyes) *n* /tɪə(r)/
teaspoon *n* /'tiːspuːn/
toilet paper *n* /'tɔɪlət ˌpeɪpə(r)/
toothache *n* /'tuːθeɪk/
toothbrush *n* /'tuːθbrʌʃ/
toothpaste *n* /'tuːθpeɪst/
traffic jam *n* /'træfɪk ˌdʒæm/
traffic warden *n* /'træfɪk ˌwɔːdn/
trapped *adj* /træpt/
trendy *adj* /'trendi/
unconventional *adj* /ˌʌnkən'venʃnl/
underwear *n* /'ʌndəweə(r)/
unlikely *adj* /ʌn'laɪkli/
videotape *n* /'vɪdiəʊteɪp/
vote *n* /vəʊt/
waiting room *n* /'weɪtɪŋ ˌruːm/
wallpaper *n* /'wɔːlpeɪpə(r)/
water *n, v* /'wɔːtə(r)/
worldwide *adv* /wɜːld'waɪd/
worth *adj* /wɜːθ/
wrapping paper *n* /'ræpɪŋ ˌpeɪpə(r)/
writing paper *n* /'raɪtɪŋ ˌpeɪpə(r)/

Unit 11

abbreviation n /əˌbri:vi'eɪʃn/
absent-mindedness n /ˌaebsənt 'maɪndɪdnəs/
affectionately adv /ə'fekʃənətli/
aggressive adj /ə'gresɪv/
anyway conj /'eniweɪ/
appear v /ə'pɪə(r)/
appointment n /ə'pɔɪntmənt/
backing vocalist n /'baekɪŋ ˌvəʊkəlɪst/
beard n /bɪəd/
bite v /baɪt/
blame v /bleɪm/
bring up (a child) v /ˌbrɪŋ 'ʌp/
campsite n /'kaempsaɪt/
caring adj /'keərɪŋ/
cartoonist n /kɑ:'tu:nɪst/
catastrophe n /kə'taestrəfi/
check in v /ˌtʃek 'ɪn/
cheerleader n /'tʃɪəli:də(r)/
chew v /tʃu:/
childbearing n /'tʃaɪldbeərɪŋ/
childbirth n /'tʃaɪldbɜ:θ/
climb v /klaɪm/
construction n /kən'strʌkʃn/
contract n /'kɒntraekt/
cope v /kəʊp/
couch potato n /'kaʊtʃ pəˌteɪtəʊ/
crate n /kreɪt/
creature n /'kri:tʃə(r)/
cross off (from a list) v /ˌkrɒs 'ɒf/
crucify v /'kru:sɪfaɪ/
currently adv /'kʌrəntli/
deduce v /dɪ'dju:s/
define v /dɪ'faɪn/
deli (= delicatessen) informal n /'deli/
dental floss n /'dentl ˌflɒs/
desk n /desk/
dinosaur n /'daɪnəsɔ:(r)/
discover v /dɪ'skʌvə(r)/
drop (sb) a line /ˌdrɒp ə 'laɪn/
drummer n /'drʌmə(r)/
emotion n /ɪ'məʊʃn/
employer n /ɪm'plɔɪə(r)/
energy n /'enədʒi/
equivalent adj /ɪ'kwɪvələnt/
eruption n /ɪ'rʌpʃn/
feelings pl n /'fi:lɪŋz/
forgetful adj /fə'getfl/
forgetfulness n /fə'getflnəs/
gadget n /'gaedʒɪt/
go back v /ˌgəʊ 'baek/
grab v /graeb/
gum n /gʌm/
halfway adj /'hɑ:fweɪ/
hammer n /'haemə(r)/
handheld computer n /ˌhaendheld kəm'pju:tə(r)/
H-bomb n /'eɪtʃ ˌbɒm/
hiccup n /'hɪkʌp/
historically adv /hɪ'stɒrɪkli/
hit n /hɪt/
hit the roof /ˌhɪt ðə 'ru:f/
hold your breath /ˌhəʊld jɔ: 'breθ/
hug v /hʌg/
in fact adv /ˌɪn 'faekt/
insane adj /ɪn'seɪn/
instinctive adj /ɪn'stɪŋktɪv/
kick the habit /ˌkɪk ðə 'haebɪt/
kick v /kɪk/
kiss (sth) goodbye /ˌkɪs gʊd'baɪ/
ladder n /'laedə(r)/
landscape n /'laendskeɪp/
lick v /lɪk/
life expectancy n /'laɪf ɪkˌspektənsi/
lifestyle n /'laɪfstaɪl/
litter n /'lɪtə(r)/
man-made adj /maen meɪd/
meat packer n /'mi:t ˌpaekə(r)/
nail n /neɪl/
natural disaster n /ˌnaetʃrəl dɪ'zɑ:stə(r)/
naturally adv /'naetʃrəli/
neglect v /nɪ'glekt/
nevertheless adv /ˌnevəðə'les/
orbit v /'ɔ:bɪt/
outlive v /aʊt'lɪv/
owner n /'əʊnə(r)/
personal trainer n /ˌpɜ:sənl 'treɪnə(r)/
philosopher n /fɪ'lɒsəfə(r)/
police officer n /pə'li:s ˌɒfɪsə(r)/
population n /ˌpɒpjə'leɪʃn/
poster n /'pəʊstə(r)/
primary adj /'praɪməri/
prove v /pru:v/
purse n /pɜ:s/
pyramid n /'pɪrəmɪd/
rainforest n /'reɪnfɒrɪst/
range n /reɪndʒ/
risky adj /'rɪski/
row n /rəʊ/
shut down v /ˌʃʌt 'daʊn/
slipper n /'slɪpə(r)/
smart (= well-dressed) adj /smɑ:t/
stare v /steə(r)/
stone n /stəʊn/
stressed adj /strest/
suggest v /sə'dʒest/
symbol n /'sɪmbl/
think v /θɪŋk/
transportation n /ˌtraenspɔ:'teɪʃn/
unfortunately adv /ˌʌn'fɔ:tʃənətli/
volcanic adj /vɒl'kaenɪk/
whistle n, v /'wɪsl/
wipe out (= destroy) v /ˌwaɪp 'aʊt/

Unit 12

add v /aed/
admit v /əd'mɪt/
all-night party n /ˌɔ:l naɪt 'pɑ:ti/
argue v /'ɑ:gju:/
ask v /ɑ:sk/
baby-sit v /'beɪbi sɪt/
blow n /bləʊ/
bow n /bəʊ/
bury v /'beri/
byway n /'baɪweɪ/
captain n /'kaeptɪn/
charter v /'tʃɑ:tə(r)/
coffin n /'kɒfɪn/
commemorate v /kə'meməreɪt/
cot n /kɒt/
cotton n /'kɒtn/
course n /kɔ:s/
crew n /kru:/
crowded adj /'kraʊdɪd/
dismantle v /dɪs'maentl/
dotted line n /ˌdɒtɪd 'laɪn/
doubt n /daʊt/
dove n /dʌv/
drum n /drʌm/
expect (a baby) v /ɪk'spekt/
feature v /'fi:tʃə(r)/
funeral n /'fju:nərəl/
get engaged v /ˌget ɪn'geɪdʒd/
groom n /gru:m/
hearing aid n /'hɪərɪŋ ˌeɪd/
helicopter n /'helɪˌkɒptə(r)/
hell n /hel/
highway n /'haɪweɪ/
honeymoon n, v /'hʌnimu:n/
invite v /ɪn'vaɪt/
judge n /dʒʌdʒ/
juicy adj /'dʒu:si/
kneel v /ni:l/
liar n /'laɪə(r)/
lifeboat n /'laɪfbəʊt/
lifeboatman n /'laɪfbəʊtmən/
mainland n /'meɪnlənd/
manage to do (sth) v /ˌmaenɪdʒ tə 'du:/
marriage guidance counsellor n /ˌmaerɪdʒ 'gaɪdəns ˌkaʊnsələ(r)/
midwife n /'mɪdwaɪf/
miss v /mɪs/
moan v /məʊn/
mourner n /'mɔ:nə(r)/
muffled adj /'mʌfld/
nappy n /'naepi/
naught n /nɔ:t/
noon n /nu:n/
offer v /'ɒfə(r)/
overhead adv /ˌəʊvə'hed/
pregnant adj /'pregnənt/
prison n /'prɪzn/
proposal n /prə'pəʊzl/
reception n /rɪ'sepʃn/
regret n /rɪ'gret/
remind v /rɪ'maɪnd/
rose-coloured adj /'rəʊz kʌləd/
say v /seɪ/
scarf n /skɑ:f/
scribble v /'skrɪbl/
selfish adj /'selfɪʃ/
spit v /spɪt/
subside v /səb'saɪd/
sweep up v /ˌswi:p 'ʌp/
take (sth) back (= return) v /ˌteɪk 'baek/
tell v /tel/
throw v /θrəʊ/
translate v /traens'leɪt/
volunteer n /vɒlən'tɪə(r)/
wake v /weɪk/
warning n /'wɔ:nɪŋ/
wedding n /'wedɪŋ/
widow n /'wɪdəʊ/
wreath n /ri:θ/